JAPAN and KOREA

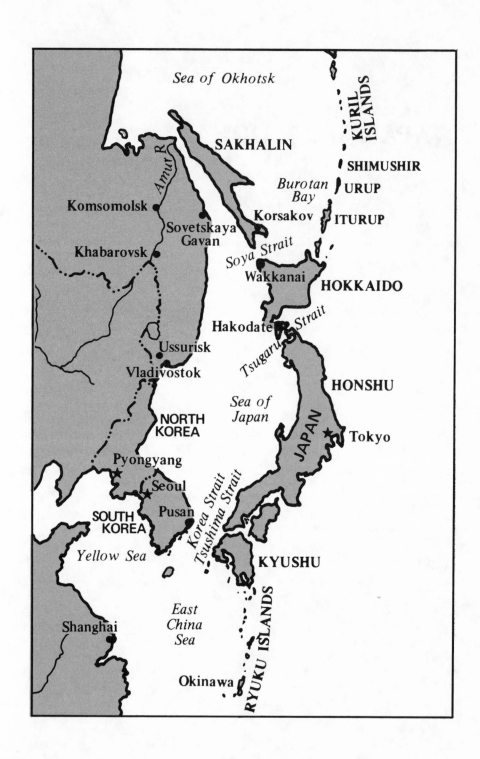

JAPAN and
KOREA

The Political Dimension

CHONG-SIK LEE

HOOVER INSTITUTION PRESS   Stanford University, Stanford, California

Hoover Press Publication 318

Copyright 1985 by the Board of Trustees of the
    Leland Stanford Junior University
First printing, 1985
Manufactured in the United States of America
89 88 87 86 85   9 8 7 6 5 4 3 2 1

Library of Congress Cataloging in Publication Data

Lee, Chong-Sik.
    Japan and Korea : the political dimension.

    Includes bibliographies and index.
    1. Japan—Relations—Korea (South) 2. Korea
(South)—Relations—Japan. I. Title.
DS849.K6L44 1985   327.5205195   85-5455
ISBN 0-8179-8181-0

Design by Lorena Laforest Bass

To
Professor Hatada Takashi
and
Dr. Key P. Yang

Contents

APPENDIXES

List of Tables

Preface

What is Korea to Japan? Where does Korea stand in the Japanese political perspective? What factors influence Japan's Korea policy? These were some of the questions I hoped to answer in this book.

The task proved more difficult than I had originally envisioned. Japan's perspective toward Korea changed significantly after 1945, when Japan was forced to abandon its former colony, and that perspective has continued to change as Japan, Korea, and their international environment have evolved. Contrary to the image of a unitary "Japan, Incorporated," there are many groups within that country that compete to affect its policy. Therefore, instead of trying to find a firm answer to all my questions, I had to confine my quest to discovering the basic characteristics of Japanese decisionmaking vis-à-vis Korea.

The task was doubly difficult for me because Japan's relations with Korea are deeply emotion-laden, as anyone even vaguely familiar with Japanese-Korean relations will know. Some scholars of both nationalities have transcended their national origins and biases in their work, but these admirable individuals have been too rare. I did strive to emulate them, but I probably did not succeed in my effort. The reader, however, should not deduce from my Korean background that this study represents a Korean viewpoint. This work may prove as disappointing to Korean readers as to the Japanese.

Another difficulty I faced was the lack of source material. A more prodigious and diligent scholar with special ties in both Japan and Korea would have had access to a wider range of materials. But, as of now, most archives of both countries are inaccessible to ordinary mortals, and I had to contend with a limited range of materials. I did consult the archival materials of the U.S. State Department, which shed much light on the early stage of negotiations between Japan and Korea, but even that material stops at 1954 or thereabouts. This study, therefore, is far from definitive. I do hope, however, that it will shed some light on its subject and stimulate further interest.

I am indebted to many individuals for guidance and support. I owe a special debt to Dr. Ramon Myers of the Hoover Institution for suggesting this study and facilitating a grant from his institution that enabled me to produce this work. Although I have been interested in exploring the relationship between Japan and Korea for many years, I would not have undertaken this study without his support and encouragement. He was also kind enough to read the various drafts and offer helpful criticisms. I am, of course, grateful to the Publications Committee of the Hoover Institution for providing me with the grant.

I am also grateful to Professors Kim Young-Ho and Ichikawa Masaaki, who acquired numerous Japanese books for me. They also ran a veritable clipping service from Tokyo to keep me abreast of events in 1982, when Japan and South Korea were engaged in loan negotiations and the textbook controversy. Their generosity is deeply appreciated. Professor Ichikawa also introduced me to Mr. Mitsutani Shizuo, the veteran diplomat, who spent many years in Korea and engaged in Korean affairs. Mr. Mitsutani kindly shared his insights, which were of enormous help to me.

I am also grateful to many Japanese scholars, journalists, and others for sharing their thoughts with me while I was visiting Japan in 1981. Mr. Hagiwara Yoshiyuki and others at the Institute of Developing Economies were not only generous hosts but were also kind enough to provide me with some of their publications, which were very helpful. I appreciated the unstinting support of the American and Japanese staffs of the International Communications Agency in Tokyo, Sapporo, Fukuoka, Osaka, and Kyoto who arranged many sessions for me with people from all walks of life. I learned a great deal about Japanese public opinion from these contacts. I wish to thank Kenneth Yates and Professor Iwashima Hisao in particular for making my stay in Japan both interesting and instructive.

A number of individuals took time off to read my manuscript and offer helpful suggestions. I am particularly grateful to Dr. Yu Chin-O and Dr. Robert T. Oliver, participants in the early stages of negotiations, who read the manuscript and shared their thoughts with me. Se-Jin Kim, astute scholar who was then the Korean Consul-General in New York, rendered me similar help, and I mourn his untimely death. I am also grateful to Professors Seki Hiroharu, Robert A. Scalapino, Claude A. Buss, Won-Mo Dong, Young C. Kim, Chae-Jin Lee, and George Ginsburgs for their criticism and advice. Members of the Columbia Seminar on Korea read and commented on Chapter 6. I am especially indebted to Professors Gary Ledyard and Gregory Henderson for their detailed comments on that chapter. My students, Yong-Ho Kim and Chat Blakeman, served as in-house critics. They also rendered yeoman's service, for Chat Blakeman edited the manuscript and Yong-Ho Kim did library research. My thanks also go to Inwon Choue and Jonathan Nathanson for their research assistance.

As always, I had to turn to Nancy Chung at the University of Pennsylvania Library for procuring the necessary materials, and she was generous with help. I also relied on Mr. Kim Sung-Ha at Harvard-Yenching Library for materials unavailable at my university.

Last, but not least, I am grateful to Tina Chen and Marla Chazin for typing numerous versions of the manuscript. I must also acknowledge the help of Carl and Lloyd Collander, and of my children, Sharon (Youngnan), Gina (Chin-a), and Roger (Chulho). They helped me to enter the computer age. Without their help, the project would have taken much longer than it did. I salute Ms. Sue E. Factor at the Hoover Institution Press for her skillful editing of the final manuscript.

To all these individuals and to many others who must remain unnamed, I offer my heartfelt thanks.

I dedicate this work to Professor Hatada Takashi of Tokyo Metropolitan University and Dr. Key P. Yang of the Library of Congress, in appreciation for their lifelong efforts to promote Korean studies in Japan and the United States. As the footnotes to this work will show, Professor Hatada has been prodigious in producing studies on Korea and the Japanese attitude toward Korea. Dr. Yang has been a teacher and guide to me and many of my colleagues in the United States. I do hope that this work is worthy of their distinguished names.

1

Legacies of the Colonial Era

The relationship between Japan and Korea is a paradoxical one. Physically, the two countries are separated only by a small body of water. The inhabitants of the Japanese archipelago came into contact with Asian continental culture via Korea long before the political entities known as Japan and Korea emerged, and the two countries maintain ties today. They share thinking and behavior patterns that stem from the same cultural heritage. Each can learn the other's language without much strain because substantial portions of Japanese and Korean are based on Chinese, and the two languages share the same syntax. (Strangely, Chinese syntax is different from that of Japanese and Korean.) All these factors have led Japan to emerge as South Korea's largest trading partner since 1966. Since that year, South Korea has alternated between the second and fourth positions on the list of countries importing Japanese products. Japanese trade with North Korea has also been steadily increasing.

Yet numerous and important negative factors plague Japanese-Korean relations. Although Japanese and Koreans can form lasting friendships and working relationships at the individual level, there is no sense of genuine friendship between the two peoples at the collective or societal level. Most Japanese are disdainful and contemptuous of Korea, do not understand and are insensitive toward the feelings of the Koreans, and simply do not wish to be involved with anything related to Korea, unless, of course, there are specific reasons for doing so.[1]

The Koreans, on their part, admire the Japanese ability to organize and accomplish important objectives, but this is also a cause for apprehension, since Japan once dominated Korea and imposed a harsh rule over the Koreans. Not only are the Japanese unrepentant, but also many are proud of their "accomplishments" in Korea. They do not understand the feelings of the Koreans and have no interest in doing so. The Japanese are indeed "economic animals" to the Koreans; the only interest Japan has in Korea is to aggrandize itself by exploiting whatever opportunity Korea provides.[2]

Not surprisingly, there is deep-seated distrust on both sides of the strait. In public opinion polls the Japanese consistently list Korea among their least-liked countries, and Koreans similarly place Japan near the bottom of their list. These attitudes and values sometimes operate in tandem and sometimes separately. Between 1948 and 1960, when President Syngman Rhee ruled South Korea, negative attitudes toward Japan prevailed. Between 1960 and 1973, through the brief democratic interlude and the first stage of General (and later President) Park Chung Hee's rule, more positive factors played a dominant role. Since 1973, the situation has been more complex, and both positive and negative factors have influenced the course of events.

Japanese-Korean relations and the attitudes of each country toward the other have been changing, just as relations among all nations vary according to alterations in internal and external environments. But memories often weigh as heavily as prevailing political and economic factors in contemporary decisionmaking. As demonstrated by the prolonged Arab-Israeli conflict, historical factors can play a far more important role than present-day environmental factors. Indeed, as we shall see in Chapter 2, Japanese–South Korean relations between 1951 and 1960 were completely dominated by a heated controversy over the record of Japanese rule in Korea between 1910 and 1945. Nor was the controversy resolved after 1960. Many events since, including the textbook controversy of 1982, clearly show how powerfully the memories of the colonial era continue to affect Japanese-Korean relations. Anyone interested in Japanese-Korean relations, therefore, must have an understanding of the contrasting Japanese and Korean perspectives on the colonial era.

Being in such close proximity, the peoples of Japan and Korea have had contacts since ancient times. Although the relationship between the Japanese and Korean kingdoms in the first millennium was not always intense, cultural and economic interaction continued through the centuries. After Tokugawa Ieyasu unified Japan in 1603 and adopted neo-Confucianism as the official philosophy (as the Yi dynasty had done in Korea two centuries earlier), the two countries maintained close diplomatic and cultural ties.

The relationship began to change in the late eighteenth century, when Korea waned and Japan prospered. The menace from Western nations brought a major political upheaval in Japan that culminated in the Meiji Restoration of 1868 and the subsequent adoption of an expansionist policy toward the continent. Japan successfully challenged China's supremacy in the Orient by defeating it in 1895; ten years later, Japan routed tsarist Russia, which had been expanding steadily southward to East Asia, intent on establishing Manchuria as a Russian colony. Having consolidated its position in the international arena by concluding an alliance with Great Britain in 1903, Japan turned the Korean kingdom into a protectorate in 1905 and annexed Korea as a colony in 1910. The colonial period lasted until 1945, when Japan was defeated by the Allied powers, who decided that Japan should lose all territories it had acquired since 1895.

Why did Koreans in the 1950s and 1960s remember the colonial period (1910–1945) with such bitterness? Why do such memories persist among a significant portion of the Korean population today and affect contemporary attitudes toward Japan?

The very fact that Japan had turned Korea into a colony was humiliating. Korea had been the most Confucian of East Asian countries outside the Chinese heartland; the Korean king and his courtiers honored the Ming dynasty (1368–1644) well into the eighteenth century, long after Ming loyalists had all but disappeared in China.[3] The Confucian cosmology and all it implied, including the relationship between states, was sacrosanct to the Koreans, and they had a fresh memory of being sought after by Japan for their superior Confucian learning. Korea had watched with repugnance the Japanese attempt to emulate the West, taking it as proof of Japanese perfidy against the very essence of Eastern culture and tradition.[4] When the Japanese applied the strength they had gained by learning Western technology to the conquest of Korea, the Koreans could not have been more humiliated.

But Koreans today understand the rules of power politics. Although they do not condone the Japanese expansionist policy that led to the takeover of Korea in 1910, they do question the wisdom of their ancestors for being ignorant about Japan and for not preparing against Japanese designs.⁵ Many reformists had warned of impending doom in the late nineteenth century, but the old elites, weighed down by centuries-old tradition, turned their backs and failed to rejuvenate the country.

Nonetheless, 36 years of Japanese rule left bitter memories. By the time the Japanese annexed Korea in 1910, the Japanese were so thoroughly convinced of their superiority over the Koreans that they found it only natural to apply their typical behavior pattern toward inferiors. Japanese treatment of those they considered inferior was brutal. Japan had long been a hierarchically oriented society, just as Korea had been. Rank and status strictly governed the behavior of individuals. Fukuzawa Yukichi, one of the most renowned Japanese intellectuals of the Meiji era (1868–1911), described the situation in 1874 in his celebrated book, *An Outline of the Theory of Civilization*:

> When we see a minor official brandishing his authority over some commoner we might think he is a very powerful person. But let this same official meet someone higher in the bureaucracy and he will be subjected to even worse oppression from his superior than he dealt out to the commoner. When some minor provincial official summons a village headman to speak to him, his overbearing attitude is hateful indeed. But when this minor official deals with his own superior, the scene would stir our pity. And though the way the village headman is roundly castigated by the minor official may elicit our sympathy, when we see him go back and just as roundly castigate the men under him he will earn our hatred. A is oppressed by B, B in turn is controlled by C; in this way there is an unending cycle of pressures and controls. Truly an amazing phenomenon indeed!⁶

After Japan annexed Korea in 1910 and imposed colonial rule, the Japanese naturally regarded the Koreans as inferiors, treating them with the same "overbearing" and "hateful" attitude they displayed toward inferiors within Japan. After all, it was not very many years after Fukuzawa wrote his account that Japan conquered Korea. Along with politicians and soldiers, the Japanese empire sent to Korea its impoverished villagers, who for centuries had been "castigated, pressured, and controlled" by their headmen, provincial officials, and the samurai. Now it was their turn to become the masters, to "castigate, control, and pressure" the newly conquered people.

What mattered most to the Koreans, however, was Japanese colonial policy. The officially enunciated policy of the Japanese emperor was to treat the newly acquired subjects on an equal basis with the

Japanese, but this ideal was not translated into action. Indeed, except for a brief period in the 1920s, Japanese rule over Korea was entrusted to a series of army generals, who ruled Korea with an iron hand. Toward the end of its rule, Japan attempted to obliterate not only the Korean identity but also the Korean language, and the Japanese used Koreans as virtual slave laborers in their struggle to win an unwinnable war. Although Japan touted its success in turning an uncivilized and underdeveloped Korea into a modern economy, the livelihood of Koreans significantly deteriorated under the two-layered economic system, which had one standard for the Japanese and another for the Koreans. I shall explore these events in some detail.

THE INITIAL STAGE

The first governor-general, Terauchi Masatake, who had been the minister of the army at the time of his assignment to Korea, set the harsh tone of Japanese rule, patterned after the policies of the Russian empire in Poland.[7] He dissolved all political organizations; prohibited all meetings and speeches; abolished all Korean newspapers; and confiscated all types of arms, including the swords and knives used by hunters. Local police chiefs, former members of the Japanese army gendarmerie, were given authority to render summary judgments. Terauchi's harsh rule led a contemporary Japanese observer to conclude that "the entire Korean peninsula was turned into a military camp" and his "extreme military dictatorship gave the impression that Korea had returned to the medieval authoritarian regime."[8] Japan at this time was no haven for liberalism, but the extent of political control in Korea was at its extreme.

Determined to eliminate all anti-Japanese thoughts at once, the governor-general and his aide fabricated a charge against Korean Christian leaders. The charge was that they had attempted to assassinate Terauchi. Some 700 Koreans were arrested, and 123 of them were subjected to more than a year of tortures too grim to describe.[9]

This reign of terror forced numerous members of the Korean elites into exile and deepened Korean animosity toward Japan. Syngman Rhee, for example, left the country in 1912. He had returned to Korea two years before with a doctorate from Princeton University and had served as an organizer, teacher, and evangelist at the Seoul YMCA. Kim Kyu-sik, also American-educated, left Korea in 1913 after pursuing a religious and educational career in Seoul. He had returned to Korea in 1904, fully aware that a Japanese victory in the impending war between Japan and Russia (1904–05) would reduce Korea to a Japanese colony. Like many other Koreans of that era, these two had hoped that the Japanese would be more humane than the tsarists. But the Japanese clearly failed the test. Many other Koreans went into self-imposed exile during the same period and spearheaded the nationalist movement abroad.

The unabashed reign of terror intensified the longing for Korean independence and led eventually to the rise of the Korean multitude (one million, according to the Japanese; two million, according to Koreans) in a nationwide demonstration for independence in March 1919. The surprised Japanese government suppressed the Koreans with a brutal force and cruelty far exceeding the limits of civilized peoples. Cold statistics reveal only a small part of the grisly scene: the Japanese army gendarmerie reported 553 Koreans killed and 1,409 injured within the first month of the uprising. Korean sources reported as many as 7,645 killed and 45,562 injured during a twelve-month period after March 1919.[10] March 1, the day the organizers of the demonstrations read their declaration of independence and thus launched the nationwide campaign, is celebrated in Korea as one of two major national holidays, the other being August 15, the day on which Korea was liberated from Japan. Every Korean child of succeeding generations has been drilled in tales of the courage and horror of this period. The March First movement has been the subject of books, articles, and motion pictures.

International pressure and changes in Japanese domestic politics led Japan to implement a more moderate rule in Korea in the 1920s. Koreans were allowed considerable latitude in organizing political groups, publishing Korean-language newspapers, organizing labor unions, and engaging in other sociopolitical activities. The colonial government also began to employ Koreans, appointing some to middle-ranking bureaucratic positions such as the prefectural governorships.

This was the period when political parties dominated Japanese politics and liberalism was in ascendance. This was also the period when an admiral rather than a general was appointed governor-general in Korea. But that decade ended with a worldwide depression that brought a drastic change in Japanese politics and Japanese policy toward Korea. Military leaders denounced the conciliatory or moderate foreign policy pursued by party politicians and launched an expansionist policy, beginning with the takeover of Manchuria in

1931. The colonial police began to impose more and more restrictions on the Koreans.

THE FINAL STAGE

Koreans remember most vividly the last phase of Japanese rule, after 1937, when Japan embarked on the conquest of China proper and eventually on a war against the United States and its allies. Korea was to serve as the "forward logistical base" in the task of Japanese expansion, together with another colony in the north, Manchuria. In preparation for the task, the military leaders assigned to Korea General Minami Jirō, who had been the minister of the army when the Japanese took over Manchuria in 1931 and had later served as commander of the Japanese army in Manchuria, known as the Kwantung (or the Kantō) Army.

The logic of the Japanese military leaders was that, in order to be self-sufficient and to rid Asia of Western control, Japan had to expand not only into Manchuria and China proper but also into Southeast Asia. The great mission ahead required that Korea and Manchuria become a combined logistical and industrial depot that would supply whatever was required for Japanese military efforts. At the same time, it was necessary for Korea to produce manpower to supplement that of Japan. Japan's 1935 population of 69 million was simply not adequate. If the 22 million Koreans could be assimilated as Japanese, they could be effectively employed in the tasks ahead. The Japanese hoped the Koreans could be assimilated as easily as the Okinawans had been several decades earlier. This was a revolutionary decision: heretofore, Korea had served only as a source of rice and mineral resources, a market for Japanese industrial goods, and lebensraum for the impoverished Japanese farmers. Although Koreans were legally Japanese subjects and some had been provided with a Japanese education, they had been taught both Japanese and Korean, and their identity had largely been left untouched. A survey conducted by the colonial government at the end of 1936 showed that only 0.8 percent of the Koreans understood Japanese.[11]

Japanization of the Koreans, of course, meant the eradication of the factors that distinguished the Koreans from the Japanese, that is, the Korean language and Korean surnames. If the Koreans spoke nothing but Japanese and had Japanese-sounding names, they would no longer maintain their identity and would be integrated as Japanese. Of course, the Koreans must be indoctrinated to believe that they truly were Japanese. If these efforts were successful, Koreans could be effectively mobilized for the holy mission of the Japanese empire. Had not the multitude of Korean immigrants to Japan in antiquity been effectively assimilated as Japanese? Could anyone distinguish their descendants from the other Japanese?[12] Why not apply the same formula for all the Koreans?

It was with these aims and assumptions that the colonial regime decided to redouble its effort to increase the number of Korean children receiving primary education. It was also for the purpose of indoctrination that the Government-General issued in October 1937 the "Oath of Imperial Subjects," a three-sentence oath that began "We are the subjects of the great Japanese empire." The oath was to be repeated by all schoolchildren daily and by all adults twice a month or more. A massive indoctrination campaign for "the general mobilization of national spirit" was launched by the colonial regime to supplement these basic measures.[13]

Colonial Policy on the Korean Language

Nowhere was Japanese policy toward Korea better illustrated than in its language policy. In his statement proclaiming Imperial Order Number 103, the New Korean Education Ordinance, on March 4, 1938, General Minami announced the "abolition of distinction between those who regularly use the national language [that is, the Japanese] and those who do not," thus "opening the way" for both Japanese and Koreans to receive an equal education under the same law. But this high-sounding statement actually meant that henceforth the Korean language would not be taught in schools and children would be punished for the use of the Korean language both at school and in their homes. Intensive efforts were also made to teach Japanese to Korean adults and, by the end of 1939, 12.2 percent of them had no difficulty in speaking Japanese; an additional 11.6 percent either spoke or understood Japanese with some difficulty.[14] This was enough for the colonial government to abolish Korean-language newspapers that year.

To a government that was determined to erase the Korean language, even scholars studying the Korean language were subversive. In 1942, the police arrested 35 members of the Korean Linguistic Society, including many of Korea's leading scholars and intellectuals of the time. They were charged with sedition and subjected to the most gruesome tortures for more than two years; two of them died. Their crime was to support the compilation of a Korean-language dictionary with the alleged intent of "advancing and developing the Korean culture, heightening Korean national consciousness, and preparing for Korean independence."[15]

The eradication of the Korean language, which had evolved through millennia, obviously meant little to those colonial elites who took pride in their achievements in Korea and the benefits they thought they had brought to Korea. These elites fortified themselves with their beliefs that Japan had ruled Korea in antiquity (a subject I shall return to later in Chapter 6) and that Japanese civilization was far superior to that of Korea. They must have convinced themselves that Korean interests would be better served if Koreans were completely assimilated as Japanese. To the Koreans, however, to lose their own language was to lose their soul. Language was one of the key elements that bound Koreans together as a nation, and they had clung to it in spite of numerous foreign invasions and occupations in the past. With the loss of the language, their whole civilization would be lost. Korea, it should be added, is a small country with a single language; Koreans did not need the language of an imperial power to communicate among themselves.

Colonial Policy on Korean Surnames

The 1939 colonial command to change monosyllabic Korean names to multisyllabic Japanese-sounding names was no less epochal. Korea was one of the few countries in the world where not only was ancestor worship an important part of life, but genealogical records had been meticulously kept and valued. Family and clan ties determined not only socioeconomic status but also who one's friends and enemies would be. Surname and clan origins were sources of pride, particularly for the *yangban* or gentry. Hence, the governor-general's demands forced all Koreans to commit a most unfilial act— denying their ancestors by assuming strange-sounding and arbitrary foreign names that bore no relationship to the past. The Koreans, in effect, were forced to break the first commandment of their culture by men from a neighboring East Asian country that Koreans had taught to honor the family and ancestors. The day of registration of a new Japanese name with the authorities was a day of mourning and sorrow for the majority of Koreans.[16] But the governor-general's edict—"permitting" the Koreans to adopt Japanese surnames—

could not be defied without risk of grave consequences. The government not only had police power but also all power over jobs, food rations, and children's education.

Imposition of Shintoism

General Minami demanded yet more. As with language, his regime attempted to force Japanese religion onto the Koreans. Koreans had to recite the "Oath of Imperial Subjects," bow daily to the east toward the imperial palace, and confirm their faith in the Japanese national polity (*kokutai*) by worshiping in Shinto shrines. Obeisance at Shinto shrines was given particular significance because Shinto worship and loyalty to the emperor were one and the same under the concept of kokutai. The national basis of Japan was found in the divine origins of the country and of the imperial household; Shinto shrines were dedicated to the divine founder and ancestor of the emperor. Therefore, as the colonial government decided to Japanize the Koreans, it redoubled its efforts to increase the number of major shrines (*jinja*) and minor shrines (*jinshi*). The number of major shrines thus increased from 51 in 1931 to 63 in 1942. Minor shrines in towns and villages increased from 186 in 1931 to 828 in 1942. Since 1936, not only were schoolchildren and college students taken to Shinto shrines for their regular monthly worship and on other occasions, but adults also were instructed to observe the bimonthly Patriotic Days by marching to the shrines in throngs.[17]

To most of the Korean public, the government order was simply another nuisance, just like the numerous "spiritual mobilization lectures" they had to endure. As the public prosecutors' bureau observed in 1938: "It is also very doubtful that those who go to worship in Shinto shrines and pray for the victory of the imperial army are doing it from their own hearts. These actions are taken because of stern instructions from the authorities or coercion of public opinion."[18] Obeisance to the Shinto shrines was an empty ritual for adults; for schoolchildren it was little more than an outing from classrooms.

But the requirement of worship at Shinto shrines met with a bitter opposition from the country's 450,000 Christians, which was to leave a deep scar, not only between Japan and Korea but also among the Koreans themselves. Obeisance at Shinto shrines came into direct conflict with the first commandment for the Christians, "Thou shalt have no other gods before me." Although there were fewer than 500,000 Christians in Korea in the mid-1930s (448,794 in 1935 and

468,514 in 1937, according to the Japanese police), they happened to be the most active, best organized, and most vocal of the religious groups.[19] The issue would have aroused intense emotions even if it had been a confrontation between church and state among the same people. But in Korea the controversy was between the Japanese colonial regime and Korean Christians, supported by most of the foreign missionaries.

Although this was primarily a religious issue, it had clear political overtones. I have already alluded to the alleged plot to assassinate General Terauchi in 1911. That charge had been advanced against more than one hundred Christian leaders in northwestern Korea because the colonial regime regarded Korean Christians and Western missionaries as the most undesirable enemies of colonialism. Indeed, in 1919, Christian leaders took a leading role in organizing the nationwide March First movement for independence that forced the Japanese government to moderate its colonial policies. The Christian church was clearly supporting the meek, the downtrodden, and the humiliated. Christianity offered a refuge and a promise for a better future, including God's judgment against the wicked. The Japanese had the upper hand in this ephemeral world, but they could not break the spirit of the Korean Christians, who believed that the day of judgment was near. For these and other reasons, the number of Korean converts continued to grow, and the group led by missionaries from the Northern Presbyterian Church of the USA grew the fastest. The number of converts belonging to that group rose from 93,000 in 1932 to 177,000 in 1935, continuing the growth to 203,000 in 1937. This group operated a college and eight secondary schools. The Southern Presbyterians had a much smaller following (36,344 in 1937), but they also operated a middle school and nine primary schools.[20] Small wonder that the colonial government decided to challenge the Presbyterians first.

The government, of course, won the match, and, by February 1938, all the educational institutions operated by the Presbyterians were closed. Rather than compromise with the government and take pupils to the shrines, the Presbyterians, who constituted 60 percent of the entire Christian population, supported the decision to close the schools. But, in September of the same year, the Korean Presbyterian General Assembly was forced to pass a resolution supporting the government view that obeisance at Shinto shrines was not a religious but a patriotic act and stating that the assembly supported such obeisance. The government turned away assembly delegates who would have opposed the resolution; uniformed police officers sitting on the platform openly interfered with missionaries who wished to present opposing viewpoints. Others at the assembly meeting, both ministers and elders, were clearly intimidated. But, subsequently, those opposing the government policy engaged in an anti–shrine worship movement, resulting in the imprisonment of seventy ministers and two thousand other Christians. Fifty ministers died in prison because of the shrine issue, and two hundred churches were closed down.[21]

The effect of the shrine issue on Korean emotions was far-reaching, for it resulted in the shutdown of private schools that had played a significant role in Korean education. No alumnus of a closed school could have been indifferent. The controversy also resulted in the imprisonment of a large number of Christian leaders and the martyrdom of many, adding sparks to the smoldering fire of resentment against Japanese rulers. In the face of these events, even those who had decided to accommodate the colonial power to retain the existence of the churches could not have been happy with the situation, particularly after the Japanese police regularly assigned detectives to monitor prayers and sermons, often ordering preachers to stop their sermons because of their subversive content. Whether they spent the years after 1938 in jail or not, Korean Christians could not help but bemoan the cross they were forced to bear or to resent the Japanese who caused so much anguish. The colonial regime that had regarded the Korean Christian church as the "fortress of Korean nationalism" may have found it necessary to bring the church under submission, but its actions inflicted as deep a scar upon Japanese-Korean relations as had Toyotomi Hideyoshi's invasion in the sixteenth century.[22]

The wounds made by the shrine issue have been kept open because of the split between Korean Christians after the liberation. The followers of martyrs were understandably bitter toward those who had transgressed against the first commandment by accommodating the Japanese persecutors. In the eyes of the imprisoned group, some of those who had spoken in favor of the assembly resolution of 1938 were no less vile than the five cabinet ministers of the old Korean kingdom who had signed away Korea's sovereignty in 1910. The Korean Christian church, which has been growing in leaps and bounds since the liberation in 1945—the number of Christians in South Korea alone was estimated at 8.5 million (1.3 million Catholics, 7.2 million Protestants) at the end of 1980—is still living in the shadow of the Shinto shrine issue. It should be noted that, although the Christians constitute a minority in terms of numbers, they are an important moral force in Korea.

Conscription of Koreans

The aim of Japan's assimilation policy, as noted earlier, was to use the Koreans in Japan's pursuit of expansion abroad, and the need to do so emerged in short order. As the war against China stretched on and casualties mounted, more and more Japanese youth were inducted into the army. Japan also feared a war against the Soviet Union after 1938, and the Japanese army in Manchuria (the Kwantung Army or Kantō-gun) expanded from three divisions in 1936 to nine in 1939. The decision to invade Indochina and the other countries of Southeast Asia in 1940 forced Japan to recruit every able-bodied man of draft age from Japanese farms, factories, and mines. Even older veterans were called up. In the meantime, the need for mineral and industrial products rose rapidly as the war front expanded.

The resulting manpower shortage was alleviated by Koreans both in the armed forces and in the labor market. The recruitment of Koreans for the armed forces proceeded cautiously from its inception in 1938, when a small number (406) were inducted under the Special Volunteer Enlistment system instituted in April of that year. The number of recruits gradually increased to 6,300 in 1943 when the system was abolished because of the implementation of the universal draft system.[23] By this time many more recruits were needed, as Japan had embarked on the war against the United States.

The draft system was announced in May 1942, but, because one-half of those reaching the age of twenty (11 of 22 million) had not received any primary education and did not speak Japanese, it was necessary to institute a crash program to teach the language. Even Japanese officials in Korea had not anticipated the implementation of the draft system before the compulsory education system went into effect in 1946, but the needs of the war were too immediate to permit postponement.[24] By July 1944, 206,057 Koreans of age twenty had gone through physical examinations. We have no figures on how many men were actually inducted, but, by the end of the Second World War, there were 186,680 Koreans in the Japanese army and 22,299 in the navy.[25] These men had been dispersed all over the Japanese war fronts.

Even more sweeping, however, was the conscription of Koreans for mines and factories in Japan and for naval construction projects and other tasks in the South Pacific. Mobilization of Korean workers for Japanese industries and mines went through three stages. Between September 1939 and January 1942, Japanese entrepreneurs received government permission to mobilize Korean workers on their own. But, as the need for Korean laborers mounted in February 1942, the year after Pearl Harbor, the colonial government directly recruited Korean workers through its administrative hierarchy, with quotas assigned to various units.

Even this system did not satisfy Japanese needs, and, in September 1944, the government instituted the compulsory labor mobilization system known as *chōyō seido*, patterned after the military draft system (*chōhei seido*). The effects of these policies can be seen from Tables 1 and 2: 40,000 to 60,000 Koreans went to Japan between 1939 and 1941, and their number doubled between 1942 and 1944. The situation became much more serious between 1944 and 1945. Whether one accepts the figures presented in Table 1, which indicate the mobilization of over 300,000 Koreans in both 1944 and 1945, or in Table 2, which reports the entry of over 500,000 Koreans to Japan for each of these years, there is no doubt that massive induction of Korean laborers took place. It should be noted that during the war years the quotas for each annual mobilization plan far exceeded the actual number of workers supplied, which suggests the kinds of pressure applied at each level of the administrative hierarchy for conscription. The nature of assignments given to these workers in Japan can be seen from a report submitted by the Korean Government-General to the Eighty-fifth Imperial Diet in August 1944:

> A great number of Korean laborers have been dispatched every year since 1939 to Japan and Southeast Asia following the national mobilization plan. These workers have been assigned to mines and industries and construction projects ... they have proven to be equal to Japanese workers in their work and, *especially in heavy* [muscular] *work, high-temperature projects, and in underground labor,* they produced good results because of their excellent physique.[26] (Italics added.)

The figures presented in Tables 1 and 2 do not include Korean laborers conscripted especially for the Japanese army and navy. Beginning in 1941, the navy required a large number of Koreans for building naval facilities in the South Pacific. The army also demanded Koreans to serve as guards for American and British prisoners of war (3,223 as of August 1944) and to perform other duties.

The number of Koreans mobilized specifically for the Japanese army and navy until August 1944 is presented in Table 3. Undoubtedly the number increased even more during the next twelve months. It is possible that some of these numbers were women.

Thus, by the end of the Second World War, Japan had mobilized approximately two million Koreans for hard labor in Japan, Sakhalin, and the South Pacific. Since there were 4.5 million Korean households as of 1942, approximately one out of every two households sent a male worker to the Japanese mines or factories. In addition, millions were mobilized for the mines and factories in Korea. Table 2 mentions "freely mobilized laborers" for Japan for 1944 and 1945, evidently indicating those mobilized by Japanese industries. But, between 1938 and 1940, the colonial government had issued various ordinances prohibiting the free movement of labor. The ordinance of August 1938 placed the employment of all technicians under government control, and an ordinance issued in August 1939 restricted the movement of those already employed by industries. Another ordinance issued in September 1940 placed the employment of males between 12 and 30 and females between 12 and 20 under government control.[27] Labor was scarce, and the government exercised stringent control to assign available labor to the places it deemed most important. "Free mobilization of labor" simply did not exist in Korea after 1940.

I have already mentioned the kinds of work assigned to these Korean laborers. The treatment accorded them by their Japanese hosts is not difficult to imagine. Japan was at war and was suffering from severe shortages of food and other materials. Even under normal circumstances, the sudden influx of thousands of foreign workers would have strained housing facilities and food supplies. These workers were not only a subject people despised as inferiors, but also most of them had little, if any, education and spoke no Japanese. They also had no experience in mines, factories, or other nonagricultural positions. The only reason they were taken to Japan was to produce the vital materials Japan needed to fight a war that it had increasingly less prospect of winning.

Such records as have been collected about the experience of these conscripted workers do not make pleasant reading. The Korean workers were essentially slaves, huddled into what amounted to concentration camps guarded constantly by Japanese men and dogs, and working long hours under abusive Japanese supervisors, with little pay and little food. These conditions explain the large number of escapees, cited in Table 2. The same table also lists a large number of

TABLE 1   KOREAN WORKERS MOBILIZED FOR JAPANESE INDUSTRY, 1939–1945

Industry	1939		1940		1941		1942	
	Source 1	Source 2[a]	Source 1	Source 2[b]	Source 1	Source 2[c]	Source 1	Source 2[d]
Coal mines	24,279	34,659	35,441	38,176	32,415	39,819	78,660	78,083
Metal mines	5,042	5,787	8,069	9,081	8,942	9,416	9,240	7,632
Civil engineering and construction	9,479	12,674	9,898	9,249	9,563	10,965	18,130	18,929
Stevedoring and transportation	—	—	—	—	—	—	—	—
Factories and other	—	—	1,546	2,892	2,672	3,898	15,290	13,207
Total	38,800	53,120	54,954	59,398	53,592	64,098	121,320	117,851
Mobilization plan	—	85,000	—	97,300	—	100,000	—	130,000

Industry	1943 Source 1	1943 Source 2[e]	1944 Source 1	1944 Source 2[f]	1945 Source 1[g]	1945 Source 2[h]
Coal mines	77,850	68,370	108,350	83,859	136,810	121,574
Metal mines	17,075	13,763	30,900	21,442	34,060	22,430
Civil engineering and construction	34,350	31,611	64,827	24,376	29,642	34,584
Stevedoring and transportation	—	—	23,820	—	15,333	—
Factories and other	19,455	14,606	151,850	157,795	114,044	86,794
Total	148,730	128,350	379,747	287,472	329,889	265,382
Mobilization plan	—	155,000	—	326,000		

[a]Includes 3,301 for Sakhalin.

[b]Includes 2,605 for Sakhalin and 814 for Southeast Asia.

[c]Includes 1,451 for Sakhalin and 1,781 for Southeast Asia.

[d]Includes 5,945 for Sakhalin and 2,083 for Southeast Asia.

[e]Includes 2,911 for Sakhalin and 2,083 for Southeast Asia.

[f]For this year, no information concerning the Koreans in Sakhalin and Southeast Asia was provided. Unlike other years, figures provided by sources 1 and 2 are widely apart. See Table 2 for another set of figures.

[g]As of March 1945.

[h]As of August 1945.

SOURCE: (1) Chosōn kyōgje t'ongge yoram (Synopsis of Korean Economic Statistics), 1949, p. 134, based on study materials (Chōsa shiryo) of Kō-sei-shō (Ministry of Welfare, Japan). (2) Tsuboe Senji, Zai-Nihon Chōsenjin no gaikyō (General Condition of the Koreans in Japan) (Tokyo, 1965), pp. 19–20, based on Dai hachijū rokukai gikai setsumei shiryō (Explanatory Materials for the Eighty-Sixth Imperial Diet) (Seoul, 1945), and Nihonjin no kaigai katsudō ni kansuru rekishiteki chōsa: Senji to Chōsen tōchi (Historical Study of the Japanese Abroad: The Wartime and Governance of Korea), 1944 and 1945. Tsuboe says that there are some discrepancies between the two sources without providing the details.

TABLE 2 KOREAN WORKERS MOBILIZED FOR JAPAN, 1944–1945

	1944			1945[a]		
	Conscripted labor	Freely mobilized labor	Total	Conscripted labor	Freely mobilized labor	Total
Approved quota	459,939	195,544	655,483	516,301	195,204	711,505
Entered Japan	402,867	148,807	551,674	455,880	148,549	604,429
Total decrease	165,336[b]	127,007[b]	292,343[b]	199,493[b]	129,074[b]	328,567[b]
Returned after fulfilling contract	13,957	31,912	45,869	19,663	32,445	52,108
Returned for defects[c]	7,481	7,247	14,728	8,664	7,137	15,801
Escapees	125,048	74,232[d]	199,280	148,316	78,181	226,497
Other	25,426	18,370	43,796	30,012	16,294	46,306
At work	244,106	26,554	270,660	264,030	24,458	288,488

[a] The figures for 1945 are as of the end of March.

[b] The total is larger than the sum of the subdivisions listed here.

[c] "Returned for defects" could mean the Koreans were returned for health reasons, physical defects, or injuries.

[d] Typographical error in the original was corrected.

SOURCE: Tsuboe Senji, Zai Nihon Chōsenjin no gaikyō (General Condition of the Koreans in Japan) (Tokyo, 1965), pp. 20–21, based on an unidentified document of Naimushō, Keihokyoku (Ministry of Home Affairs, Police and Security Bureau).

TABLE 3   KOREAN WORKERS CONSCRIPTED FOR THE JAPANESE ARMY AND NAVY, 1939–1944

Year	Japan	Korea	Manchuria	China	Southeast Asia	Total
1939	—	—	145	—	—	145
1940	65	—	656	25	—	746
1941	10,291	1,085	284	13	9,249	20,922
1942	8,042	1,903	293	50	16,294	26,582
1943	7,032	2,624	390	16	5,242	15,304
1944[a]	12,097	15,415	1,617	260	4,833	34,222
Total	37,527	21,027	3,385	364	35,618	97,921

[a]The figures for 1944 are as of August 22, 1944.

SOURCE: Chōsen Sōtokufu (Korean Government-General), *Dai hachijūgokai Teikoku Gikai setsumei shiryō* (Explanatory Material for the Eighty-fifth Imperial Diet), reprinted in "Taiheiyōsen ka shūmatsuki Chōsen no chisei" (Administration of Korea During the Pacific War: The Last Period), *Chōsen kindai shiryō: Chōsen Sōtokufu kankei jyūyō bunsho senshū* (Historical Materials on Modern Korea: Principal Documents of the Korean Government-General), ed. Kondō Kenichi (Tokyo, 1961), no. 2, p. 156.

workers lost by reasons other than escape or return to Korea. Contemporary accounts reveal frequent and large-scale accidents—particularly in mines—and murder and suicide. There is no way to determine how many Koreans died of consumption, hunger, accidents, or simple murder. A Korean scholar in Japan ascertained the death of 2,175 Koreans in Japanese mines between 1943 and 1945. Many also became casualties of war. As of August 1944, 2,142 Korean laborers were reported killed and 735 missing in the South Pacific.[28] Undoubtedly, many more suffered a similar fate as General MacArthur's forces pounded Japanese fortifications toward the end of the Pacific war. Many of those assigned to guard American and British prisoners were later tried and convicted by the Allied forces as war criminals. Some 40,000 were detained on Sakhalin Island by the Soviet Union, never to be allowed to return home. Until the late 1970s, the Japanese government made no serious attempt to return these unfortunate Koreans to their original homes in Korea.[29]

Japanese conscription, particularly labor conscription, touched at least half of the Korean households and severely affected the Korean image of the Japanese rule in Korea. Undoubtedly, those who were fortunate enough to survive the ordeal and return home after August 1945 recounted their tales of inhuman suffering.

Many of the survivors, however, could not openly relate their experiences. These were the young women inducted into what was called Joshi Teishin-tai, literally, Women's Submit Body Units. Between 1943 and 1945 the colonial government recruited some 200,000 Korean women between the ages of 12 and 40, according to one estimate. Some 50,000 to 70,000 of them were assigned to various war fronts as prostitutes.[30] Those Koreans who remained in Korea suffered from diminishing food rations and ever-tightening government control, but those who were conscripted for the war abroad had visited a living hell.

The Economic Effect of Japanese Colonial Rule

Japan had touted economic progress in Korea, and, indeed, Japan vastly altered Korea's landscape by building numerous industrial complexes. But the overall effect of Japanese development on the Koreans was negative. Landownership among Koreans substantially decreased,[31] those classified as "the poor and indigent" increased (from 11.2 percent of the total population in 1926 to 25.5 percent in 1937),[32] the number and proportion of tenant farmers or sharecroppers among farmers increased (from 35.2 percent in 1914 to 53.8 percent in 1942),[33] and per capita consumption of food grains declined (from 2.0 koku in the 1910s to the 1.6 koku mark in the 1930s, and eventually to 1.2 koku between 1943 and 1945).[34] Industry was in the hands of the Japanese; the Koreans' share of total industrial capital in Korea in 1942 was only 1.5 percent of the total.[35] Government policy, differential interest rates for the two peoples, and other factors simply made it impossible for the Koreans to make headway in their own land.

The Conflict in Japanese and Korean Perspectives

Although the colonial government had succeeded in converting a significant number of Koreans into loyal subjects of the emperor, many others remained defiant. The dichotomy of Japanese and Korean views regarding the status of Koreans under Japanese rule was clearly displayed in 1936, when two Korean athletes, Son Ki-jŏng and Nam Sŭng-yong, won the first and third places, respectively, in the marathon at the Berlin Olympic Games. Even though the Japanese government treated their feat as a victory of the Japanese Olympic team of which the two were members, the Korean public and newspapers noted the fact that both champions were Koreans rather than Japanese; Korean newspapers devoted large columns to the event and used the occasion to boost national pride and praise the superiority of the Korean race. The Koreans were clearly unwilling to identify themselves as Japanese. Champion Son Ki-jŏng reportedly gave autographs to foreigners in Germany by signing his name "Son Ki-jŏng, Korea." Two Korean newspapers deliberately deleted the Japanese flag emblem from the photograph of Son Ki-jŏng's uniform when advertising a newsreel.[36] The police arrested several staff members of *Tong-a Ilbo*, detained them for 40 days of intensive questioning, and suspended the paper for nine months. Although the police had not detected the similar action of *Chosŏn Chung'ang Ilbo*, the paper voluntarily suspended publication.

The Japanese perspective was that the Koreans should have been grateful that Japanese rule had facilitated the champions' victory. The Koreans proclaimed, however, that the champions had reached the apex in spite of Japanese rule. The Koreans were Japanese from the conquerors' point of view, even though they could not be equal to the Japanese. But many Koreans continued to treat the Japanese as foreign oppressors who had wronged the Korean nation. It is noteworthy that the Berlin Olympic Games took place in 1936, 26 years after Japan annexed Korea and 9 years before Korea's liberation from Japan.

The crux of the matter was that Korea had been a means to an end for the Japanese empire, and the end justified the means as far as the Japanese were concerned. The Korean reaction was of incidental concern to the Japanese. This perspective could not be reconciled with the Koreans, whose principal concern was their own welfare and the integrity of their nation.

CONCLUSIONS

Koreans of all strata had reason to feel relieved and vindicated by the Japanese defeat in August 1945. Japanese colonialism had brought Korea degradation, deprivation, and suffering, and the experience after 1938 had been particularly nightmarish. Japan had been taken over by a demonic frenzy that seemed to know no limit in human endurance.

This was not the view shared by the Japanese, however. As Maruyama Masao commented in 1946, "Ultra-nationalism succeeded in spreading a many-layered, though invisible, net over the Japanese people, and even today they have not really freed themselves from its hold." In his opinion, "The Empire of Japan came to be regarded *per se* as the 'culmination of the True, the Good, and the Beautiful,' and was by its very nature unable to do wrong; accordingly the most atrocious behavior, the most treacherous acts, could all be condoned."[37]

The colonialists in Korea who had internalized the government's official slogan regarding the unity of Japan and Korea (*naisen ittai*), therefore, felt no compunction about using whatever resources Korea had—both human and material—for the cause of serving the emperor. For them, what was good for Japan was good for Korea. To quote Maruyama again, "In order to spread the just cause it is necessary to act; conversely, when the nation acts, it is *ipso facto* in the just cause."[38] And the Japanese authorities had acted on behalf of the empire. Everyone had to bear the burden of the empire, doing the best they could at the station of life to which fate had assigned them. It was unfortunate that the Koreans had to be at the lowest level of the organic whole, but then, millions of Japanese had to erase their youthful lives on the war front. Why should a Japanese moan for the fate of Korean young men slaving in the Japanese mines and war fronts and Korean women pushed into the gutter when Japanese men were being killed in throngs for the cause of the emperor? Were the "compatriots of the peninsula" (*hantō dōhō*), as the Japanese referred to the Koreans, asked to bear heavier burdens than the Japanese themselves?

To the Koreans, however, Japan's holy war was not theirs. Nor was the Japanese national polity (kokutai) their own. In spite of the incessant propaganda about the unity of Japan and Korea and "the eight corners of the world under one roof" (*hakkō ichiu*), there was no sign that the Japanese empire was dealing fairly with Korea. The colonial authority was an object of fear; contacts with it brought nothing but suffering and humiliation to ordinary Koreans, particularly after Japan embarked on the war against the United States.

These conflicting views, unfortunately, were not reconciled even after the two nations began to interact as independent nations. Indeed, the emotional clash between the two peoples prevented them from establishing diplomatic relations until 1965.

2

The Clash of Emotions:
Japan and Syngman Rhee

Japanese and Korean emotions clashed between 1945 and 1960 because the two nations collided over the assessment of Japanese colonial rule in Korea and also because they held completely different perspectives on the modern history of northeast Asia. The key question was whether Japan ought to apologize for what had transpired between 1905 and 1945. The Koreans regarded it as a matter of course that Japan must acknowledge the pain it had inflicted; the Japanese, however, felt that Japanese rule in Korea had been dictated by Japan's—indeed, the yellow race's—need to protect itself against Western encroachment. In the process, some Japanese argued, they had done Korea a favor by developing the country. Hence the Japanese not only saw no reason to apologize for their conduct, but also they were chagrined that the Koreans did not appreciate the efforts they had made "on behalf of Korea." Since admission of guilt could have been used by Koreans as a justification for demanding reparations, the Japanese were all the more adamant.

All these factors prevented Japan from establishing diplomatic relations with South Korea and resolving some of the more pressing problems between the two countries. The diplomatic stalemate, in turn, prevented the two peoples from establishing a dialogue that could bring mutual understanding and reconciliation. The interactions between Japan and South Korea during this period clearly demonstrate the potent effect emotional conflicts may have on international relations.

As is well known, Korea was divided in two at the end of World War II. By delaying the surrender until August 15, 1945, the Japanese not only experienced the horrors of Hiroshima (August 6) and Nagasaki (August 9) but also opened the door for the entrance of the Soviet Union into the Pacific war (August 8), which ultimately led to the division of Korea. This was a development Japanese leaders had not foreseen, and few Koreans held the Japanese responsible for it, but, nonetheless, it affected Koreans more than any other action Japan had taken during the 36 years of colonial rule. The division of Korea in 1945 led to the emergence of two rival regimes on the Korean peninsula in 1948, the horrendous war between North and South Korea between 1950 and 1953, and the continuing tension between the two Korean states. The division of Korea was the most damaging legacy the Japanese empire left the Koreans.

Initially, Japanese postwar contacts were limited to South Korea or the Republic of Korea (ROK), with whom the Japanese government began its official relations in 1951. But, until 1960, Japanese–South Korean relations were marked by high tension and the baring of raw emotions on both sides. Japanese–South Korean relations in this period deserve special attention because during this time the two sides openly articulated their deep-seated emotions and because, by failing to resolve their differences, the two sides set the stage for emotional outbursts in later periods.

Most contemporary observers of Japanese-Korean negotiations, particularly those in the West, have attributed the clash to President Syngman Rhee's truculent anti-Japanese attitude. There is no doubt that Rhee felt a strong animosity toward Japan and that his attitude affected Japanese-Korean relations. He was angered not only by what he considered intransigent Japanese policies against Koreans in Japan (which he viewed as a reflection of the Japanese attitude toward Koreans in general) but also by Japan's refusal to acknowledge its misdeeds in Korea.

More than Rhee's nationalism or pugnacity was involved in the impasse, however. Had Rhee's hostility been the only stumbling block, Japan and South Korea would not have seen the recurrence of emotional outbursts after Rhee's demise. President Rhee, like a large number of Koreans, wanted a "spiritual reconciliation" to pacify the national soul that had been trampled by the Japanese. Korea's approach to Japan was spiritual, moral, holistic, and Oriental, whereas the Japanese approach was legalistic, pragmatic, piecemeal, and

Western. The Koreans talked of human sufferings and indignities, and the Japanese talked of material benefits they had brought to the Koreans. The conflict between these two approaches ruffled emotions on both sides of the strait during the Rhee era; the same situation prevailed in subsequent periods to lesser degrees. Strange as it may seem, a cultural gap did exist between the Japanese and the Koreans.

THE POSTWAR JAPANESE ATTITUDE TOWARD KOREA

Maruyama Masao's explanation for the Japanese tendency to condone and accept the conduct of imperial Japan was that the empire was just and imperial actions were beyond criticism—either from within or without. The Meiji leaders had transformed the feudal nation into a modern world power and, by doing so, not only prevented Japan from following the dismal fate of China but also propelled it to a position as a leader of the Orient. Any failings of the empire had to be ignored.

Although many Japanese intellectuals tried to liberate public opinion from the grip of ultranationalist doctrine, others turned to Marxism as a way of redemption. This new trend, however, did not influence the postwar political leadership. Even though Japanese political institutions were revamped under the aegis of American occupation from an emperor-centered authoritarian system to a party-centered democracy, the metamorphosis did not extend to the political leadership and its values. By 1947, the United States had shifted the goal of Japanese occupation policy from demilitarization and reform to rehabilitation. Rather than concentrating on the creation of a Japan that would be democratic in both content and form, the new policy called for the creation of a stable and self-confident society that would rebuild its armed forces to the point where Japan could make a more significant contribution to the defense of the Western camp.[1] Japan, in short, was to be turned into a principal American ally in East Asia. The bitter enemy that had perpetrated the perfidy of Pearl Harbor had to be utilized in the struggle against a new foe.

U.S. Policy and Japanese Political Leadership

The new American policy toward Japan soon had a direct and important impact on the future of Japanese–South Korean relations, for U.S. policy permitted and even encouraged the restoration of personalities of the previous era and the resurgence of traditional Japanese values. The U.S. occupation, governed by the Supreme Commander of the Allied Powers (SCAP), called for a political structure led by those Japanese who had proven their political and administrative ability by their service under the imperial system. Those who had been at the forefront of power during the militarist era were unacceptable, but SCAP needed experienced administrators of conservative leaning.

Yoshida Shigeru quickly emerged as the single most important political figure of postwar Japan; he served as the head of the Liberal Party and as premier for 86 months between April 1946 and December 1954 (excluding 18 months in 1947 and 1948). Yoshida not only led the Japanese people during a crucial era when they laid new foundations and set new directions, but also he trained many postwar leaders such as Ikeda Hayato, Satō Eisaku, and Ohira Masayoshi. These new leaders occupied key posts in successive cabinets, including the premiership, and they were regarded as disciples of the so-called Yoshida school. Satō Eisaku served as premier for the longest tenure in Japanese history, a period of 92 months between 1964 and 1972. The previous record holder, Itō Hirobumi (1841–1909), set the model for Yoshida and other postwar leaders.[2]

Yoshida had opposed the war against the United States in 1941 and had attempted to solicit the emperor's active support in bringing the war to a close in early 1945, but he was also a "great loyalist, and a firm defender of Japanese empire." His postwar regenesis as a man of political power and influence "involved no personal *volte-face*, no sacrifice of basic values and priorities, no belated kindling of progressive ideals," according to his biographer.[3] No metamorphosis occurred in the conservative leader's perspective on Japan's relations with its neighbors. In his long memoirs, published in 1961, Yoshida justified Japan's past actions as follows:

> Though my country had become industrialized, it possessed no natural resources to speak of; we had turned our nation into a modern state, but the rest of Asia was still composed of countries which through wars and famine attendant upon misgovernment remained in that stage of development which was barely sufficient to enable them to maintain their independence, so that, whatever we ourselves might have become, their backward condition acted as a drag on us which prevented Japan from putting itself on anything like the same level as the other major world powers. In addition to this, the worldwide depression of 1929 caused the precariousness of our po-

sition to be still more acutely felt, while at the same time the vitality of our people which had been responsible for our national development continued to seek some further outlet—and it was only natural that this should have been found in China, from Manchuria southwards, and in the Pacific area.[4]

In Yoshida's view, Japan had acted out of necessity; its neighbors' backwardness sapped Japan's strength and made the nation vulnerable to outside forces. Naturally, according to Yoshida, the energy or "vitality" of the Japanese people sought an "outlet" in China and elsewhere. Yoshida was succeeded as premier by Hatoyama Ichirō (December 1954–December 1956) and Ishibashi Tanzan (December 1956–February 1957), both of whom SCAP had purged as undesirable elements for their involvement in the militarist government. I shall have more to say about Kishi Nobusuke, who followed Ishibashi as premier between 1957 and 1960. These early postwar leaders shared the outlook that the policies of the Japanese empire had been proper and justified.

The Japanese Attitude Toward Korea

The top leaders were not alone in their pride in Japan's past. Most of those involved in colonial affairs found it simply impossible to accept the notion that Japanese conduct before 1945 deserved Korean condemnation. This view was articulated by Yagi Nobuo, who had spent twenty years of his life in Korea as an official of the Korean Government-General between 1926 and 1945 and who played an important role in restoring Japanese–South Korean ties in 1965. In his memoirs-cum-essay, published in 1978, Yagi strongly denied that Korea had been a Japanese colony. The annexation of Korea in 1910, he noted, was brought about "in the form of mutual consent" between the old Korean government and Japan and, hence, Korea could not be considered a colony. The fact that the Japanese had to dethrone the Korean emperor in 1907 for his objection to Japanese aggrandizement or the opposition of his cabinet to the protectorate treaty of 1905 were immaterial to Yagi. Korea simply became an extension of the inner empire of Japan, like the islands of Shikoku and Kyūshū, and had to be ruled in the "spirit of equality in the eyes of the emperor" (*isshi dōjin*), as enunciated in the imperial rescript on Korean annexation. Although Japanese policy had been "misunderstood" as assimilation policy, he argued, the basic aim underlying Japanese rule in Korea had been to establish a "total harmonious whole" (*konzen ittai) of the two peoples at a very high level, with complete equality and without discrimination.[5]

Yagi considered deplorable the widespread emphasis placed on Japan's "errors and misgovernment" in the course of moving from the stage of "absorption-annexation" to that of "complete merger on an equal basis" and the concentration on the heavy pressures of the war period. Such outlooks, he felt, denied the basic principle of Japanese rule, thus leading to the incorrect conclusion that Japan had been pursuing colonialism or an assimilation policy. To so conclude, he argued, was to distort the history and damage the future of Japanese-Korean relations. The history of Japanese rule in Korea, according to Yagi, was a continuing forward movement toward the attainment of a noble goal. Many prominent Koreans, he argued, enthusiastically supported that goal.[6] No remorse can be found in Yagi's writing— only regrets that the noble goal had not been attained in time or had been pursued with the wrong methods, as well as sorrow that the efforts he made for his cause had been ignored and even condemned.

Yagi was not alone in slighting or ignoring the negative aspects of colonial expansion and in taking pride in what had been accomplished in former colonies, particularly Korea and Manchuria. Yagi and others like him looked back to the development of these lands against all odds and concluded that the results had been positive. They did not see themselves as part of a colossus that had imposed itself on foreign lands; even those who recognized the atrocities committed by the military segregated themselves from the military, thus absolving themselves of all blame.

This attitude was graphically revealed in the project initiated in 1980 to erect a monument commemorating the "founding of Manchukuo" (Manshū kenkoku no hi). Former colonial officials wished to "accurately inform posterity about the ideals and accomplishments of Manchukuo," the puppet regime that the Japanese had established in northeastern China in 1932.[7] When questioned by the press, Kishi Nobusuke, the head of the group soliciting funds for the monument, told the press that "the founding of Manchukuo is a fact that cannot be denied and the ardent desire of the civilian officials at that time was to establish an ideal state where five races [the Japanese, Manchu, Mongolian, Chinese, and Korean] would live in harmony. There was absolutely no thought of [establishing] a colony."[8]

Kishi, brother of Premier Satō Eisaku, had been a powerful force in the Liberal Democratic Party since his return to politics in 1952, and he served as premier between 1957 and 1960. He had played a key role in the colonization of Manchuria between 1936 and 1939, having served as de facto vice premier of Manchukuo. He returned to Japan in 1939 to assume responsibilities for the production of war materials as minister of commerce and industry and vice minister of munitions in the Tōjō cabinet. To leaders like Kishi, the intent and reasoning behind Japan's expansion abroad since 1894 was eminently justifiable even in hindsight.[9]

The opinion that the Japanese rule of Korea and Manchuria had had a positive effect on those lands and that Japan had had good intentions toward the native peoples was broadly shared by all Japanese. As we shall see presently, Kubota Kanichirō made a statement to that effect in 1953 at a Japanese–South Korean negotiation session, precipitating the rupture of talks, which did not resume until 1958. The retraction of the statement in 1957 caused a group of men who had held top positions in the colonial structure to hold a round-table discussion on the Japanese record in Korea before 1945. Their views were identical to those of Yagi, Kishi, and Kubota. Mitarai Tatsuo, former publisher of *Keijō Nippō* (Seoul Daily), the organ of the colonial government, for example, praised General Terauchi Masatake, the first governor-general in Korea, as a "benevolent governor" because he "built the Korean National Museum with his private funds" [his own money?] and had five copies of prints made from the Tripikata Koreana woodblocks for preservation. The woodblocks contained a complete Chinese manuscript of the Buddhist scripture, and the Japanese had been trying to obtain a copy of them since the fourteenth century. Mitarai was referring to a man who, as he himself noted, was "spoken of as if he were the incarnation of the devil himself." Terauchi was the governor who had replicated the tsarist rule of Poland in Korea, as I noted in the previous chapter.[10] Mitarai also proudly proclaimed that Japan had provided education to some 70 percent of all Korean children of school age. Had he checked the relevant statistics, he would have discovered that, as of 1944, only 7.1 percent of the Korean population had graduated from elementary school and less than 1 percent (0.8 percent) had finished middle school.[11]

Tanaka Tetsusaburō, former governor of the Bank of Chōsen, the central bank of the colonial regime, stated that "there had never been a moment when we were not thinking about the welfare of the Korean people"; he cited the leprosarium in Chŏlla Namdo as the "most advanced for its time" and said that it was for "no one but the Koreans."[12] But Professor Yokota Masaburō of Tokyo University interjected a more sober note when he admitted that "it must be realized that the primary objective was to benefit ourselves, not the Koreans," yet he still declared himself to be "one of those who believe that the Japanese helped the Koreans during the years of Japanese rule."[13]

Nor were such views limited to the 1950s. Premier Tanaka Kakuei sent a shock wave through South Korea when he told the lower house of the Japanese Diet on January 24, 1974, that Japan's rule of Korea had brought "spiritual benefits" to the Korean people. He argued that the Japanese had introduced a system of compulsory education that was still well maintained and had taught the Koreans how to cultivate laver, an edible seaweed that is highly prized in both countries.[14] Premier Tanaka, who had spent some years in Korea before 1945, had just returned from a tour of Southeast Asian nations, and thought that Japan should bring such benefits to the people of that region. Japan, it should be noted in passing, had not instituted a compulsory education system in Korea before its capitulation, and, as we noted earlier, the Japanese record in Korean education was not something they could be proud of. Tanaka's statement, along with Mitarai's statement on education quoted earlier, shows how ignorance can breed prejudice and ill-feelings. Exaggerated impressions of benefits bestowed can easily turn into contempt or worse when the beneficiary does not show gratitude for the favor granted. The beneficiary, in turn, resents the benefactor for demanding gratitude for an act that had been taken to satisfy the benefactor's own need.

Other examples abound. Takasugi Shin'ichi told a press conference after he had been appointed a delegate to Japanese-Korean negotiations in March 1979 that "if Japan had ruled Korea for a little longer, Japan would have turned Korea's naked mountains green."[15] Sakurada Takeshi, the president of the Japanese Federation of Economic Organizations (Keidanren), caused a furor in 1979 when he said, in his keynote speech at an international seminar sponsored in Seoul by the federation's Korean counterpart, the Korean Association of Managers (Han'guk Kyŏngyŏngja Hyŏphoe), that the "amazing economic progress in Korea was made possible by the excellent education provided during the Japanese colonial era."[16] Sakurada would have been surprised to learn that less than 1 percent of the Korean population had graduated from secondary schools during the colonial era.

The opinions of political leaders and former colonials had not changed, and the attitude of the Japanese general public toward Korea turned from bad to worse between August 1945, when Japan surrendered Korea to the United States and the Soviet Union, and October 1951, when Japanese and South Korean representatives first met to discuss their future relationship. This worsening of relations occurred because of the continuing presence of a large number of Koreans in Japan.

The Korean Minority in Japan and the Japanese View of Korea

I have already alluded to the Japanese recruitment and conscription of Korean laborers for Japanese industries and mines after 1939. Even before such programs had been instituted, a great number of impoverished Koreans had gone to Japan in search of work, their number reaching 300,000 by 1930 and doubling to 625,000 in 1936.[17] Although the U.S. military governments in Japan and Korea facilitated the repatriation of nearly two million Koreans between 1945 and 1949, some 600,000 decided to remain in Japan.[18] Most had probably migrated to Japan before labor conscription began. They had uprooted themselves from Korea by abandoning their ancestral homes and most had nowhere to go. Although their lot in Japan may have been harsh, they found it preferable to the uncertain prospects in Korea. The restrictions placed on baggage and the amount of cash each repatriate was permitted to carry out of Japan also discouraged the Koreans.

Even before 1945, the Japanese had regarded these Koreans in their midst with contempt, if not hatred. Since most of the Koreans arriving in Japan were impoverished, uneducated, and unskilled farmers pushed out of their land by unscrupulous colonialists or natural calamities, they had no alternative but to work in lowly positions and live in ghettos. The rapid infusion of Koreans created massive housing, sanitation, health, and social problems, and, more than once, the Japanese government placed restrictions on immigration.

Maltreated Koreans, on their part, harbored deep resentments against the Japanese, and, after Japan was defeated, pent-up emotions surfaced. The Koreans believed that they were a liberated people and the Japanese a conquered nation, and they behaved accordingly. When SCAP orders directed the Japanese government to impose a capital levy tax on both the Japanese and Koreans (1947), subject the Koreans to an alien registration law (1947), and apply the school education law and other Japanese education regulations (1948) to the multitude of Korean schools that had sprung up (requiring, among other things, the use of the Japanese language in all curricula other than extracurricular Korean-language instruction), violence flared in some Japanese cities and emotions raged on both sides of the Tsushima Strait. The Japanese press and officials retaliated with a fierce propaganda campaign against the Koreans, which focused on Korean black-market activities, hooliganism, and the menace posed by the illegal entry of Koreans into Japan.[19]

A Japanese Diet member, Shiikuma Saburō from Hokkaidō, said the following in his speech of August 17, 1946:

> We refuse to stand by in silence watching Formosans and Koreans who have resided in Japan as Japanese up to the time of surrender, swaggering about as if they were nationals of victorious nations. We admit that we are a defeated nation but it is most deplorable that those who lived under our law and order until the last moment of the surrender should suddenly alter their attitude to act like conquerors, posting on railway carriages "Reserved" without any authorization, insulting and oppressing Japanese passengers and otherwise committing unspeakable violence elsewhere. The actions of these Koreans and Formosans make the blood in our veins, in our misery of defeat, boil.[20]

Seoul Shinmun on April 26, 1947, responded by spreading the following across its front page when SCAP closed the Hakata Liaison Office of the U.S. Military Government in Korea: "Behold Japan Has Not Yet Relinquished Aggressive Intentions . . . Food Ration Restricted, Shipment of Property Obstructed . . . Public Opinion Boiling on Hakata Liaison Issue . . . Petition for Continuance Being Drawn Up . . . Interim Legislative Assembly Drafts Protest to SCAP."[21]

JAPAN'S REORIENTATION TO THE WEST

The situation might have improved had there been some prominent Japanese intellectuals earnestly working toward the improvement of understanding between the two peoples. But Japanese intellectual attention was focused elsewhere until at least the late 1950s. Emperor Hirohito's surrender message of August 15, 1945, had signaled the end of Japan as a continental power. Japan's survival and recovery required its reorientation toward the United States, not only because Japan was placed under U.S. occupation but also because the United States was regarded the best model for development. Interest in Asia waned, and concern for Korea all but disappeared. The Korean War, of course, brought Korea back to the news, particularly since the Japanese economy boomed as a result of a vast procurement program implemented by the United States armed forces. Nevertheless, the Japanese were not involved with Korea emotionally, politically, or militarily. All that mattered to Japan was the policies of the United States, which reconstructed Japan's economy, rebuilt its army, and procured Japanese goods for the war in Korea. U.S. spending in Japan in connection with the Korean War constituted 37 percent of total foreign exchange receipts in 1952 and 1953.[22]

Intellectual efforts in Japan, therefore, were directed toward the United States and the West and, as Japanese nationalism began to reassert itself, focused on Japanese history and tradition. Few demanded knowledge about Korea. Despite the four decades of Japan's involvement in Korea, few Japanese had learned the Korean language, and not more than a handful of scholars specialized in Korea (most of them were students of Korean history). Not a single definitive study of the colonial experience in Korea was published by a Japanese scholar in the 1950s or the 1960s, and only a few scholars authored general surveys of Korean history. The vast majority of the Japanese public, therefore, continued to rely on the knowledge it had acquired before 1945. That knowledge, of course, had been implanted by those who had directed or participated in the colonial administration, and it presumed the justice and fairness of the empire.

KOREAN POLITICS

Korea, meanwhile, was led by those who had distinguished themselves as foes of Japanese imperialism. Many had exiled themselves to China, Siberia, and the United States and, upon returning home, became heroes. In Korea they naturally assumed leadership positions. The phrase used so often by the Koreans, *"il-je sam-sip ryuk-nyŏn"* (36 years of Japanese imperialist rule), was synonymous with hardship, humiliation, and indignity; life under the Japanese had always been hard but particularly so during the last decade of Japanese rule. The Japanese defeat was celebrated in Korea not only because it put an end to the suffocating Japanese police and the political system that had attempted to eradicate Korea's identity, but also because it meant the end of the economic stringency imposed by the Japanese. For those who had been conscripted for the Japanese armed forces or for hard labor, it was a liberation in every sense of the term. It seemed only just that those who had dedicated their whole lives to the anti-Japanese struggle should lead the liberated nation.

The United States and the Soviet Union created two Koreas instead of one, and a traumatic political struggle between the separate political regimes broke out in 1948. Even so, leaders like Kim Il-sŏng in the north and Syngman Rhee in the south shared a common anti-Japanese attitude, which bordered on a desire for revenge. They would have heartily agreed with the U.S. policy of 1945, which stated that Japan should "not again become a menace to the peace and security of the world." Even the Korean War did not diminish anti-Japanese feelings in either Korea. When the possibility of using Japanese troops against North Korea was mentioned in 1951, Syngman Rhee sharply retorted that in such an event he would conclude a truce with the North Korean Communists to repel the Japanese.

Opportunities for contacts between Japan and Korea, however, did not arise until the United States prepared to end its occupation of Japan and to restore Japanese independence with the signing of the peace treaty in San Francisco in September 1951. The Republic of Korea did open a diplomatic mission to Tokyo in April 1949, but it was attached to SCAP under General MacArthur rather than to the Japanese government. A small quantity of goods had been traded between Japan and South Korea since 1946, but they were regulated by agreements between SCAP in Tokyo and the U.S. Military Government in Seoul. The ROK government also concluded trade and financial agreements with Tokyo in 1949, but they were with SCAP.

JAPANESE–SOUTH KOREAN NEGOTIATIONS

The Soviet Union refused to sign the San Francisco treaty that officially ended the Second World War, and its ally, the Democratic People's Republic of Korea (DPRK), did not gain the recognition of the Allied powers participating in the conference. But the ROK government showed an active interest in the peace treaty, thus initiating establishment of a new relationship with Japan. When the United States referred its draft of the treaty to the ROK government, President Rhee sought to have the ROK included among the Allied powers signing the treaty because he wished to press "certain legitimate residual claims for reparations against Japan as a result of the Japanese occupation of Korea."[23] The ROK government also wished (1) to secure the rights of the 600,000 Koreans remaining in Japan, (2) to prevent Japan from developing armament that would constitute a threat to Korean security, and (3) to gain Japanese acceptance of the MacArthur Line as a boundary for fishing purposes.[24] The MacArthur Line referred to the outer limits for Japanese fishermen established by SCAP in September and October 1945, and it ran midway through the waters between Korea and Japan.

The United States government opposed the reparations hoped for by the ROK government because, as the occupation power that had financed Japanese rehabilitation and recovery, the funds would essentially have come from U.S. taxpayers.[25] The ROK was not granted a seat at the San Francisco conference because Korea had not been at war against Japan. Although the Korean government in exile in Chungking, China, had declared war against Japan in 1941, that government had failed to win international recognition, and hence Korea could not be treated as one of the belligerent powers. The ROK government's request, however, led to the inclusion of certain provisions in the San Francisco treaty that later directly affected Japanese–South Korean relations. The most important provision was Article 4, paragraph (b), which read: "Japan recognizes the validity of dispositions of property of Japan and Japanese nationals made by or pursuant to directives of the United States Military Government in any of the areas referred to in Article 2 and 3."[26] This paragraph was important because the U.S. Military Government in Korea had confiscated all Japanese properties in Korea in December 1945 and had transferred them to the ROK government in 1948. Other issues (but not Japanese rearmament) were to be negotiated between Japan and South Korea.

Although South Korea could not be a party to the San Francisco conference, President Rhee still wanted to conclude a peace treaty with Japan.[27] Therefore, the South Korean government requested SCAP's good offices for Japanese-Korean talks soon after the San Francisco treaty was signed on September 8, 1951.[28] Since the U.S. government had been urging South Korea to conclude a fishery agreement with Japan before the peace treaty went into effect, SCAP was more than willing to accommodate.[29] The Japanese were also eager to settle the status of the Koreans in Japan, hoping, perhaps, to relocate a substantial number of them in Korea.[30]

Japanese and South Korean representatives met on October 20, 1951, six weeks after the signing of the San Francisco treaty and five months before the treaty went into effect. Japan and the ROK, however, were not to reach an agreement until fourteen years later, in 1965.

The long and intermittent process of negotiations showed the depth of the emotions that separated Japan and Korea and their contrasting outlook on the colonial era. Even though the U.S. intent in facilitating Japanese–South Korean talks was to settle the fishery question and the status of Koreans in Japan, the Japanese and Korean governments locked horns in an emotional battle over what had happened between 1905 and 1945. The concrete issues at hand were set aside without resolution. Instead of improving the understanding between the two peoples, the Japanese–South Korean talks exacerbated the existing tensions.

It is unfortunate in many ways that Japan and South Korea rushed into talks in 1951, not only because the two peoples were far apart in their feelings toward each other but also because their attendance at the talks was not based on the same premises. South Korea's intention clearly was to conclude a peace treaty that would resolve long-standing emotional issues and begin a new relationship. Japan, however, was interested only in the immediate issue of the Koreans in Japan.[31] Although the San Francisco treaty had been signed, it had not yet taken effect, and Japan was still technically under U.S. occupation. Japan, therefore, insisted on delaying the resolution of complicated issues until it was fully sovereign.

Given the outlook of Premier Yoshida and the Japanese elites concerning Japanese-Korean relations in the past, it is doubtful that the Japanese and Korean representatives could have arrived at a meeting of minds even if the talks had been delayed until a later time. Obviously, Japan and Korea needed a large-scale intellectual dialogue to narrow the gap between them. But, for reasons discussed earlier, few Japanese paid any attention to the problem or worked toward its resolution. In the meantime, the Japanese–South Korean talks inflamed both the Japanese and Koreans even further, creating more obstacles along the way.

President Syngman Rhee wrote the following in his confidential memorandum to Korean diplomatic representatives abroad after the first two months of talks with Japan had exposed the divergent motives of Japan and the ROK:

> Our delegates went to Japan with open minds and with a strong hope of finding out what are the true sentiments of Japan toward our Government and our people. Have the Japanese abandoned their arrogant and domineering attitude toward us? Have they finally and

completely renounced their expectation of dominating us? These are the fundamental issues which, from our point of view, have to be decided before there is any hope of bringing the two nations together into peaceful and harmonious relationships. Any commercial and diplomatic relations are impossible so long as the Japanese still fail to respect the rights of Koreans as citizens of a free and independent nation . . .

However, the Japanese delegates insisted on restricting considerations wholly to the question of Korean nationals residing in Japan. This problem, which they consider presents a hardship to them and which they want to solve to their own advantage, is the only problem they will accept on the agenda. They insist upon postponing any consideration of other matters until after the Japanese Peace Treaty has been ratified. They apparently have given no thought to the seriousness of the psychological barriers between our two peoples which their attitude is erecting. They show no desire to work toward a removal of the difficulties that exist or to take positive steps toward bringing our two peoples into friendly relations . . .

The following paragraph represents Rhee's minimum requirement from Japan:

What we most need from Japan is not an offer to send soldiers onto our shores, but a concrete and constructive evidence of repentance for past misdeeds and of a new determination to deal fairly with us now and in the future. Convincing evidence that this change of heart has occurred and has become deeply rooted in Japan would not only strengthen us but would also greatly improve the situation in Japan itself . . . We are still waiting and hoping that this evidence will be shown.[32]

Having concluded that the Japanese attitude toward Korea had not changed, the ROK government proclaimed on January 18, 1952, its sovereignty over waters 50 to 60 miles off the Korean coast. The ROK government's rationale was that the move was required to protect maritime and mineral resources in and above the continental shelf and to protect Korean fishermen from Japanese fishermen and their advanced equipment. Since the MacArthur Line would have been nullified when the peace treaty took effect in April and since there was no prospect of Japan and South Korea reaching an amicable agreement on the fishery question, Korea took unilateral action to protect its resources. The Japanese government naturally protested, and the Japanese mass media were agitated. The proclamation of the new Rhee Line was the political equivalent of war as far as the Japanese were concerned.[33]

Each of the subsequent sessions generated more highly emotional issues. At the second half of the first session, held between February and April 1952, the two sides confronted each other over the issue of property claims. The South Korean side was determined to elicit penitence from Japan and the return to Korea of gold reserves and art treasures taken during the 36 years of colonial rule. The ROK also requested payment for the funds transmitted from Korea to Japan after August 9, 1945, compensation for stocks and bonds and other promissory notes owned by the Koreans, payment of the sums accrued to conscripted laborers, and so on. The Japanese side responded by stating that Japanese nationals retained the right to claim compensation for properties they had abandoned in Korea. The Japanese were cognizant of Article 4 (b) of the peace treaty cited above, which was unequivocal on the issue, but they argued that the right of the victor to confiscate private property was not recognized by international law and that outright confiscation of the private property of a defeated nation was contrary to the precedents of international law.[34] Angered by the Japanese attitude, President Rhee ordered his navy to capture Japanese fishing boats violating the Rhee Line, which was now called the Peace Line, and some one thousand Japanese fishermen were sentenced to prison terms on October 13.[35]

The United States government was anxious for the Japanese–South Korean talks to resume, and it dispatched Ambassador Robert Murphy from Tokyo to Seoul to persuade Rhee to moderate his stand. Washington clearly opposed the Rhee Line and adhered to the three-mile limits for territorial waters even though it did not officially announce its position on the Rhee Line for fear of aggravating the situation. But the U.S. had concluded that Rhee "wanted no harmony with the Japanese."[36] Having failed to mollify Rhee, General Mark Clark, the U.N. commander, and Ambassador Murphy invited Rhee to Tokyo in January 1953 in the hope that Rhee and Yoshida would arrive at an understanding. President Rhee was willing to continue the talks, but he wanted the Japanese to "show some endeavor towards creating good will" between the two nations. Premier Yoshida, however, had such an intense personal dislike for Rhee that he abstained from a luncheon arranged by the American ambassador for the two leaders. He was afraid that he could not conceal his personal dislike even in a brief meeting and would make matters worse if he appeared at the luncheon.[37] Clearly, there was no possibility for a reconciliation.

ESCALATION OF EMOTIONAL CONFLICT

It is not surprising, therefore, that Japan and South Korea reached a total impasse after the brief encounter between October 6 and October 21, 1953, known as the third round of talks. What began as a discussion of Japanese claims to private property in Korea turned into an altercation on the colonial era, with predictable result. In requesting the Japanese withdrawal of property claims, the Korean side noted that no reparation had been demanded of Japan in spite of all the ills suffered under the Japanese occupation. This brought forth a rebuttal from the Japanese chief delegate, Kubota Kanichirō, whose response inflamed the Koreans. Kubota stated that the Japanese occupation of Korea was not an "unmixed evil." For example, Japan had reforested the denuded hills of Korea; reclaimed land; constructed irrigation facilities that greatly expanded Korea's rice production; built railroads, highways, schools, and government buildings; and poured millions of yen into Korean investments.[38]

Kubota also made other comments that enraged the Koreans; for example, he remarked that Korea had not actually become independent in Japan's eyes until the effective date of the Japanese peace treaty, that the phrase "enslavement of the Korean people" used in the Potsdam and Cairo declarations was generated in the heat of wartime and "reflected on the dignity of the Allied nations," and that the forced repatriation of Japanese from Korea and the seizure of their properties were contrary to international law.[39] When the Korean delegation reacted violently against his statements, a spokesman for the Japanese Foreign Ministry charged that the Korean side "deliberately distorted some trivial remarks made by our side."[40] Neither Premier Yoshida nor his successors, Hatoyama or Ishibashi, saw the need to retract the Kubota statement, and the ROK and Japan did not hold another round of talks for four and a half years (until April 1958), in spite of repeated U.S. attempts to bring the two sides together. Japan formally withdrew the Kubota statement and the property claims on December 31, 1957.

The Koreans in Japan, and Japanese handling of them, was to snarl the ROK-Japan talks once more, however. In March 1959, the Japanese cabinet under Premier Kishi decided to permit voluntary repatriation of Korean residents to North Korea on "humanitarian" grounds. Even though Japan conducted the repatriation program through the Red Cross societies of Japan and North Korea, the action was tantamount to open provocation as far as South Korea was concerned. The ROK was still at war with North Korea even though a truce agreement had been signed by the United States, China, and North Korea in July 1953. President Rhee had refused to participate in the truce talks at Panmunjom, insisting that Korea must be unified under ROK control. For Japan to have any ties with South Korea's enemy was bad enough—repatriation of Korean residents to what the South Koreans believed to be a gigantic prison camp was a mortal sin. When the Syngman Rhee regime came to an end in April 1960 in the aftermath of a student revolt, the Japanese and South Korean viewpoints were still miles apart.

JAPAN AND SOUTH KOREA IN THE RHEE ERA: SOME OBSERVATIONS

The nine years of contacts between Japan and South Korea only aggravated the hostility between the two countries. Clearly, normal ties between the two peoples could not be established until Japan mollified the deep anger Koreans felt toward Japan, at least while Syngman Rhee headed the South Korean government.

Besides the dichotomy of the two peoples' views about the colonial era, the Japanese and Korean confrontation during the Rhee era manifested the long-standing emotional conflict over the Oriental or Confucian tradition. As noted in the previous chapter, Koreans of the nineteenth century watched with repugnance the Japanese attempt to emulate the West. Consciously or unconsciously, Syngman Rhee and his representatives displayed the same attitude when they rejected Japanese claims based on Western international law. In the disputes over Japanese properties in Korea, repatriation of the Japanese from Korea, and the Rhee Line, the Koreans simply dismissed these legal arguments as irrelevant. Although South Korea later defended its position by citing provisions in the San Francisco peace treaty and other international precedents, most Koreans found legal arguments repugnant and shallow.

The Korean side demanded above all a properly repentant posture by the Japanese. The Koreans were angered that Japan, an Oriental nation steeped in Confucian teachings, had ignored the spiritual dimension in interstate relations and simply advanced legal arguments over material issues. In spite of his Western education and long exile in the United States, Syngman Rhee was the epitome of the Confucian literati. Japan, furthermore, was a defeated nation in the eyes of Rhee and his compatriots. For it to renounce U.S. disposition of Japanese properties in Korea and to cast doubt on the integrity of the new republic was unthinkably inappropriate.

Such differences, however, did not necessitate the harsh confrontation. Indeed, what Japan and Korea needed most during this period was a dialogue toward mutual understanding and reconciliation, and an ample number of Japanese and Korean intellectuals were willing and able to bridge the gap. But President Rhee's forte was not dialogue and reconciliation. He was a man steeped in the zero-sum game of confrontation, and the Japanese had forced him into a 33-year exile. Rhee saw Japan as a monolith centered on its government leadership, and he wanted a formal apology from the Japanese before any dialogue was established. Rhee, therefore, would not think of permitting Korean intellectuals and officials to engage in discourse with their Japanese counterparts. He even prohibited Japanese reporters from landing on Korean soil. The issues involved were truly complicated, but Rhee's personality clearly played an important role in prolonging the Japanese–South Korean confrontation.

Given the nature of the Japanese-Korean conflict, business-minded Americans who focused their attention on the immediate issues at hand understandably found the Japanese more reasonable. Ambassador John M. Allison, Murphy's successor in Tokyo, had this to say about the impasse:

> The Koreans, under the instigation of Rhee, adopted a most intransigent line, and in the opinion of most of us in Tokyo, were being completely unreasonable. The Japanese had offered many concessions on [the] fishing problem, and we believe that if Korea showed any good will, the Japanese could be persuaded to offer more in the general financial and economic talks being conducted at the same time as those in the fisheries problem.[41]

The Americans could not and would not understand the historical and moralistic arguments of the Koreans. It was easier to blame Syngman Rhee for not wishing to compromise with the Japanese.

Unmitigated confrontation also continued during the Rhee era because neither side had an urgent need to improve the strained relationship. South Korea's primary concern was defense against the communist regime in the north and economic rehabilitation from the war, and both of these tasks required support from the United States rather than Japan. Japan itself was only on the road to recovery from the devastation of the Second World War and had little to offer Korea. South Korea's economic goal was to control inflation and achieve stability, and this did not require much contact with Japan. And, in spite of political strain, South Korea did maintain a trade relationship with Japan.

Japan also had no urgent needs other than the desire for a resolution to the fishery question. The Japanese economy made a rapid recovery due to U.S. procurements for the Korean War, and the United States continued to support the Japanese government in almost every sphere of its activities. This was all that mattered to the Japanese leaders. South Korea's trading capacity was limited, and such trade as existed did not require an improvement in political relations. Having determined that the fishery question could not be resolved soon and lacking other motives to woo the South Korean government, the Kishi government decided to resolve the other Korean problem, that is, the problem of the Korean minority in Japan, by repatriating those who wished to go to North Korea. The Japanese government felt no need to heed the South Korean protest. That, in turn, aggravated the already strained relations with South Korea. This situation, however, changed after President Rhee was forced out of the government in April 1960.

3

Normalization and Economic Symbiosis

The fall of Syngman Rhee brought momentous changes to South Korea and had a direct impact on Japanese–South Korean relations. As the character of the South Korean leadership altered, so did its priorities and modes of operation. Japanese political and business leaders responded to the changes in Korea with eagerness and sought to maximize their interests. The Japanese–South Korean normalization of 1965 and the trade boom that followed displayed the possibilities of a cooperative relationship between the two countries in spite of the unsettled emotional conflict.

POLITICAL CHANGES IN KOREA

Korean politics went through kaleidoscopic changes between 1960 and 1961. When Syngman Rhee resigned the presidency in the wake of the student uprising, his long-time associate Huh Chung took over as acting president for the interim between April and August 1960. The constitution was revised and a July election ushered in the Democratic Party and elected Chang Myun (or John M. Chang) premier. In May 1961, however, a junta headed by Major General Park Chung Hee toppled the Democratic government and established a military regime.

The Democrats and the military junta, however, shared similar problems and concerns that affected their outlook toward Japan. Both regimes' foremost priority was economic development, which they required to gain legitimacy and support for their governments. But, in view of declining U.S. economic aid and the shortage of domestic savings, they needed an alternative source of investment capital.[1] U.S. aid had steadily increased from a low of $108.4 million in 1954 to $368.8 million in 1957, but it plummeted to $219.7 million in 1959 and $245.2 million in 1960. Since American aid had paid for over 70 percent of South Korea's imports since 1955, the U.S. action called for an immediate response.[2]

The U.S. action was triggered not only by its responsibilities elsewhere but also by the declining condition of the American economy. The United States had enjoyed a pre-eminent position in the world until the mid-1950s, in both the political and economic realms, but it began to lose ground in the late 1950s. U.S. trade suffered deficits in 1958 and 1959, to such an extent that international concern was aroused about the strength of the dollar. The U.S. government responded by adopting a fiscal retrenchment policy in 1959 and calling on European countries and Japan to share the burden of aiding underdeveloped countries.[3] The United States continued to reduce its economic aid to South Korea and urged closer cooperation between Japan and South Korea.

It was not for economic reasons alone that the United States urged Japanese–South Korean cooperation. Strategic considerations required it. This point was clearly articulated by John M. Allison, assistant secretary of state for Far Eastern affairs between 1951 and 1953 and ambassador to Tokyo between 1953 and 1957. He said:

> [I have] recommended to the State Department that we make clear to him [President Rhee] that we endorsed what General [John E.] Hull had told his superiors in Washington, namely, we must face up to the fact that Korea is a small nation surrounded by three powerful neighbors, only one of which, Japan, was friendly to the free world, and it is therefore essential that Korea realize that its safety and future progress, as well as that of the West, depends upon the renewal of friendly relations with Japan, and this can only come about through compromise and cooperation on both sides.[4]

Although the U.S. government could not use such an argument publicly, Secretary of State Christian Herter stated in his speech of September 8, 1960, that "cooperation between Japan and Korea would be in the interests not only of the two nations but of the United States and the Free World as a whole."[5]

The outlook of the new Korean leaders toward Japan was also very different from that of Syngman Rhee. Unlike Rhee, whose entire life had been dedicated to the cause of driving Japan out of Korea, both Chang Myun and Park Chung Hee had worked under the Japanese during the colonial era, the former as principal of a Catholic secondary school and the latter as a graduate of the Manchukuo and Japanese military academies and a first lieutenant in the Japanese army. Whatever animosity they may have felt toward Japan during the colonial era, they had successfully climbed the ladder of success under the colonial regime. Syngman Rhee was a revolutionary fighter; the new leaders were pragmatists. Rhee spent 33 years as an exile in the United States fighting for Korea's cause; the younger leaders had lived under the Japanese and had learned to accommodate them. They spoke Japanese, knew the Japanese way, and had many Japanese friends. For Rhee, Japan had been the principal enemy; for the younger leaders, Japan was a model.

Despite their similar attitudes, the Democratic and military regimes were different in one important respect. The Democrats came to power because of the student uprising, not because they had won the political struggle against Syngman Rhee and his Liberal Party. Through illness, the Democrats had lost two of their most dynamic leaders, Shin Ik-hui and Cho Pyŏng-ok, and the party was badly divided. Hence the Democrats were highly susceptible to the pressure of public opinion, particularly of student groups. The military junta, however, had taken over by force and did not owe its existence to public support. Although it could not ignore public opinion altogether, it had much more latitude in decision making. These differences were crucial in the two groups' dealings with Japan.

INITIAL CONTACTS

Chang Myun and his Democrats sought to normalize Japanese-Korean relations as soon as they had settled into power. The importance attached to the problem by both the Democratic regime and the Japanese government can be seen from the fact that Foreign Minister Kosaka Zentarō visited Seoul on September 6, 1960, exactly two weeks after Chang Myun had formed his first cabinet. Premier Chang had sent his close friend and supporter, Pak Hŭng-sik, a successful businessman during the colonial era, to Tokyo to confer with Cabinet Secretary Ōhira Masayoshi and other Japanese leaders.[6] Kosaka, incidentally, was the first Japanese official to visit Korea since 1945.

His visit led to the opening of the fifth round of Japanese–South Korean talks on October 25. The Chang government publicly enunciated its willingness to compromise with Japan on certain issues, and both Premier Chang and Foreign Minister Kosaka talked of economic cooperation. On August 17, 1960, the Korean government issued visas to representatives of the Mitsubishi Trading Company, the first of thousands of businessmen to visit Korea. Although the Chang regime reaffirmed on September 17 its policy of capturing fishing boats that violated the Peace Line, it decided to chase them off rather than seize them. The Japanese government, on its part, strove to speed up the repatriation of Korean residents in Japan to North Korea in order to reduce points of friction when official talks began.[7]

Each side, however, had different priorities and political concerns, and, as a result, official talks progressed slowly. When the "preliminary session" of the fifth round of talks began under the Democratic regime, the Korean side focused its attention on the issue of financial compensation, just as it had in 1951; the Japanese side stressed the need to resolve the fishery question before all other issues. The Liberal Party in Japan had just undergone a major political crisis between May and June 1960, regarding the issue of the revision of the United States–Japan Security Treaty. The affair had resulted in the resignation of Premier Kishi. A new election was scheduled for December, and Premier Ikeda was understandably cautious on Japanese–South Korean negotiations lest they precipitate another political crisis. Only the resolution of the fishery issue would bring political advantage. In Seoul, Premier Chang had to contend with vociferous domestic opposition to "hasty retreats." His image had already been tarnished by a series of compromises with the Americans. The Democrats had announced in September that the size of the army would be reduced by 50,000 troops, but by November they had scrapped the plan under American pressure. Rightly or wrongly, President Rhee had resisted American pressure to revise the inflated hwan-dollar exchange rate, but the Democrats found it necessary to revise the rate from 500 to 1,000 hwan per dollar in January 1961, and the rate increased to 1,300 to one in February.[8] Yielding on as emotional an issue as the Peace Line would cripple the Democratic government. The National Assembly's February 3 resolution on Korean-Japanese relations indicated the kind of pressure the politicians were under. It stated that (1) diplomatic ties with Japan should be expanded gradually, (2) the Peace Line should be defended, (3) official ties should be restored after Japan "clarified" the damages and pains inflicted on the Koreans, and (4) economic cooperation beyond the current trade should be expanded only if it would not harm domestic industries.[9]

The Japanese and Korean leaders, however, established an informal network of communications to resolve the impasse. According to Yagi Nobuo, the former colonial official in Korea, Premier Chang sent his close associate, Yu Tong-jin, to Tokyo in February 1961 to establish contacts with Japanese leaders. The premier, a devout Catholic, also enlisted the services of a Catholic priest in establishing contacts. These emissaries mobilized the support of former colonial officials such as Yagi to establish ties with former premiers Yoshida and Kishi, Speaker of the House Ishii Mitsujirō, and others, who established on April 26 the Round Table on the South Korean Problem (Nik-Kan Mondai Kondankai).[10] This was the beginning of the so-called pro–South Korean group in Japan. That group dispatched an eight-man parliamentary delegation headed by Diet member Noguchi Uichi and accompanied by the chief of the East Asia Bureau of the Foreign Ministry to Seoul on May 6 for a week-long visit. The two sides decided to open official talks in September. Meanwhile, the Chang government referred to the "establishment of a Korean-Japanese economic cooperative system" with increasing frequency. The first five-year economic development plan (1962–1966) anticipated considerable Japanese aid and loans.[11] This was the situation on May 16, 1961, when General Park ousted the Democrats.

THE JAPANESE PERSPECTIVE

The emergence of the military regime in Seoul only spurred the Kishi group to work more diligently for a positive South Korean policy. The coup was regarded as a blessing for Japan. "Fortunately," Kishi said:

> South Korea is under a military regime where a small number of leaders under Park Chung Hee can decide things [on their own]. Even if Japan exerted itself and gave a great sum of money, South Korea will never be satisfied on the compensation issue. So, if [we] persuaded Chairman Park at a certain level, [that will be all]. They have no National Assembly. Even if the newspapers opposed it, Chairman Park can seal them off.[12]

Kishi Nobusuke, the veteran of Manchukuo and the Tōjō cabinet, was no sentimentalist. Under his administration Japan had repatriated its Korean residents to North Korea; now it was time for Japan to normalize relations with South Korea. Political developments in South Korea demanded it. A democratic government in South Korea was compelled by public opinion to demand more and yield less. Clearly the situation was more favorable for Japan under a junta regime.

Kishi was not alone in rejoicing at the fortuitous opportunity. According to Ōoka Eppei, the veteran political commentator in Tokyo, Kōno Ichirō, the leader of a major faction within the Liberal Party and a serious contender for the premier's position, expressed the same thought when Premier Ikeda consulted him about the Korean question. He supposedly told Ikeda that "This is the greatest opportunity since the end of the war to solve the Japanese–South Korean problem. It is because South Korea is undergoing a serious economic crisis now and they need money most urgently. This is the time to haggle down the price." Kōno recommended Sugi Michisuke, the financial magnate of the Kansai area and incumbent chairman of the Japan External Trade Organization (JETRO), as the chief delegate for negotiations with the Park regime. Sugi was Kōno's most influential financial supporter.[13]

Former premier Kishi also stressed the close linkage between Japanese security and the settlement of the Korean problem. The military group under Park Chung Hee was the last chance for a "Free Korea," according to Kishi. He feared that the failure of the Park regime could bring a communist advance to the southern edge of the Korean peninsula, with grave consequences for Japan. Kishi saw a parallel between his concern and that of his ancestors:

> The reason that our forefathers [senpai] worked so laboriously before was not because of their imperialist designs but because they thought that Japanese security would be jeopardized if anti-Japanese forces emerged in Korea or if forces against Japan occupied Korea. This is why the Sino-Japanese War, Russo-Japanese War, and various Korean incidents took place. This is Japan's fate. So, Japan must normalize its relations with the Republic of Korea, provide economic aid in conjunction with the United States, and thereby build South Korea's economic foundation. If we leave the South Korean people's livelihood to such a strained condition and do nothing politically, and if the Park regime fails as a result, a very serious situation would develop. This is not the time [to sit idly by].[14]

In one stroke Kishi had defended Japanese policy of the past and rationalized his policy of close cooperation with the military regime in Seoul.

Kishi not only led the movement within Japan for close ties with the Park regime but also exerted a strong influence on U.S. support for the junta. When the military toppled the Democratic government on May 16, General Carter M. Magruder, commander of the United Nations forces in Korea, and Marshall Green, chargé d'affaires of the U.S. embassy, had strongly denounced the junta and called for the restoration of democratic government.[15] When Premier Ikeda visited Washington in late June, the Kennedy administration still had misgivings about the political situation in South Korea, which became one of the principal topics of discussion between American and Japanese leaders. Premier Ikeda and Foreign Minister Kosaka reportedly persuaded President Kennedy and Secretary of State Dean Rusk that "Japan and the United States must intensify economic aid to South Korea in order to bring about political stability there."[16] The Kennedy-Ikeda joint communiqué of June 22, 1961, stated:

> The President and the Prime Minister stressed the importance of development assistance to less developed countries. The Prime Minister expressed a particular interest in this connection in development assistance for East Asia. They agreed to exchange views on such assistance and agreed that both countries would make positive efforts to the extent of their respective capacities.[17]

The Kennedy administration issued a statement in support of the junta on July 28, dispatched Secretary of State Dean Rusk to Seoul on November 5, and invited General Park to the White House on November 14.[18] In the meantime the U.S. government worked actively behind the scenes to normalize Japanese–South Korean relations.

THE SETTLEMENT

The military junta in Seoul was eager to sustain the momentum created by the Democrats and continued talks both at official and unofficial levels. Various emissaries from Seoul sought out members of the Kishi group and leaders in the Japanese financial and business world.[19] Perhaps the most important emissary was Kim Yu-t'aek, deputy premier and chairman of the Economic Planning Board, who met Foreign Minister Kosaka in early September and indicated that Korea was willing to compromise on the Peace Line if Japan was willing to provide a large sum of money. Kim reportedly mentioned $2 billion, but later lowered the sum to $800 million. Kosaka, however, spoke of $50 million. Obviously, the two sides were far apart on the sum of money involved, but the South Korean retreat on the fishery issue brought the two sides closer than ever before. Cordiality prevailed on November 12 when General Park visited Tokyo on his way to Washington and was given a royal reception. Park and Ikeda agreed to expedite the negotiations.[20] General Park then left to confer with President Kennedy, who was most eager for Japanese–South Korean cooperation.

Normalization of Japanese–South Korean relations, however, required much more than the eagerness of the two sides. Although Foreign Minister Ōhira and the Korean Central Intelligence Agency director Kim Jong-pil (Kim Chong-p'il) reached an agreement on the money to be provided to South Korea in their talks of October and November 1962, other issues remained unresolved.[21] South Korea adopted a new constitution in December and prepared to restore a civilian government. In March 1963, General Park attempted to prolong military rule by four years but had to scuttle the plan because of strong opposition from the Kennedy administration.[22] Park left the army in August 1963 and ran for president in October, narrowly defeating former president Yun Po-sŏn. Although the new president was in firm control of domestic politics, particularly because of the elaborate control mechanisms, including the KCIA, he had established after the coup, he confronted the strong and vociferous opposition of politicians, intellectuals, and students, who launched a pan-national movement against "humiliating diplomacy with Japan" in March 1964. Seoul and other major cities were virtually paralyzed by student demonstrations between March and June, and Park's cabinet, under Premier Ch'oe Tu-sŏn, resigned on May 9. Park proclaimed martial law on June 3, ordering four army divisions to move into Seoul to maintain order.[23]

The emotional explosion in Korea was directed not so much against Japan as against the identity and manner of the Korean negotiators. As noted earlier, the Japanese preferred the military regime as a negotiating partner, but a large segment of the aroused Korean public felt that the Park regime was the wrong one to negotiate with the Japanese and that it was dealing with the situation in an inappropriate manner.[24] The prominent role played by KCIA director Kim Jong-pil in the negotiations particularly inflamed the opposition. Kim had used his unchecked power to illicitly import a vast amount of flour, sugar, cement, and more than two thousand Japanese cars for huge profits. He had also directed a project to milk a huge sum of money from the stock market and, in doing so, had ruined thousands of innocent investors.[25] The ostensible reason for the 1961 coup had been the elimination of corruption from the army and the body politic, but, evidently, the KCIA director was unscrupulous in gathering political funds. As these scandals surfaced and the opposition against the settlement with Japan gathered momentum, President Park found it necessary to send Kim into an eight-month exile between February and October 1963.

Suspicion and anger among the Korean public heightened even further when Foreign Minister Ōhira revealed, on January 29, 1963, the content of the secret agreement on property claims. The situation was exacerbated when Kim Jong-pil continued his direct involvement in the Japanese negotiations after his return from exile. Kim and Ōhira announced in Tokyo on March 23, 1964, that all outstanding issues would be resolved by the end of March and that an agreement would be signed by May. Fear and suspicion of a sellout by the Park regime were fueled by a comment of Ōno Banboku, vice president of the Japanese Liberal Democratic Party (LDP), that his relationship with President Park was a paternal one and that he had attended Park's presidential inaugural with the joy of a father attending his son's inaugural.[26] The more the Japanese expressed their intimate feelings for the Park regime, the more the Korean opposition suspected collusion. The opposition parties demanded a nonpartisan foreign policy based on the concurrence of substantial elements of the national leadership, and they warned against excessive concessions to Japan. They regarded the reparations amount agreed to by Kim Jong-pil and Ōhira ($300 million of grant, and up to $300 million of loan) as dismally low; the opposition's demand was for $2,700 million. As rumors spread that Kim had agreed to a 12-mile limit off the Korean coast for Japanese fishermen, the opposition insisted on a 40-mile limit. President Park recalled Kim Jong-pil from Tokyo and sent him into his second exile in June 1964.[27]

Japanese leaders also faced serious opposition from the Socialist Party and left-wing elements. The Socialists had pledged in their action platform of 1962 to carry out a "people's movement" against the conclusion of an agreement with South Korea, and they were expected to engage in obstructive tactics in and out of the Diet.[28] Since nearly half of the Koreans residing in Japan supported North Korea and opposed South Korea, they could easily be mobilized in any street demonstration against Japanese–South Korean rapprochement.

Various statements of Japanese government leaders revealed their serious concern about the Socialist opposition. Foreign Minister Kosaka's comment on the occasion of General Park's Tokyo visit was most revealing. He said:

> Of course it is a matter of grave concern for Japan that red flags might be posted in Pusan, which is only across the Korea Strait from Japan. In this sense I can understand the motives of the positivists [such as former premier Kishi] who wish to bring about a quick turn of events through the Ikeda-Park meeting [of November 12, 1961]. But would it not be more serious for today's government to have the Diet Building surrounded by red flags and demonstrators as a result of hurrying the negotiations with South Korea?[29]

Economic advantages and U.S. encouragement, however, outweighed the risk of domestic political crisis. Resolution of the fishery problem with South Korea would be of obvious advantage to Japan, and would improve the LDP's political position. In addition to economic opportunities provided by South Korea's second five-year economic development plan (1967–1971), normalization of the political relationship was expected to facilitate more bilateral trade since it would permit the government to guarantee loans and credits. Even before the political relationship had been normalized, 60 major Japanese trading and industrial companies had established offices in Seoul and a great number of businessmen had been visiting Seoul.[30] Japanese business leaders eagerly pushed for normalization.

Japanese businessmen had a special reason to be eager for the opening of the Korean market in the early 1960s. As is well known, Japan had achieved the world's highest growth rate in both production and exports since 1952, sustaining an average rate of growth of more than 9 percent per year in its gross national product (GNP). But, beginning in 1961, Japan experienced the problems of a rapidly expanding economy. Consumer prices rose by 5.3 percent in 1961, 6.8 percent in 1962, and 7.6 percent in 1963, very high rates by Japanese standards. Tight monetary control imposed by the Bank of Japan created a mild stagnation, and the rate of growth plummeted from 14.4 percent (an inflation-adjusted rate) in 1961 to 5.7 percent in 1962 and 4.7 percent in 1965. Although the growth rates in 1963 and 1964 were very high (12.8 and 13.7 percent, respectively), economic fluctuations were very damaging to small and medium businesses. During 1964, 4,212 businesses, a record number, went bankrupt. In 1965, the number increased to 6,141. The bankruptcy of the Sanyō Special Steel Corporation in 1965, the largest enterprise to declare bankruptcy since the end of the Second World War, caused a stir in the business world.[31] Clearly, apart from political and security perspectives, Japanese businesses needed the expanded South Korean market.

The United States had reason to prod both the Japanese and the Koreans to normalize their relationship. The situation in Indochina was deteriorating rapidly in the early 1960s, and the United States was deeply involved there. Secretary Rusk visited Tokyo and Seoul in January 1964 for the specific purpose of encouraging Japanese–South Korean normalization. Assistant Secretary of State William Bundy paid another visit in October. American ambassadors in Seoul and Tokyo were publicly involved. The visible U.S. involvement was useful to both Japanese and South Korean leaders for deflecting domestic opposition in their respective countries.[32]

The seventh and final round of talks began in late December 1963, but the final details were worked out by the cabinet headed by Satō Eisaku, younger brother of former premier Kishi. Satō replaced ailing Premier Ikeda in November 1964. There is little doubt that Premier Satō supported his brother's views vis-à-vis Korea. He appointed Shiina Etsusaburō his foreign minister and sent him to Seoul on his first mission abroad on February 17, 1965. Shiina had been a close follower of Kishi since the 1930s and had served under Kishi in the Ministry of Commerce and Industry and in the Manchukuo regime. When Kishi was appointed minister of commerce and industry in the Tōjō cabinet in 1941, Shiina was his vice minister.[33] Thus, although Kishi held no official position in the government, he was in a position to formulate Japanese policy toward Korea. Kishi had maintained an alliance with Ikeda throughout the Kishi and Ikeda administrations, that is, while they each headed the cabinet as premier, but the two did not necessarily agree on all policy matters, including the Korea issue. As noted earlier, Ikeda was much more cautious on Korean rapprochement than Kishi, just as he and the men in his faction were critical of Kishi's "high-handed tactics" in pushing through the security treaty in 1960.[34] The situation changed when Satō became premier. It is significant in this connection that Premier Satō stayed in power for 92 months, until July 1972, breaking the previous record of 90 months held by Itō Hirobumi during the Meiji era.

Foreign Minister Shiina settled all the outstanding issues by April 1965. President Park had appointed a young politician, Yi Tong-wŏn (Dong Won Lee), as foreign minister, with the specific mission of normalizing Japanese–South Korean relations, and both sides were ready. On his arrival at the airport, Shiina issued a statement "deeply reflecting (or apologizing—*hansei*) for the unfortunate past with Korea," an attempt to placate the opposition within Korea.[35] During his four-day stay, Shiina and Lee hammered out the first of many documents, the Treaty on Basic Relations. The most important element in the treaty was Article 3, which affirmed that the Republic of Korea was "the only lawful government in Korea as specified in the Resolution 195 (III) of the U.N. General Assembly."[36] The second part of Article 3 contained the seeds of future frictions, as we shall see. The South Korean side had hoped to be recognized as the only legitimate and sovereign government of all Korea, but, by including a proviso in the second part of Article 3, the Japanese side in effect limited its recognition of the ROK as the government of South Korea only.

By April 3, all other issues were resolved. The Peace Line was replaced by a twelve-mile exclusive fishery zone plus a jointly regulated fishing area. As for the property claims, Japan was to provide South Korea with $45 million over a ten-year period. But Japan was also to provide more funds as a "gesture of good will": a grant-in-aid of $300 million in Japanese products and labor for South Korea's economic development over a ten-year period, a $200 million government loan from the Overseas Development Aid fund (ODA) over the same period at 3.5 percent interest per annum, and $300 million in commercial loans, of which $90 million was to be allocated for Korean purchases of Japanese fishing boats. Japan also agreed to return a number of old Korean books and art objects. Koreans who had resided in Japan before August 1945 and their descendants were to be granted permanent resident status.[37] The Treaty on Basic Relations and four agreements were initialed on June 22. Fourteen years of intermittent and embittered negotiations were thus brought to a close.

As anticipated, opposition forces in Japan and Korea rejected the settlement. When the Park government convened a special session of the National Assembly on July 29, only a month after the documents were initialed, the opposition parties boycotted the ratification process by resigning from the assembly en masse. As the government rammed the documents through the National Assembly, the opposition took the issue to the streets, where students and intellectuals joined in protest. The treaty was quickly labeled the Second Ŭlsa Treaty, since the year 1965 happened to be the year of Ŭlsa in the Chinese cyclical calendar. In Korean history, the Ŭlsa Treaty refers to the treaty of 1905, by which Japan turned the old Korean kingdom into a Japanese protectorate. It had been exactly 60 years, or one calendar cycle, since that treaty was signed.[38]

The opposition had much to protest. South Korea had yielded on every issue, as it turned out. Nowhere in the documents was there any reference to a Japanese apology for their past conduct, and, instead of reparations due Korea, Japan was to provide economic aid as a show of generosity. Notwithstanding the text of the ROK's constitution, which defined the territory and jurisdiction of the ROK as the entire Korean peninsula and adjacent islands, the treaty limited Korea's jurisdiction to South Korea. The Peace Line was abolished, subjecting Korean fishermen, with their primitive equipment, to the competition of aggressive Japanese fishermen with the most advanced equipment. But the main causes of opposition were fear of renewed Japanese economic and political exploitation, distrust of the Park regime, and the allegedly submissive attitude of the Park government toward Japan. According to a survey conducted by South Korea's leading newspaper, *Tong-a Ilbo*, which leaned more toward the opposition than the government, 45 percent of respondents favored normalization of relations with Japan, 28 percent opposed it, and another 27 percent were undecided.[39]

Japanese Socialists vigorously opposed the settlement. They argued that the treaty was a prelude to an anticommunist alliance among Taiwan, South Korea, and Japan and that it would impede the unification of North and South Korea. When the treaty was presented to the Diet for ratification in November, the Socialist Party resorted to violence in the Diet to prevent ratification, but, in the end, the LDP prevailed without the Satō government's suffering undue damage.[40]

PROLIFERATION OF ECONOMIC RELATIONS

The Japanese-Korean settlement marked a major new departure in the economic relations of the two nations. In the context of the already extensive bilateral trade between Japan and South Korea, in which the latter continued to suffer huge trade deficits, the $500 million provided by Japan in ten installments was not large. But the availability of $500 million and the active Japanese interest in Korean trade encouraged South Korean leaders who were intent on rapid economic development. The government suppressed student opposition by dispatching troops to two major universities in August 1965 and expelling a number of student leaders and professors. The government also imposed martial law in Seoul for two weeks in late August in a display of its determination to enforce its decision. The opposition parties that had formed an alliance against the treaty in May soon split apart, and organized opposition dissolved.[41]

The Park government, meanwhile, acquired considerable experience in the economic sector, and, by early 1964, the South Korean economy had recovered from the recession of 1958–1962. Its GNP rose by 9.1 percent in 1963 and 8.3 percent in 1964. The new chairman of the Economic Planning Board, Chang Key-young, undertook some bold moves to prepare for the second five-year economic plan (1967–1971): adopting the floating exchange-rate system, easing import restrictions, and raising the interest rate to attract private savings to the banks. The Park government had decided to stress an increase in exports as the principal means of developing South Korea's economy.

South Korea's condition, however, was not conducive to rapid growth in exports. Its industry was still woefully underdeveloped; its mineral resources were not abundant; and its farms produced a barely adequate supply of food for the rapidly increasing population, even in good crop years. Since the ROK had suffered from trade deficits for so long, its ability to buy foreign plants was severely limited. But the government's strategy required foreign capital—either in investment, loans, or credit—and foreign technology. South Korea did have educated manpower in abundance, thanks to the stress placed on education by the Koreans. The number of Koreans who had completed elementary school jumped from 1.7 million in 1944 to 5.5 million in 1962, and middle and high school graduates increased from 200,000 in 1944 to over 1.8 million in 1962.[42] The marriage of South Korea's labor to foreign capital and technology was to propel South Korea's economy.

Japanese exports to South Korea began to rise at a phenomenal rate once the political issues were settled. The annual average for the four preceding years (1961–1964) had been $133 million. Exports jumped to $180 million in 1965 and reached an annual average of $586 million between 1966 and 1970. They spiraled to an average of $1,765 million a year between 1971 and 1975 (see Table 4). The rate of growth of South Korean exports to Japan was even faster, but, because Korean exports to Japan had constituted less than a quarter of all Japanese imports between 1961 and 1964 (a total of $119 million as against $652 million in Japanese exports to Korea during those years), it would have required a quantum leap in Korean exports to balance the trade accounts. This did not happen, as Table 5 graphically shows, and South Korea accumulated an increasingly large trade deficit.

South Korean trade was enormously profitable to Japanese businessmen. Chang Key-young (Chang Ki-yŏng), South Korea's deputy premier and chairman of the Economic Planning Board, who played a key role in promoting South Korea's economic relations with Japan, depicted the situation vividly. He said:

> There is a saying in Korea that one not only eats the pheasant but its egg too. [That is, one may have a cake and eat it too.] But Japan not only eats the pheasant and eggs but the chicks hatched from the eggs. Japan loans South Korea the dollars Korea paid for commodities purchased from Japan. This loan has a string attached to it because it is tied to Korea's purchase of Japanese goods. Japan exports plants and intermediate goods to South Korea; in order to maintain the plants, Korea must continue to import parts. The products of these plants suit Japanese tastes, and hence they are exported to Japan, but at low prices. This is the state of the South Korean–Japanese cooperative relationship.[43]

The comment was made in front of former premier Kishi and fellow members of the Japan–South Korea Cooperation Society (Nik-Kan Kyōryoku Iinkai) in December 1975, and drew no objection. This organization had been established by high-level pro–South Korean Japanese political and business leaders in February 1969 to "promote friendship between Japan and South Korea."

In addition to geographic proximity, Japanese businessmen found the South Korean market attractive for a number of reasons. As should be clear from previous chapters, Japan and Korea have maintained close cultural ties since antiquity and the Confucian behavioral pattern is deeply rooted in both societies. The Japanese, therefore, could operate in Korea without painful behavioral adjustments. They could easily understand the meaning of subtle gestures and expressions. Chances of misunderstanding due to cultural differences were not high. Further, many Japanese knew Korea intimately, either because they were born and raised there or because they had spent years there as adults. They could establish personal ties very easily since many Koreans had worked under the Japanese or had studied or worked in Japan. Facility in establishing personal connections was of enormous advantage because those lacking proper introduction were treated as outsiders, whereas insiders were granted preferential treatment depending on the degree of intimacy of the relationship.

Another advantage for Japanese businessmen in Korea was ease in communicating with the Koreans. Although few Japanese spoke or understood Korean, most Koreans in their forties and above—the generation of Koreans engaged in business or in leading positions in

TABLE 4   JAPAN'S TRADE WITH SOUTH KOREA AND THE WORLD, 1953–1983
(IN MILLIONS OF U.S. DOLLARS)

Year	JAPANESE IMPORTS				JAPANESE EXPORTS			
	From World	From ROK	Percentage ROK	ROK Ranking	To World	To ROK	Percentage ROK	ROK Ranking
1953	2,410	9	0.4	34	1,275	107	8.4	2
1954	2,399	8	0.3	34	1,629	69	4.2	5
1955	2,471	10	0.4	32	2,011	39	1.9	10
1956	3,230	11	0.3	41	2,501	64	2.6	8
1957	4,284	12	0.3	37	2,858	57	2.0	16
1958	3,033	11	0.4	38	2,877	57	2.0	13
1959	3,599	12	0.3	39	3,456	62	1.8	14
1960	4,491	19	0.4	33	4,055	100	2.5	11
1961	5,810	22	0.4	37	4,235	126	3.0	6
1962	5,636	28	0.5	32	4,916	138	2.8	7
1963	6,736	27	0.4	38	5,452	160	2.9	4
1964	7,938	42	0.5	33	6,674	109	1.6	18
1965	8,169	41	0.5	33	8,452	180	2.1	13

Year								
1966	9,523	72	0.8	25	9,776	335	3.4	3
1967	11,663	92	0.8	23	10,442	407	3.9	2
1968	12,987	102	0.8	24	12,972	603	4.6	2
1969	15,024	134	0.9	25	15,990	767	4.8	2
1970	18,881	229	1.2	17	19,318	818	4.2	2
1971	19,712	274	1.4	16	24,019	856	3.6	4
1972	23,471	426	1.8	14	28,591	980	3.4	4
1973	38,314	1,207	3.2	7	36,930	1,789	4.8	2
1974	62,110	1,568	2.5	9	55,536	2,656	4.8	2
1975	57,863	1,308	2.3	10	55,753	2,248	4.0	4
1976	64,799	1,917	3.0	9	67,225	2,824	4.2	2
1977	70,809	2,114	3.0	9	80,495	4,080	5.0	2
1978	79,343	2,591	3.3	8	97,543	6,003	6.2	2
1979	110,672	3,359	3.0	9	103,032	6,247	6.1	2
1980	140,528	2,996	2.1	13	129,807	5,368	4.1	3
1981	143,290	3,389	2.4	8	152,030	5,658	3.7	4
1982	131,931	3,254	2.5	7	138,831	4,881	3.5	4
1983	126,393	3,365	2.7	8	146,927	6,004	4.1	3

NOTE: FOB prices for exports and CIF prices for imports.

SOURCE: Research and Statistics Department, The Bank of Japan, *Economic Statistics Annual*, 1968–1982, annual volumes, and Japan Tariff Association, *The Summary Report Trade of Japan*, December 1983. Ranking is from ibid., and the United Nations, *Yearbook of International Trade Statistics*, 1956–1981.

TABLE 5   SOUTH KOREA'S TRADE BALANCE WITH JAPAN AND THE WORLD, 1955–1983 (IN MILLIONS OF U.S. DOLLARS)

Year	ROK Exports		ROK Imports		Trade Deficit		Japanese Percentage of Total Deficit
	To World	To Japan	From World	From Japan	With World	With Japan	
1955	18	7	341	19	323	12	3.7
1956	25	8	386	21	361	13	3.6
1957	22	11	442	34	420	23	5.5
1958	17	10	378	50	361	40	10.1
1959	20	13	304	32	284	19	6.7
1960	33	20	344	70	311	50	16.1
1961	41	19	316	69	275	50	18.2
1962	55	23	422	109	367	86	23.4
1963	87	25	560	159	473	134	28.3
1964	119	38	404	100	285	62	21.8
1965	175	44	463	167	288	123	42.7
1966	250	66	716	294	466	228	48.9
1967	320	85	996	443	676	358	53.0
1968	455	100	1,463	624	1,008	524	52.0

Year							
1969	623	133	1,824	754	1,201	621	51.7
1970	835	234	1,984	809	1,149	575	50.0
1971	1,068	262	2,394	954	1,326	692	52.2
1972	1,624	408	2,522	1,031	898	623	69.4
1973	3,225	1,242	4,240	1,727	1,015	485	47.8
1974	4,460	1,380	6,852	2,621	2,392	1,241	51.9
1975	5,081	1,293	7,274	2,434	2,193	1,141	52.0
1976	7,715	1,802	8,774	3,099	1,059	1,297	122.5[a]
1977	10,047	2,121	10,810	3,923	763	1,802	236.2[a]
1978	12,711	2,627	14,972	5,981	2,261	3,354	148.3[a]
1979	15,055	3,353	20,339	6,657	5,284	3,304	62.5
1980	17,505	3,039	22,292	5,858	4,787	2,819	58.9
1981	21,254	3,503	26,131	6,374	4,877	2,871	58.9
1982	21,853	3,388	24,251	5,305	2,398	1,917	79.9
1983	24,445	3,404	26,192	6,238	1,741	2,835	162.3[a]

NOTE: Exports are valued at FOB and imports at CIF, except before March 1958, where the value of both exports and imports is based on the face value of the drafts involved. Error in addition is due to the rounding of numbers for imports and exports.

[a] South Korea's trade deficit with Japan in these years was larger than its total deficits. At first sight this appears logically impossible, but the large trade deficit with Japan was compensated by favorable trade balances with other countries, reducing the total amount of deficits.

SOURCE: The Bank of Korea, *Economic Statistics Yearbook*, 1961–1983, and *Monthly Bulletin*, May 1984. When data were inconsistent in different editions of the yearbook, the data from later editions were used.

government—spoke Japanese or had a good understanding of the language. Except for Taiwan, which had been ruled by the Japanese between 1895 and 1945, Korea was the only country where the Japanese could easily establish communication without any understanding of the native language. Korean businessmen who sought to establish business relationships with the Japanese were, of course, eager to please. Politics was outside their realm, if not their concern. Those without previous connections built them, in spite of their initial disadvantages.

Not only did the Koreans understand the Japanese, but also they were very familiar with conditions in Japan. Since the mid-1950s, increasing numbers of the Korean elites had been exposed to Japanese publications and mass media as they sought to broaden their perspectives in business, management, and specialized fields of knowledge. Korea was behind Japan not only because the Japanese colonial government afforded little opportunity to receive higher education but also because the internecine war deprived it of human and material resources. When Koreans recovered from the war and sought to rebuild their society, they naturally turned to Japan for publications because they had a command of the language and Japan had an abundance of literature in every field. Although most of the younger generation went to the United States or Europe for new knowledge (and a small number of them began to play a role in society after the late 1950s), the younger men were a minority clustered mostly in academic circles. English publications were readily available, but the linguistic and cultural barriers were formidable. Korean elites of the 1960s, therefore, acquired the new or Western knowledge through the prism of the Japanese and in the process became familiar with prevailing conditions in Japan.

Politics, of course, favored close cooperation between Japan and South Korea. Not only did President Park favor ties that increased trade, but also he was a Japanophile who adopted the developmental model of the Meiji era (1868–1911) as his own. (The chief features of this model were political power concentrated in the hands of the few; government leadership in economic development; and stimulation of economic growth through the nurturing of capitalist enterprises.) Moreover, Park closely studied the post–World War II pattern of Japanese economic growth and emulated it. Although he was strongly nationalistic, he admired Japan for its powerful emergence as a modern nation.

Park's affinity with Japan was reinforced by his resentment of the

United States. He had become strongly anti-American while working as a communist activist between 1945 and 1948, since the Korean Communist Party was at the forefront of the anti-American struggle. Even though he received a year's training in the United States as a South Korean military officer, Park was not able to or did not wish to adapt to the American pattern of behavior. The United States was strongly suspicious of Park's ideology when he spearheaded the coup of 1961 and withheld its support for a considerable length of time. Even after Park visited President Kennedy in Washington in 1961 and won the latter's approval, the United States exerted pressure against his plan to prolong military rule. On one occasion, the U.S. went so far as to delay the unloading of flour, provided through the Public Law 480 program in August 1963, even though the cargo ships were anchored in Inchon harbor and South Korea was undergoing a serious food crisis. This forced Park to send an emissary (Chang Key-young, who was later to become the deputy premier and chairman of the Economic Planning Board) to the Mitsui Trading Company in Tokyo to seek a special favor. Mitsui sold Park, on credit, 100,000 metric tons of flour.[44] The eagerness of the Japanese to cooperate with Park's regime contrasted sharply with the aloof, condescending, and suspicious American attitude.

The effect of the Park government's adoption of an export-oriented growth strategy is well known. Benefiting from strong encouragement and aid from the government, including government-guaranteed, low-interest foreign loans (in a society where the interest rate has often exceeded 30 percent per annum), Korean businessmen competed among themselves to import machinery and whole plants and to increase the production of exportable commodities. As a result, industry altered the country's landscape and drew millions of laborers to urban manufacturing centers. Many sleepy farm communities were turned into bustling industrial cities. South Korea attained one of the world's highest rates of growth in gross national product, as shown in Table 6. The content of the rapidly growing exports also changed drastically. Manufactured goods constituted less than 20 percent before 1962, but increased to 44.5 percent in 1963, and to 73.5 percent in 1968.[45]

Although it is difficult to determine the exact role played by Japanese capital and technology in South Korea's economic growth, there is no doubt that they played a prominent role. Japanese loans, particularly the commercial loans provided by Japanese financial magnates, permitted Korean businessmen to build new plants and to purchase the necessary resources to produce export products. The

TABLE 6 SOUTH KOREA'S ANNUAL GROWTH RATE IN GNP AND EXPORTS, 1954–1983
(PERCENTAGE)

Year	GNP	Primary Exports	Secondary Exports		Tertiary Exports	Total Exports
			Total	Manufacturing		
1954	5.5	7.6	11.2	18.7	2.5	—
1955	5.4	2.6	21.6	22.9	5.7	—
1956	0.4	−5.6	16.2	17.3	4.0	—
1957	7.7	9.1	9.7	8.2	5.8	—
1958	5.2	6.2	8.2	9.1	3.2	−25.7
1959	3.9	−1.2	9.7	9.2	7.5	20.0
1960	1.1	−2.1	10.9	8.2	2.3	65.7
1961	5.3	12.2	4.4	4.0	−0.5	24.7
1962	2.2	−6.0	13.4	11.7	8.6	34.0
1963	8.3	9.5	14.2	16.1	7.5	58.4
1964	8.7	15.6	10.5	9.9	3.5	37.2
1965	5.5	−1.0	18.3	20.5	9.7	47.0
1966	11.3	11.6	15.3	17.3	13.0	42.9
1967	6.2	−5.9	20.2	21.6	14.6	27.9

Year						
1968	10.1	1.3	23.4	27.2	15.3	42.2
1969	12.1	10.5	19.2	21.6	14.2	36.7
1970	7.1	1.7	19.6	19.9	9.5	34.2
1971	8.6	0.6	17.3	18.8	9.8	27.8
1972	5.5	2.0	12.9	14.0	5.0	52.1
1973	13.0	6.3	28.6	29.2	13.6	98.6
1974	7.4	6.7	15.2	15.8	5.0	38.3
1975	6.7	5.3	12.6	12.6	5.1	13.9
1976	13.1	10.7	21.5	22.6	13.7	51.8
1977	12.7	2.6	15.7	16.0	15.8	30.2
1978	9.7	-9.2	20.2	21.3	12.1	26.5
1979	6.5	6.7	9.3	10.3	5.0	18.4
1980	-5.2	-21.7	-1.5	-1.1	-1.8	16.3
1981	6.2	14.5	7.6	7.2	0.6	21.4
1982	5.6	4.1	3.6	4.0	7.3	2.8
1983	9.3	6.9	10.6	10.8	9.4	11.9

NOTE: The data for 1954–1959 are based on 1970 constant price data. The percentage growth in total exports is not available for 1954–1957. The data for 1960–1982 are based on 1975 constant price data. Export data for all years are based on current price data. The data for 1983 are preliminary.

SOURCE: Bank of Korea, *Economic Statistics Yearbook*, 1973, 1979, 1983.

government provided additional local currency loans at favorable terms to pay for labor and other costs. Fruitful negotiation of Japanese loans and the winning of government approval was the quickest way for an entrepreneur to acquire wealth.[46] Little wonder that businessmen were eager to compete in the race for more and larger production facilities.

Although the new opportunities provided by the 1965 normalization of relations spurred the growth of the Korean economy, they also began to change the character of the relationship between Japan and Korea. As more and more Japanese capital was injected into South Korea in the form of loans and direct investment, Japanese business and government assumed proportionally larger roles in Korea's economic decisionmaking. The Koreans could not build or operate new plants without Japanese approval and cooperation. By 1969, South Korea had acquired $400 million in commercial loans, and these continued to grow in size. Although Deputy Premier Chang Key-young called for "perpetual coprosperity and mutual benefit" in the relationship between the two countries and the implementation of the principles of free trade and free movement of capital, South Korea continued to accumulate huge trade deficits.[47]

In a speech before the inaugural meeting of the Japanese–South Korean Cooperation Committee in 1969, Chang expressed his fear that the mounting trade imbalance might become a source of political friction in the future, and he was not far off the mark. South Korea requested the lowering of tariffs and the elimination of import quotas and other trade barriers to bring about a trade balance, but, as can be seen from Table 5, South Korea's deficit continued to mount. An "organic international division of labor" between the two countries remained the elusive goal of the Park regime.[48] The huge trade deficit with Japan added tremendous pressure to South Korea's economy, for Korea either had to incur more foreign debts or to increase exports to other markets in order to correct the situation.

Japanese–South Korean trade and other financial transactions were highly profitable to entrepreneurs in both countries and contributed significantly to South Korea's economic growth. But the huge deficits and the ever-present need to expand exports to meet debt obligations made South Korea's economy highly susceptible to the vicissitudes of international markets. This created such serious side effects as a high rate of inflation, steep rises in wages, and a shortage of consumer goods. In time, these developments adversely affected South Korea's exports and destabilized its politics. I shall turn to these events in subsequent chapters.

CONCLUDING REMARKS

Thus, economic motives on both sides of the strait brought Japan and South Korea together in 1965. Since then, Japan and the Park regime have established a symbiotic relationship. Perhaps the Park government needed Japanese cooperation more than its Japanese counterpart needed Korea, because Park's survival depended largely on economic development, which required Japanese capital and technology. Japanese businessmen, however, were no less eager, since huge profits were to be made. Japanese business circles, which already had close ties with their politicians, had a powerful ally in Kishi Nobusuke, the power behind the throne. The close relationship aspired to by both the Park government and Japanese business circles also coincided with the interests of the U.S., which was in a position to exert a strong influence on both Japan and South Korea.

In their eagerness to pursue their respective aims, however, both sides pushed aside their historical animosity and emotional conflicts. Detractors were unwelcome, and Japanese and South Korean leaders made no attempt to build a bridge of genuine understanding. President Park was in the key position to initiate such a process, but he was absorbed with technocrats who could plan and implement rapid economic advancement. Park set the tone for bilateral relations. And, as the South Korean economy expanded in an unprecedented manner in the aftermath of Japanese–South Korean normalization, the opposition within Korea dissipated. But the surging economic relationship had only masked deep-seated emotions.

4

Groping for a Korea Policy in the Détente Era

The election of Richard M. Nixon as U.S. president in 1968 and the ushering in of the détente era caused momentous changes in international politics. In rapid succession, Nixon enunciated the Guam Doctrine in July 1969, established détente with China, improved relations with the Soviet Union, and terminated U.S. involvement in Vietnam.

Nixon's new strategy sent tremors around the world, but Japan and South Korea were among the nations most directly affected. Japanese and South Korean leaders scurried to study his famous 1967 article on "Asia After Viet Nam" even before Nixon's election was confirmed and tried to adjust their policies accordingly. Nixon called for "Asia for the Asians" and for a reduced U.S. role there. Japan, the region's most powerful industrial and financial nation, was called upon to assume a new role. Nixon not only recognized the Japanese desire to play a greater role in Asia but also argued that it was necessary for Japan to take up the responsibility of "helping secure the common safety of non-Communist Asia." He called for the removal of the no-war clause from the Japanese constitution (Article 9) and urged Japan to build its own armed forces and assume responsibility for its own defense. A Pacific community had to be built among the nations in the region to coordinate their military defenses and strengthen their economies.[1] The United States clearly expected Japan to undertake greater responsibility for Asian affairs, including economic development, political stability, and even security.² Nixon intended to build a "structure of peace" by Soviet-American and Sino-American détente that would reduce tension throughout the world. Japan's new role would then be assured.

Nixon's détente strategy and subsequent actions taken by his government profoundly affected Japanese policy toward the Korean peninsula and Japanese–South Korean relations. U.S. actions revealed the situational and reactive character of Japanese foreign policy and the fragility of Japanese–South Korean ties built upon a foundation of economic symbiosis. Japan's Korea policy had been dictated by Japan's assessment of its position in East Asia as a whole—particularly its relations with the superpowers—not by any special relationship with South Korea. Japan had coordinated its policy with South Korea only when it served the interests of both nations. Nixon's policies also confirmed the consensual nature of Japanese foreign policy decisions. The disposition of individual leaders played little role in the face of overwhelming changes in the international arena. The loyalty of "pro–South Korean" groups proved ephemeral.

THE NIXON DOCTRINE AND THE KOREA CLAUSE

As is well known, the Guam Doctrine or Nixon Doctrine was corollary to the prolonged Vietnam War. That war destroyed the myth of U.S. invincibility and undercut America's role as gendarme against world communism. As the antiwar movement encouraged isolationist tendencies, political leaders began to seek retrenchment. The era of Pax Americana came to an end, removing the central pillar from the structure that had enabled Japan to concentrate on economic growth alone.

In the meantime, Japan had achieved a spectacular economic growth, surpassing West Germany in 1967 as the second largest economic power in the noncommunist world. In 1965, for the first time in postwar history, Japan's exports to the United States exceeded its imports, manifesting Japan's superb industrial capability. These phenomena naturally boosted the morale of the Japanese and encouraged the resurgence of nationalism. Increasingly frequent calls for an independent diplomacy were heard in Japan, and the country's intellectuals sought a new role for Japan in the world arena. The Japanese could not be content with the role of a second-rate power dependent on the United States.

The Japanese were also becoming more and more disillusioned by the United States' policy in Vietnam. Vietnam showed not only the limits of U.S. power, on which Japanese security depended, but also the questionable wisdom of American leaders, who chose to involve the entire nation in what had begun as a mere counterinsurgency operation. The Japanese also questioned the U.S. containment policy that presumed the monolithic unity of communist countries, since the Sino-Soviet split after 1957 had clearly shown the potency of nationalism even among communist countries.

American involvement in Vietnam had a direct impact on South Korean security and Japanese–South Korean relations in that the United States was unable to respond to North Korean provocations. On January 23, 1968, the North Koreans captured a U.S. intelligence ship, the USS *Pueblo*, off the North Korean coast. President Park was already agitated by an attempted raid on the presidential palace two days before by 31 commando troops dispatched by North Korea. He urged U.S. retaliation against North Korea, but to no avail.[3] The United States dispatched a flotilla spearheaded by the USS *Enterprise*, but it chose to negotiate for the release of *Pueblo* crewmen rather than take military action. The United States was virtually immobilized by the Tet offensive of January 30, only a week after the capture of the USS *Pueblo*; it was, in any event, unprepared to open a second front in East Asia. These American actions raised grave doubts in South Korea about U.S. resolve to defend the peninsula.

Evidently the South Korean government pressed the Japanese for closer cooperation in light of declining U.S. credibility and might, and the Japanese leaders shared Korean concerns. At the second annual joint ministerial meeting, held in August 1968, the two sides declared that "the security [*anzen* in Japanese and *anjŏn* in Korean] and prosperity of South Korea have a grave [*jūdiana* or *chungdae han*] influence on that of Japan." This clause was repeated at subsequent meetings in 1969 and 1970, but was dropped at the fifth annual meeting in August 1971.[4] South Korean misgivings about U.S. resolve heightened in 1969 when the United States made no retaliatory move against North Korea after its MIG fighters shot down an American reconnaissance aircraft (EC-121) in April.

The practical meaning of the clause was delineated by Chang Key-young, the South Korean deputy premier, in February 1969, at the inaugural conference of the Japanese–South Korean Cooperation Committee. Chang defined the term "security" after predicting that the day would come when the security of South Korea was linked directly to that of Japan. He told Japanese leaders that the "security of South Korea can be attained through its economic stability, growth, and prosperity," and he implored them to "earnestly render a political decision" on the matter.[5]

In this context Richard Nixon enunciated the Guam Doctrine in July 1969. The doctrine called for a linkage between Japanese and South Korean security, and, in November 1969, when Premier Satō visited Washington for a summit talk with President Nixon, a phrase was inserted into the Nixon-Satō joint communiqué stating that the security of the Republic of Korea was "essential to Japan's own security." This phrase came to be known as the Korea clause, and it had significant political and military implications.

The Korea clause was a culmination of prolonged Japanese-American negotiations on the reversion of Okinawa to Japan. Although the United States recognized the residual rights of Japan in Okinawa, it continued to administer the islands after the Second World War; the islands were of crucial strategic value to the United States simply because of their location in the western Pacific. In the late 1960s, the United States was prepared to accede to intense nationalistic feeling in Japan and give the islands back, but in turn it requested that Japan grant the United States the unrestricted right to use American bases in Okinawa for the defense of Korea, Taiwan, and Vietnam.[6] The long negotiations ended with the Satō visit, when the two sides agreed on the reversion of Okinawa to Japan in 1972 in return for the inclusion of the Korea clause in the joint communiqué.

The practical meaning of the Korea clause was delineated by Premier Satō in his speech at the National Press Club after the summit meeting: if South Korea or Taiwan came under attack, Japan would regard it as a threat to the peace and security of the Far East, including Japan, and would take prompt and positive measures so that the United States could use its military bases and facilities within Japan (which would include Okinawa after 1972) to meet the armed attack.[7] This Japanese commitment was necessary for the United States because, without it, U.S. ability to provide support for South Korea would be severely limited. As Kubo Takuya, chief of the Defense Bureau of the Japanese Self-Defense Agency, put it:

> If the United States could not use Japanese [territory for the defense of Korea], it would be like going up to the second floor and having the ladder removed. Only if there is a Mutual Security Treaty between Japan and the United States, and if the U.S. could use Japan, could the U.S. provide military support to Korea. Under such a situation, there will be no war on the Korean peninsula. Therefore, the security of the Korean peninsula is essential to Japan.[8]

Thus, a close cooperation between the United States and Japan was a pillar in the "structure of peace" that Nixon envisioned. But a series of U.S. actions taken after the Nixon-Satō meeting cast doubt on U.S. policy in East Asia. President Nixon's unilateral withdrawal of 20,000 U.S. troops from South Korea in 1970, his decision not to consult Japan on his contacts with China, and his actions in the economic arena (such as the embargo of soybean exports to Japan; the floating of the dollar in 1971, which led to the revaluation of yen; and the surcharge imposed on Japanese exports to the United States) created the impression that the United States would no longer treat Japan as an ally and that the interests of the United States no longer coincided with those of Japan. The United States had nurtured Japanese true believers in the cold war world order centered on the United States, but now they were cut loose into the uncharted open sea and told to find their own bearings.[9]

Uncertainty in Japan was heightened by the Watergate affair (1973–74) and the surge of liberal and neoisolationist forces in the United States that followed it. When the Japanese economy was teetering on the brink because of the oil crisis of 1973, the United States government enacted a law prohibiting the export of newly found Alaskan oil to Japan. This was certainly not an ally that Japan could rely on. Between 1969 and 1975, therefore, Japanese leaders groped to find an "independent foreign policy." As former foreign minister Ōhira told a television audience in January 1972, Japan wanted to "get out of this military dependence on the United States and attain political independence in world affairs, just as Japan has done in the economic field."[10]

Japan did find the idea of building a "structure of peace" appealing. Heavily dependent on foreign resources and trade for its economic well-being and having spent little on defense since 1945, the Japanese found that the structure of peace offered many advantages. Although still shocked and humiliated by U.S. refusal to consult Japan, Premier Tanaka Kakuei followed Nixon's footsteps to Beijing in September 1972 and established diplomatic relations with the People's Republic of China (PRC). His government also initiated talks with the government of North Vietnam in January 1973, and, in September 1974, Tanaka journeyed to a number of countries in Southeast Asia to improve ties with them. Many of his lieutenants and colleagues toured the Middle East and Latin America in 1975 in pursuit of "resource diplomacy."[11]

As for the security issue, Japanese leaders were not prepared to tackle thorny Article 9 of the constitution, which prohibited the maintenance of "land, sea and air forces, as well as other war potential." It was too sensitive an issue in Japanese domestic politics, and the LDP simply could not withstand the domestic uproar a reevaluation would cause. But, in drawing up the fourth defense buildup plan, covering the years 1972–1976, a significant step was taken to bolster Japan's defense capability. Although the third plan (1967–1971) had called for defense capabilities that could "deal most effectively with an aggression lower in scale than a local conventional war," the fourth plan aimed at the creation of an autonomous defense capacity. Japanese security relations with the United States were to be reversed: the Mutual Defense Treaty was to supplement Japan's own autonomous defense capability rather than the other way around. Japan was to maintain an air and sea capacity sufficient to deal with any crises.[12] Whereas the third plan called for an expenditure of $7.2 billion, the fourth plan required $16.6 billion. Clearly these changes reflected the new U.S. strategy, but they also reflected Japanese doubts about U.S. intentions. Many Japanese believed that Japan should bolster its defense capability for its own sake regardless of U.S. intentions.

TURBULENCE IN KOREA

Changing U.S. strategy also created uncertainty in South Korea. The United States had withdrawn 20,000 troops from Korea in 1970, and South Korea did not know how far and how fast the United States would proceed with the withdrawal of its remaining 38,000 troops.[13] The ROK could not be certain at what level of conflict between North and South Korea the United States would see fit to commit its military power against the enemy as stipulated in the Mutual Defense Treaty of 1954—if, indeed, the United States would enter the conflict at all. Answers to these questions were vital to South Korean policymakers because Seoul's reliance on the United States was absolute, and the challenge from the north was perceived as imminent. U.S. inaction after the North Korean seizure of the USS *Pueblo* and the shooting down of the EC-121 plane made the South Koreans more wary of U.S. commitment.

It was clear, however, that the United States' reduction of its Asian commitments would require a decrease in the prevailing level of tension in Asia. U.S. allies were expected to redirect their efforts toward accommodation rather than confrontation. Beginning in August 1970, the South Korean government implemented a policy of approaching North Korea and other communist countries. The result was the historic July 4, 1972, joint communiqué between representatives of the North and South Korean regimes, which pledged to find ways to attain peaceful unification. In the euphoria that followed, delegates from Pyongyang and Seoul established the North-South Coordinating Committee and deliberated on the means for achieving unification.

The talks, however, snagged quickly, and, by the spring of 1974, the two sides had reached an impasse. North Korea insisted that tension on the Korean peninsula must be reduced and trust built through the removal of U.S. forces from South Korea; the South Korean side was adamant that the two sides must first undertake economic, scholarly, and cultural exchanges. Only then could the two sides deal with the more difficult military matters. Neither side trusted the other's motives and there was no room for compromise. The two Koreas returned to the posture of belligerent confrontation.[14]

JAPAN AND THE THAW IN KOREA

Thus the euphoria in Korea proved short-lived and illusory. But the atmosphere of détente galvanized Japanese intellectuals, who argued that Japan should pose no obstacles to the Korean effort at unification. Mushakōji Kinhide, a widely respected liberal intellectual, summed up this position well:

> The two Koreas announced in July 1972 to bring about unification through independent Korean efforts, through peaceful means, and by transcending differences in policies, ideologies, and systems. This situation behooved Japan to abandon policies that tied Japan too closely to South Korea, thereby rigidifying the cold war structure. Only if the two sides in Korea were loosened from the restraints of the cold war could they achieve unification based on the three principles cited above.[15]

This was the intellectual rationale for an equidistance policy favored by many liberal and left-wing intellectuals and politicians, the same rationale they had advanced in opposing the 1965 treaty between Japan and South Korea.[16]

The advocates of the equidistance policy could also justify their policy on strictly strategic grounds, by citing the American policy of reducing tension in the region. They could quote the following passage from Nixon's 1967 article to buttress their argument:

The world cannot be safe until China [read North Korea] changes. Thus our aim, to the extent that we can influence events, should be to induce change. The way to do this is to persuade China [North Korea] that it *must* change: that it cannot satisfy its imperial ambitions, and that its own national interest requires a turning away from foreign [or South Korean] adventuring and turning inward toward the solution of its own domestic problems.[17]

More immediately, détente between the two Koreas offered many advantages to Japan. It would provide a securer environment by reducing the need for Japan to expend more resources on defense; it would render the urging by the United States to share responsibility of regional security less convincing. Détente would also enable Japan to increase its trade with North Korea. North Korea had traded very little with noncommunist countries and was eager to buy Japanese ships, factories, machinery, and other products. The Japanese had been trading with North Korea since 1961 (indirectly since 1956), but political barriers had severely restricted commerce. Even so, business groups in Japan were eager to expand the North Korean trade. Whatever their motives or rationale, various groups in Japan began to step away from past policies and to approach North Korea. Obviously it was not the liberal intellectuals alone who thought it desirable to remove Japan from the "cold war structure," for it was Foreign Minister Fukuda Yoshio, a solid conservative and mainstream LDP leader, who opened the new trend by urging that the Korea clause be revised.

Fukuda on the Korea Clause

Fukuda was eager to rid Japan of the responsibility it had assumed in the Korea clause, which he viewed as not only unnecessary but also detrimental to Japanese interests. Its cancellation would remove Japan from the anticommunist structure. At the Japanese-American ministerial meeting held in September 1971 Fukuda advocated a revision of the Korea clause. In October, after Beijing was accepted as the official representative of China at the United Nations, Fukuda invited reporters to his residence and revealed the content of his proposal at the September meeting.[18] He told the Diet on May 16, 1972, that the Korea clause had in fact lost its validity because of the new, stabilized situation on the Korean peninsula.[19]

As I noted earlier, the fifth Japanese–South Korean joint ministerial conference of August 1971 omitted reference to the "close relationship between the security and prosperity of the two countries." Fukuda clearly took the lead in detaching Japan from the Korea clause. Premier Satō held similar views. Pressed on the issue at a press conference in Tokyo on January 8, 1972, after the summit meeting with President Nixon at San Clemente, Satō said, "This particular expression is not necessarily valid in describing the situation today," adding that "a communiqué is not a treaty."[20] Clearly Satō regarded the Korea clause as no longer binding. When the U.S. government requested a clarification of the premier's remarks, however, Foreign Minister Fukuda retracted the premier's statement on January 9, saying that the premier had misinterpreted the question.[21] The U.S. government had more than a casual interest in Satō's remark; in spite of the thaw, the entire U.S. defense strategy in East Asia depended on the use of the Okinawan bases.

JAPAN AND NORTH KOREA

The Japanese leaders' move toward an equidistance policy can be seen from their attempt to improve relations with North Korea. In the wake of Sino-American and Sino-Japanese rapprochement, the North Korean regime tried to establish an economic and cultural beachhead in Japan, penetrate Japanese domestic politics, and build a united front against the "reactionaries." At the same time North Korea was attempting to create tensions between Japan and the South Korean government. In September and October 1971, the government of the Democratic People's Republic of Korea (DPRK) invited influential Japanese journalists like the managing editor of *Asahi Shimbun* to visit the country. Premier Kim Il-sŏng assured the editor that the DPRK had "always striven to have friendly and good-neighborly relations with Japan, wanted to develop trade relations with Japan, and hoped to arrange with Japan mutual visits of journalists, technicians, and other people as often as possible."[22] North Korea appeared particularly eager to increase trade with Japan, because it desperately needed Western technology and Japanese capital for its economic advancement.

Premier Kim's remarks found eager listeners. In November, Japanese politicians from various parties, including the ruling Liberal Democratic Party, established a "Dietmen's League for the Promotion of Japan–[North] Korean Friendship." The league claimed a roster of

234 upper and lower house members, and Kuno Chūji, a LDP member, was provisional chairman. In late 1972, a 13-member delegation from this group, headed by Kuno, visited Pyongyang, and, on January 23, this group and a DPRK Committee for the Promotion of International Trade signed a trade agreement. The terms stipulated that total trade would expand to between 150 and 200 million British pounds by 1976, large export items could be paid for within eight years, trade exhibits would be held in Pyongyang and Tokyo, personnel exchanges would be promoted, and trade missions would be exchanged. Although Premier Satō had objected to the mission, ruling LDP politicians warmly greeted Kuno upon his return to Tokyo.[23]

Business leaders were no less eager. When the DPRK government approached Japanese business leaders through the pro–North Korean Federation of Korean Residents in Japan (Chō-sō-ren) in 1972, top business and financial leaders in the Keidanren (Federation of Economic Organizations), Chambers of Commerce, and other associations responded with enthusiasm and began to organize a visiting delegation of business (*zaikai*) leaders. They also united to organize a giant trade consortium, the Kyō-a (Asian Cooperation) Trading Company, which was to serve as a channel for exporting whole plants to North Korea.[24]

Of course, this was not a simple business operation; former Diet member Fukuya Jun'ichi of the Fukuda faction and Yatsugi Kazuo, one of the key lieutenants of Kishi Nobusuke in the Japan–South Korean Cooperation Committee, actively worked behind the scene to bring the venture to fruition. Yatsugi's involvement in this venture was particularly noteworthy because of his close ties with Kishi and his previous enthusiasm for promoting economic ties between Japan and South Korea. He had drawn considerable attention in South Korea in the spring of 1970 when he presented the so-called Yatsugi Plan, which called for the establishment of an Economic Cooperative Zone (*keizai kyōryokuken*) linking the southeastern part of Japan with the southern part of Korea.[25] The Kyō-a Trading Company, which failed to make much progress for various reasons, revealed the situational character of the so-called pro–South Korean groups in Japan.

Japanese–North Korean trade rose at a phenomenal rate even though the amount of trade had been very low before 1972. Total annual trade figures are presented in Table 7. If we use the annual average between 1968 and 1971 as a base for comparison, Japanese exports to North Korea had increased 3.85 times in 1972 (an increase of 285 percent), 4.12 times in 1973, 10.37 times in 1974, and 7.44 times in 1975. Japanese imports from North Korea meanwhile in-

TABLE 7   JAPAN'S TRADE WITH NORTH KOREA, 1961–1983
(IN THOUSANDS OF U.S. DOLLARS)

Year	Japanese Exports	Japanese Imports	Total Trade	Trade Balance
1961	4,938	3,976	8,914	962
1962	4,781	4,553	9,334	228
1963	5,347	9,430	14,777	−4,083
1964	11,284	20,231	31,515	−8,947
1965	16,505	14,723	31,228	1,782
1966	5,016	22,692	27,708	−17,676
1967	6,370	29,606	35,976	−23,239
1968	20,748	34,032	54,780	−13,284
1969	24,159	32,186	56,345	−8,027
1970	23,344	34,414	57,758	−11,070
1971	28,907	30,059	58,966	−1,152
1972	93,443	38,311	131,754	55,132
1973	100,160	72,318	172,478	27,842
1974	251,914	108,824	360,738	143,090
1975	180,630	64,839	245,469	115,791
1976	96,056	71,627	167,683	24,429
1977	125,097	66,618	191,715	58,479
1978	183,347	106,862	290,209	76,485
1979	283,848	152,027	435,875	131,821
1980	374,305	180,046	554,351	194,259
1981	290,995	139,476	430,471	151,519
1982	313,162	152,026	465,188	161,136
1983	327,077	126,149	453,226	200,928

SOURCE: Japan External Trade Organization, *White Paper on International Trade* (Tokyo, 1961–1983).

creased 2.2 times (an increase of 120 percent) in 1973, 3.3 times in 1974, and 1.9 times in 1975.

It should be noted also that the DPRK maintained a trade surplus with Japan until 1971, but, since 1972, it has incurred large deficits. Japan has extended credit, mostly in the form of extended payment; 40 percent of Japanese exports in 1974 were in this form. A large part of Japanese exports, 70 percent in 1974 and 60 percent in 1975, went to North Korea's industries in the form of plants, machinery, steel, and metal products. As early as 1968, the Satō government was willing to extend long-term, low-interest loans from the government-sponsored Export-Import Bank to North Korea. In 1971, two such requests were approved, but they were later rescinded because of strenuous objections from the South Korean government. In 1973, however, the Export-Import Bank allowed Japanese exporters to use its funds for a transaction involving 500 million yen.[26]

The increase in trade also brought numerous North Korean personnel into Japan, which, of course, required government permission. In 1972, a seven-member delegation from the DPRK Committee for the Promotion of International Trade visited Japan for the first time. This was followed in 1973 by some half-dozen delegations of North Koreans involved in radio and television broadcasting, steel, iron, cement, and so on. In 1974, a trade, industrial, and commercial delegation visited Japan for wide-ranging talks.[27] For all intents and purposes, the Japanese government encouraged a broad range of exchanges between Japan and North Korea.

Not only were these exchanges and trade given extensive coverage by the Japanese mass media, but a large retinue of Japanese newspaper, radio, and television reporters visited North Korea and returned with glowing accounts. They were impressed by North Korea's orderliness, discipline, and intense efforts in agriculture, industry, and education. These reports and texts of interviews with the North Korean leader were given prominent space in Japanese newspapers, magazines, radio, and television. Unmistakably, the era of the equidistance policy had arrived, or so it seemed.

Given the context of the continuous North Korean barrage against Japanese "reactionaries," "aggressors," "monopoly capitalists," "militarists," and the like, the Japanese exhibition of enthusiasm toward North Korea was little short of miraculous. In sharp contrast to the endless criticism of the South Korean government and society, Japanese visitors to North Korea, including the LDP politicians, made nothing but laudatory remarks in public after their return. It was paradoxical that in the context of such intense historical animosity, the Japanese would "hit it off" so well with North Korea when their relations with South Korea had been marred by so many complex emotions. Japanese journalists would report statements made by the North Korean leader with reverence and comments made by their official guides were depicted as the whole truth. There was no trace of the exercise of independent judgment.

A South Korean reporter commenting on this phenomenon attributed it to a number of psychological factors: many Japanese were infatuated with socialism and communism and wished the North Koreans would vicariously fulfill their unfulfilled "revolutionary romanticism," and, he theorized, this "illusion" was combined with a feeling of "penitence" about 36 years of colonial rule and the discriminatory attitude toward Koreans that still existed in Japan. In addition, information from the "closed society" was at a premium for the Japanese mass media and hence, for commercial reasons, they adopted friendly and submissive attitudes toward North Korea. Also, to criticize North Korea would be to reduce blame for the Park regime in the south, which was unacceptable.[28]

Whether one accepts or rejects this analysis, there was a marked contrast in the nature of Japanese–North Korean relations and Japanese–South Korean relations. The image projected by the continuous stream of laudatory comments about North Korea was that of a remote and sanitized society centered on a resolute and omnipotent leader. Such a society was held in respect and was not to be tampered with by Japanese commercialism or decadence. Japan's relationship with the DPRK was not extensive, but some sort of official relationship needed to be established.

Tanaka-Kimura on the Korea Clause

The trend away from the "cold war structure" accelerated after Tanaka Kakuei succeeded Satō as premier in July 1972. In July 1974, the new foreign minister, Kimura Toshio, revealed his government's intention to redirect its Korea policy. Soon after his appointment as foreign minister, Kimura stated that the "peace and security of the entire Korean peninsula" rather than just the Republic of Korea was essential to Japan. He also stated on August 31 that there was no threat to South Korea from the north.[29] These statements were interpreted as a sign of the Tanaka cabinet's attempt to alter its relationship with the two Koreas. Kimura's reinterpretation of the Korea clause cast doubt on the legality of the U.S. use of Okinawan bases for the defense of South Korea. The denial of a threat from North Korea by the foreign minister aroused concern in South Korea because it buttressed North Korean demands that U.S. forces be withdrawn from South Korea.

Another indication of the Japanese inclination toward an equidistance policy was the September 5 statement of Foreign Ministry officials, including Kimura, which declared that the Republic of Korea was not the only legal government in Korea.[30] The statement was made by the chief of the Treaty Bureau in response to a query from a

Diet member, and his position was endorsed by the foreign minister. In a strictly legal sense, of course, the Foreign Ministry's view was in accordance with the agreement signed between Japan and the ROK in 1965, as noted in Chapter 3. Nonetheless, it was the first time that Japanese officials had articulated the meaning of the phraseology of Article 3 of the treaty in public in so stark a manner. Given the background of Kimura's previous statements on Korea and the timing of the statement, there was no doubt about the general intention behind it. The South Koreans took the September 5 remark as a sign of Japanese perfidy and held massive demonstrations; some of the demonstrators broke into the Japanese Embassy in Seoul and ransacked it.

STRAINS WITH SOUTH KOREA

Japan's eagerness to promote friendly ties with North Korea contrasted sharply with the intense animosity between Japan and South Korea triggered by the kidnapping of Kim Dae-jung from a Tokyo hotel in August 1973 and the attempted assassination of President Park by a Korean resident of Japan in August 1974. These incidents so strained Japanese–South Korean relations that diplomatic ties between the two governments nearly reached a breaking point in late 1974. By early 1975, the two governments had arrived at a settlement, but the Kim Dae-jung affair was destined to remain an unresolved issue that flared up time and time again.

The Kim Dae-jung Affair

The Kim Dae-jung affair began when President Park Chung Hee proclaimed martial law in October 1972 and, in November, adopted a new constitution ensuring the perpetuation of his dictatorship. The previous constitution, adopted in 1963 under Park's aegis, considerably restricted presidential powers, granted legislative powers to the popularly elected National Assembly, and required that the president be elected by popular ballot. But Park had the constitution revised in 1969 to permit him to hold office indefinitely, and he rammed a National Emergency Law through the National Assembly in December 1971 to give him complete power to control, regulate, and mobilize the people, the economy, and the press whenever he deemed it necessary. Park still found the constitutional provisions constraining. Under the new constitution, the president was elected indirectly by an electoral college (which elected Park to a fourth term in December 1972 without a dissenting vote), and he was given the power to appoint one-third of the National Assembly members.

President Park had his own perception of the international environment and did not share the euphoria that prevailed in Japan and among the populace in South Korea. The talk of thaw had a sense of unreality for him. I have already alluded to the seizure of the USS *Pueblo* in January 1968 and the shooting down of an EC-121 reconnaissance aircraft in April 1969. South Korean intelligence continued to report the imminence of an all-out attack from North Korea in 1970 and 1971. In short, the South Korean leadership was caught in a vise between the extremely belligerent state across the truce line and the strong current of Sino-American détente. If the sudden change in the structure of international relations in East Asia provided new challenges and opportunities to Japan, the fluid new environment presented enormous risks for South Korea, whose policy options had been greatly constricted by its traditional and extraordinary dependence on the United States and by its rigid anticommunist ethos.

Unlike the leaders of North Korea, who had the advantage of an intensely mobilized and monolithic political system that permitted them to adjust to environmental needs without fear of disrupting the ongoing operation of the system, South Korean leaders were obliged to calculate carefully the effect of their actions upon their quasi-open political system as well as upon their two close allies, the United States and Japan. President Park's statement of December 1971, when he proclaimed a state of national emergency and reported that the Republic of Korea was "faced with grave crisis," certainly had a ring of truth.

The president was evidently stung by public criticisms expressed by some opposition politicians concerning the manner in which North-South dialogue had been conducted before the historic joint communiqué of July 4, 1972. Some politicians had questioned the constitutionality and legality of the North-South dialogue as well as the high-level travels between Pyongyang and Seoul. Under the Anticommunist Law enacted in July 1961 by the military junta, of which Park Chung Hee was the leader, any form of contact with a Communist was made a criminal offense. The president evidently decided that he must have absolute power if he was to steer the country out of the domestic and international crises.

Kim Dae-jung had run against President Park in 1971 as the opposition candidate and was narrowly defeated, winning 5,395,000 votes to President Park's 6,342,000 votes. When President Park declared martial law, Kim was abroad. Upon hearing the news, he issued a strident denunciation of Park's action and attempted to rally American and Japanese politicians and intellectuals against President Park. The South Korean government then charged that Kim Dae-jung was plotting to form a provisional Korean government in Japan to attack the legitimacy of the ROK. Officials also charged that Kim had contacted various elements in Japan with ties to the North Korean regime. Kim strenuously denied these charges.

On August 8, 1973, a group of men kidnapped Kim from a Tokyo hotel, drove to a boat, and transported him to Seoul. According to Kim's own later account, the kidnappers had planned to dump him in the Sea of Japan but scuttled the plan when they received new instructions from an unidentified source. He was released unharmed near his home in Seoul five days after the kidnapping. The Japanese police later found the fingerprints of Kim Tong-wun (Dong Woon Kim), the first secretary of the South Korean Embassy in Tokyo, at the Tokyo hotel where Kim had been kidnapped.

An uproar soon followed. The Japanese government was greatly embarrassed. Although a Korean citizen, Kim Dae-jung was on Japanese territory when kidnapped, an act that clearly violated Japanese sovereignty. Japanese officials demanded Kim's return, without success. Finally, in November, the Japanese and South Korean governments reached a "political settlement" whereby the ROK government assured Kim Dae-jung's freedom, including his right to depart from Korea, and promised that he would not be tried for any action he had taken while in Japan. In return, the Japanese government agreed to drop the issue.[31]

The Kim Dae-jung incident gravely damaged the image of South Korea in Japan and destroyed whatever favorable image the regime of Park Chung Hee had built there through phenomenal economic growth. The affair reinforced the strong anti-Korean prejudices held by that large segment of the Japanese population who scorned Koreans as uncivilized people. It strengthened the conviction of the intellectuals who had argued against Japan's close ties with South Korea. The incident also provided opposition parties and the North Korean–supported Federation of Korean Residents in Japan (Chō-sō-ren) with a golden opportunity to attack the South Korean government and denounce the LDP government.

The incident added considerable momentum to anti-Park forces in Japan. Kim Dae-jung came to personify the opposition forces in South Korea suppressed by the Park regime, and the confrontation between the president and the South Korean opposition forces did not abate. Beginning in October 1973, South Korean students, Christian leaders, newspaper reporters, and intellectuals engaged in a vigorous and sustained movement against the Park government in spite of the government's severe measures against them. The Japanese mass media gave prominent attention to these developments, particularly the actions and reactions surrounding Kim Dae-jung. The dark and turbulent image of South Korea portrayed in the Japanese mass media contrasted sharply with the bright picture painted of North Korea.

The Park government chose to battle not only the South Korean press but also an important segment of the Japanese and American presses. The government pressured large advertisers not to place advertisements in *Tong-a Ilbo*, the most prominent newspaper in Korea, because of its defiance of the government. *Asahi Shimbun*, a "progressive" Japanese newspaper with one of the largest national circulations, was banned from South Korea in February 1974. Elizabeth Pond, a foreign correspondent for the *Christian Science Monitor*, was barred from South Korea in June. The government had already closed the Seoul office of *Yomiuri Shimbun*, another major Japanese newspaper, in September 1972 for its publication of a special supplement on North Korea that was laudatory of North Korea and overtly defamatory of South Korea.

The Mun Se-gwang Incident

President Park won considerable sympathy in and out of Korea and gained a foothold for an offensive against Japan in August 1974, when Mun Se-gwang, a second-generation Korean living in Japan, attempted to assassinate him while he was delivering a message commemorating the anniversary of Korea's liberation from Japan. President Park was protected by a shield, but Mun's bullet killed his wife, who was sitting behind the president on the stage.

The Korean government held the Japanese government responsible for Mun's action because Mun, a permanent resident of Japan, went to Korea under a forged Japanese passport, used a Japanese identity, prepared for the assassination in Japan, and killed Mrs. Park with a pistol stolen from a police substation in Osaka, Japan. When Japanese officials disclaimed moral and legal responsibility for Mun's action, Korean officials were infuriated. The Japanese reasoned that Mun was a Korean and had committed the crime in Korea. Furthermore, he had entered Korea with a visa issued by a Korean consulate and had passed through elaborate security checkpoints not only at the airport but also at the National Theater, where the crime was committed.

The anger in Seoul was heightened further when Japanese editorials blamed the Park government for inflicting the outrage on itself by suppressing freedom.[32] Foreign Minister Kimura's comments minimizing the threat North Korea posed to the south (August 29) and denying that the ROK was the only legitimate government on the Korean peninsula (September 5) came at just this time, thus aggravating the situation even more. The Koreans held massive demonstrations, and, on September 6, some of the demonstrators ransacked the Japanese Embassy in Seoul. The Japanese interpreted the raid on the Embassy as instigated or tacitly approved by the Korean government.

The Park government demanded that Japan apologize for the incident and pledge to regulate the Federation of the Korean Residents in Japan, regarded by the Korean government as the headquarters of anti–South Korean operations in Japan. The Japanese government was willing to express regret over the incident, and Premier Tanaka personally attended Mrs. Park's funeral, but it saw no reason to offer an apology. As for the Korean residents' federation, the Japanese government would interfere with it only if it violated Japanese laws. An impasse was reached, and the possibility of diplomatic rupture was frequently mentioned. But U.S. mediation brought the two sides together again, and, on September 19, the Japanese government dispatched Shiina Etsusaburō, vice president of the Liberal Democratic Party and a close associate of the premier, to Seoul to tender two statements of regret, one written and the other oral. The written version adhered to the Japanese position whereas Shiina's oral statement—written down as an aide-mémoir and signed by Shiina—was much closer to what the South Korean government demanded.[33]

The Effect on Economic Relations

Thus Japanese–South Korean relations weathered a number of storms between 1972 and 1974, each of which would have been sufficient to disrupt normal relations for a long time. Had emotions and public opinion polls been the only factors determining international relations, Japanese–South Korean relations would certainly have ruptured sometime between 1973 and 1974. But the interests of the two nations were too closely intertwined to let even the most outrageous incidents completely break relations. The national interests of both Japan and South Korea dictated that the two parties mend their relations and find a modus vivendi. The deteriorating political relations did have an effect on economic relations, although private trade continued to flourish.

As discussed in Chapter 3, Japanese–South Korean trade began to gather momentum after the 1965 normalization, and, in 1966, Japan became the largest trading partner of South Korea, surpassing even the United States. It has continued to occupy that position since. Although the United States remained the largest purchaser of South Korean products until 1972, Korean exports to Japan in 1973 ($1,242 million, or 38.5 percent of total exports) surpassed exports to the United States ($1,021 million). Japan has been a major source of public and private loans to South Korea, having provided $674 million in commercial loans and $416 million in government loans between 1965 and 1973. The Japanese also had invested $42 million by 1971 (35.4 percent of total foreign investment), with the figure reaching $634 million (54.4 percent of the total) by 1981.[34] Details are provided in Tables 8 to 11.

These transactions indeed had played an important role in the rapid growth of South Korea's export-oriented industries, which had won President Park a considerable degree of support and legitimacy. Export expansion required plants, equipment, and intermediary goods that Korea could not produce but Japan did. Therefore, economic ties with Japan were always important to President Park. But they were most important to Park in the early 1970s. In 1972 Park launched the ambitious third five-year economic development plan (1972–1976), which emphasized the agricultural sector. It sought to redress the imbalance caused by the first two five-year plans (1962–1971).[35] The third plan also called for the development of heavy and chemical industries to better prepare South Korea for the intensified competition in the world market. All this required a massive dose of foreign capital, and, at the sixth Japanese–South Korean ministerial talks held in September 1972, South Korea requested $2.3 billion in public loans for the five-year plan period. The Japanese were reportedly receptive.[36]

But the Kim Dae-jung affair of August 1973 dampened Japan's enthusiasm and led to the postponement of the seventh ministerial talks scheduled for early September. Even though the Tanaka cabinet did hold the seventh round of talks in December, notwithstanding strong opposition from within the ruling LDP and from the opposition parties, the Japanese government was far from eager to cooperate with the South Koreans. The worldwide oil crisis had intervened between September and December, and the skyrocketing cost of oil and its shortage, coupled with galloping inflation, brought a major crisis in the Japanese economy and provided a plausible excuse for reducing Japan's commitment to South Korea. The Japanese loan for the year 1973 was reduced from the $170 million of the previous year to $45 million, although the Koreans had requested $300 million.[37]

The Japanese government also reversed its position on assistance for the expansion of Pohang Steel Mill by not granting the government's yen funds for the project. This obliged the Korean government to depend on private investment by Japanese corporations. The same applied for Korea's development projects in heavy and chemical industries.[38] At the 1972 ministerial talks, the Korean government had expressed its hope that the Japanese would provide low-interest government loans until the third five-year plan was completed in 1976, when Japanese-Korean economic cooperation would shift to private transactions.[39]

Thus the Park regime paid a high price in financial terms for the Kim Dae-jung affair. There was, of course, more to the Tanaka cabinet's effort to distance itself from the South Korean government's developmental plan than the emotional and political conflict over Kim Dae-jung or the oil crisis. The Tanaka cabinet was clearly swayed by the changing international and domestic political climate of the period. Reducing the Japanese government's involvement in South Korean economic development was one way of laying the ground for an equidistance policy between the two Koreas. There is no doubt, however, that the outrage of the Kim Dae-jung affair forced Japanese politicians to put a distance between themselves and the Park government regardless of their private emotions. Although President Park stayed in power for several more years after the bizarre affair, he was not able to recover from the damage done by the tragedy.

THE VIETNAM DEBACLE AND THE REASSESSMENT OF THE KOREA POLICY

The Japanese wavering on Korea abruptly ended in the summer of 1975 in the wake of the debacle of South Vietnamese forces in the spring of that year. The U.S. decision to "Vietnamize" the war and the manner in which the denouement was brought about forced the Japanese to seriously re-evaluate the implications of the change in U.S. policy toward Asia. Even though Gerald Ford succeeded Richard Nixon as president in August 1974 and paid a two-day visit to Seoul

TABLE 8   SOUTH KOREA'S TRADE WITH JAPAN, THE U.S., AND THE WORLD, 1956–1983
(IN MILLIONS OF U.S. DOLLARS)

Year	JAPAN			UNITED STATES			WORLD TOTAL		
	Exports	Imports	Total	Exports	Imports	Total	Exports	Imports	Total
1956	8	21	29	11	87[a]	98	25	386	411
1957	11	34	44[b]	4	110[a]	114	22	442	464
1958	10	50	60	3	209	212	17	378	395
1959	13	32	45	2	148	150	20	304	324
1960	20	70	91[b]	4	134	137[b]	33	344	376[b]
1961	19	69	89[b]	7	143	150	41	316	357
1962	23	109	133[b]	12	220	232	55	422	477
1963	25	159	184	24	284	308	87	560	647
1964	38	110	148	36	202	238	119	404	524[b]
1965	44	167	211	62	182	244	175	463	639[b]
1966	66	294	360	96	254	349[b]	250	716	967[b]
1967	85	443	528	137	305	443[b]	320	996	1,316
1968	100	624	724	237	449	686	455	1,463	1,918
1969	133	754	887	316	530	846	623	1,824	2,446[b]
1970	234	809	1,044[b]	395	585	980	835	1,984	2,819

Year									
1971	262	954	1,216	532	678	1,210	1,068	2,394	3,462
1972	408	1,031	1,439	759	647	1,406	1,624	2,522	4,146
1973	1,242	1,727	2,968 [b]	1,021	1,202	2,223	3,225	4,240	7,465
1974	1,380	2,621	4,001	1,492	1,701	3,193	4,460	6,852	11,312
1975	1,293	2,434	3,727	1,536	1,881	3,417	5,081	7,274	12,355
1976	1,802	3,099	4,901	2,493	1,963	4,455 [b]	7,715	8,774	16,489
1977	2,148	3,927	6,075	3,119	2,447	5,566	10,047	10,811	20,857 [b]
1978	2,627	5,981	8,609 [b]	4,058	3,043	7,101	12,711	14,972	27,683
1979	3,353	6,657	10,010	4,374	4,603	8,976 [b]	15,055	20,339	35,394
1980	3,039	5,858	8,897	4,607	4,890	9,497	17,505	22,292	39,797
1981	3,503	6,374	9,876 [b]	5,661	6,050	11,710 [b]	21,254	26,131	47,385
1982	3,388	5,305	8,693	6,243	5,956	12,199	21,853	24,251	46,104
1983	3,404	6,238	9,642	8,245	6,274	14,520 [b]	24,445	26,192	50,637

NOTE: Exports are valued at FOB and imports at CIF, except through March 1958, where the value of both exports and imports is based on the face value of the drafts involved.

[a] Figures for 1956 and 1957 do not include foreign aid imports. When these are included, imports from the U.S. in 1956 were $290 million; in 1957, $330 million. Total world trade includes foreign aid imports.

[b] Error in addition is due to rounding of numbers for imports and exports.

SOURCE: The Bank of Korea, *Economic Statistics Yearbook, 1961–1983*. When data were inconsistent in different editions of yearbooks, the data from later editions were used.

TABLE 9   JAPANESE AND AMERICAN ROLES IN SOUTH KOREA'S TRADE, 1955–1983 (PERCENTAGE)

Year	JAPAN			UNITED STATES		
	Export	Import	Total	Export	Import	Total
1955	38.9	5.6	7.2	38.9	75.7 [a]	73.8 [b]
1956	32.0	5.4	7.1	28.0	75.1 [a]	73.2 [b]
1957	50.0	2.5	9.7	18.2	74.7 [a]	72.0 [b]
1958	58.8	13.2	15.2	17.6	55.3	53.7 [b]
1959	65.0	10.5	13.9	10.0	48.7	46.3 [b]
1960	60.6	20.3	24.2	12.1	39.0	36.4 [b]
1961	46.3	21.8	24.9	17.1	45.3	42.0 [b]
1962	41.8	25.8	27.9	21.8	52.1	48.6 [b]
1963	28.7	28.4	28.4	27.6	50.7	47.6 [b]
1964	31.9	24.8	28.2	30.3	50.0	45.4 [b]
1965	25.1	36.1	33.0	35.4 [c]	39.3	38.2 [b]
1966	26.4	41.1	37.2 [b]	38.4	35.5	36.1
1967	26.6	44.5	40.1 [b]	42.8	30.6	33.7
1968	22.0	42.7	37.7 [b]	52.1	30.7	35.8
1969	21.3	41.4	36.3 [b]	50.7	29.1	34.6
1970	28.0	40.8	37.0 [b]	47.4	29.5	34.8
1971	24.5	39.8	35.1 [b]	49.8	28.3	35.0
1972	25.1	40.9	34.2 [b]	46.7	25.7	33.9
1973	38.5	40.7	39.8 [b]	31.7	28.3	29.8
1974	30.9	38.3	35.4 [b]	33.5	24.8	28.2
1975	25.4	33.5	30.2 [b]	30.2	25.9	27.7
1976	23.4	35.3	29.7 [b]	32.3	22.4	27.0
1977	21.4	36.3	29.1 [b]	31.0	22.6	26.7
1978	20.7	40.4	31.1 [b]	31.9	20.3	25.7
1979	22.3	32.7	28.2 [b]	29.1	22.6	25.4
1980	17.4	26.2	22.4	26.3	21.9	23.8 [b]
1981	16.5	24.4	20.8	26.6	23.2	24.7 [b]
1982	15.5	21.9	18.9	28.6	24.6	26.5 [b]
1983	13.9	23.8	19.0	33.7	24.0	28.7 [b]

[a]Includes foreign aid imports.

[b]Indicates South Korea's largest trading partner.

[c]In 1965, the United States became South Korea's largest export market. Japan had occupied that status until then.

SOURCE: Calculated from Table 8.

TABLE 10   INVESTMENTS IN SOUTH KOREA BY JAPAN, THE U.S., AND THE
WORLD, 1962–1981[a] (IN THOUSANDS OF U.S. DOLLARS)

Year	U.S.	Japan	World[c]
1962–66	15,987	4,663	21,263
1967–71	32,664	37,373	96,354
1972–76	87,536	395,473	557,040
1977	11,797	52,759	102,286
1978	13,832	45,014	100,457
1979	29,857	55,022	126,977
1980	60,353	29,799	96,177
1981[b]	45,931	13,803	64,417
Total	297,957	633,906	1,164,971
%	25.6	54.4	100.0

NOTE: By 1981, U.S. investors had withdrawn $81,976; the Japanese had withdrawn $117,324,000. The biggest withdrawals by U.S. investors occurred in 1980; Japanese withdrawals reached their height in 1979.

[a]Arrival basis.

[b]The figures for 1981 are probably up to June.

[c]World figures include Japan, the U.S., and all other countries.

SOURCE: Economic Planning Board, Republic of Korea, *Oeguk'in t'uja paeksŏ* [White Paper on Investment by Foreign Nationals] (Seoul, July 1981), pp. 126–29, 136–37.

in November to reaffirm U.S. determination to abide by the 1954 treaty with South Korea, a grave doubt was cast on U.S. ability to bear the burden.[40] Would the United States, so deeply wounded in Vietnam and with its people so divided and disillusioned, be able to commit its armed forces to another Asian war? Would the United States not be forced to take a loss in Korea as it had in Vietnam? If not, how much support would the United States be able to provide South Korea in the event of an all-out attack from the north? What is stopping North Korea from attacking the south? These questions carried a sense of immediacy for Japanese decisionmakers. Vietnam was located thousands of miles away, and developments there had no immediate effect on Japan, but Korea was a different matter. The Korea clause in the Nixon-Satō communiqué suddenly came to have real meaning.

Conservative leaders in Japan were concerned about the possibility of another war in Korea for a number of reasons. Some feared that turmoil in Korea, where national interests of the United States, the Soviet Union, China, and Japan are involved, could further unsettle the uneasy balance of power in Asia. Moreover, they feared that

TABLE 11   CUMULATIVE JAPANESE AND U.S. INVESTMENTS IN SOUTH KOREA, 1966–1983

IN THOUSANDS OF U.S. DOLLARS

	1966	1971	1976	1977	1978	1979	1980	1981	1982	1983
U.S.	15,987	48,651	136,187	147,984	161,816	191,673	252,026	314,236	374,186	409,691
Japan	4,663	42,036	437,509	490,268	535,282	590,300	620,557	651,707	672,990	711,770
Total[a]	21,236	117,617	674,657	776,943	877,400	1,004,377	1,101,012	1,206,460	1,307,058	1,408,492

PERCENTAGE OF TOTAL INVESTMENTS

	1966	1971	1976	1977	1978	1979	1980	1981	1982	1983
U.S.	75.3	41.4	20.2	19.0	18.4	19.1	22.9	25.6	28.6	29.1
Japan	22.0	35.7	64.8	63.1	61.0	58.8	56.3	54.4	51.5	50.5

[a]Total figures include investments by the U.S., Japan, and all other countries.

SOURCE: Economic Planning Board, Republic of Korea, *Oeguk'in t'uja paeksŏ* [White Paper on Investment by Foreign Nationals] Seoul, July 1981); and Ministry of Finance, Republic of Korea, *Chaejong Kumyung t'ongge* (Fiscal and Financial Statistics), 1983–1984.

a unified Korea under the Communists would be a potential threat to Japanese security and economic interests. Others feared that a conflict in Korea, and North Korean dominance of the peninsula, would sharpen the conflict between left and right political groups within Japan and could destroy Japan's democratic system. A war in Korea, either through direct North Korean assault on South Korea or after North Korea's support of insurgency in South Korea, would bring an outcry for rearmament in Japan that was sure to set up a titanic struggle between left and right, a civil war. A right-wing victory and decision for massive rearmament would surely aggravate Japanese relations with China, the Soviet Union, and possibly other neighbors. Still others were concerned about the consequences of turbulence in Korea for Japanese economic interests. Not only would trade with South Korea be affected, but Japan would lose its huge sums of loans and investments there.[41]

President Kim Il-sŏng's visit to Beijing in April 1975 intensified apprehension. The Japanese, along with the South Koreans and Americans, were particularly concerned about the following paragraph in Kim's statement made in Beijing on April 18:

> If a revolution takes place in South Korea, we of the same nation will not just watch it with folded arms but will strongly support the South Korean people. If the enemy recklessly ignites a war, we shall resolutely answer it with war and completely destroy the aggressors. In this war we will lose only the military demarcation line and will gain the country's reunification.[42]

The moderate language employed by the Chinese hosts in their addresses and the text of the joint communiqué issued by the Chinese and North Koreans at the end of Kim's visit considerably mollified the fears of another Korean war, but the situation could not be the same as before.[43]

The United States was clearly alarmed by the prospect of another war in Korea. In May Secretary of State Henry Kissinger repeatedly reaffirmed U.S. commitment to defend South Korea. Secretary of Defense James R. Schlesinger went a step further in June when he confirmed the presence of American tactical nuclear weapons in South Korea and promised to strike the heart-point of the enemy should North Korea attack the south.[44] In this atmosphere Premier Miki authorized in June a Defense Agency study of contingency planning for cooperation with U.S. forces in the event of emergency.[45] No such planning had taken place before because the LDP government would have been liable to opposition charges that the security treaty with the United States was a military alliance.

Not all Japanese shared the alarmist view of the government. Leftist elements refused to admit anything other than peaceful intentions on the part of the DPRK. Citing the experience in Vietnam, they stressed the inability of the "U.S.–Japan–South Korean pseudo-state" to stem the tide of "people's war," which they viewed as a principle of national self-determination.[46] For many others, Korea was America's problem. They suggested letting "Washington do what is necessary to see that trouble does *not* brew and boil over, and desist from seeking to needle Japan into action." Most Japanese, including government leaders, probably shared the sentiment of the *Asahi Shimbun* cartoonist who drew his hero carting baskets of dirt across the land, west to east, from the Sea of Japan to the Pacific Ocean, to move Japan eastward.[47] The prospect of war in Korea did not draw Japanese closer to Koreans. The government had its own imperative.

MIKI AND THE KOREA CLAUSE

In April the Miki cabinet dispatched Foreign Minister Miyazawa to Washington to ascertain U.S. intentions. Miyazawa reaffirmed the validity of the Korea clause in the Nixon-Satō communiqué.[48] In early May, Tokyo invited South Korean premier Kim Jong-pil for a series of talks with Premier Miki Takeo and Foreign Minister Miyazawa. Miki reportedly affirmed on this occasion that South Korea's security was essential to that of Japan and expressed his willingness to reopen ministerial talks.[49] Pro-Seoul Diet members of the LDP and the Democratic Socialist Party (DSP) were also galvanized. Between late May and mid-July, they renamed the Friendship Society of the Japanese–[South] Korean Diet Members (Nikkan Giin Kanshinkai), which had existed since May 1972, as the Federation of Japanese–[South] Korean Diet Members (Nikkan Giin Remmei). The pro-Seoul faction enlisted the support of 30 DSP members, who joined approximately 170 LDP members in the new federation. The pace of traffic between Japanese and Korean politicians intensified in May and June.[50]

The Miki government also took measures to reduce its own ties with North Korea while offering to serve as an intermediary between North Korea and the United States. Thus, in mid-May, it rescinded permission for the use of Export-Import Bank funds for exports to North Korea and applied restrictive measures against the Federation of Korean Residents in Japan (Chō-sō-ren); foreign delegations and reporters invited to the society's twentieth-anniversary gathering were either denied entry or prohibited from attending the conference. By doing this, the Japanese government for the first time publicly articulated its position that the federation was a political group supported by the DPRK rather than a simple organization of Korean residents in Japan.[51]

The Miki government, however, did dispatch LDP Diet member Utsunomiya Tokuma to Pyongyang in July for consultation with President Kim Il-sŏng. During the same month, it also approved a visit to North Korea by a group of LDP Diet members headed by Tamura Hajime. The delegation was given a cordial welcome in Pyongyang, and Premier Miki conferred with Utsunomiya and Tamura upon their return. He apparently transmitted President Kim's desire to conclude a peace treaty with the United States when he went to see President Ford in August.[52]

In any event, the Miki government was anxious to restore normalcy to Japanese–South Korean relations. In July, Foreign Minister Miyazawa visited Seoul to remove the last obstacle to closer ties, namely, the ancillary issues of the Kim Dae-jung incident. Miyazawa agreed to drop the issue of Kim Tong-wun, former first secretary of the South Korean Embassy in Tokyo, whose fingerprints had been discovered in Kim Dae-jung's hotel room. The Japanese decided to close the book on the case with the dismissal of Kim Tong-wun from his government post, even though the Korean government insisted that there was no evidence linking him to the Kim Dae-jung case.

The vociferous opposition within Japan regarded the settlement as a capitulation, but the Miki government found it imperative to settle the Kim Dae-jung affair in light of security concerns. Miki was scheduled to go to Washington in August for a summit meeting with President Ford, and the United States had been urging Japan to normalize its relations with the ROK. Seoul could not yield on the Kim Tong-wun case because a full-scale investigation for the satisfaction of the Japanese would have involved Kim's superiors in Seoul.

Miki's summit meeting with Ford in August confirmed Japan's return to its previous position of 1969–1971. Although the wording of the Ford-Miki joint communiqué was contorted, as if its authors had attempted to combine the 1969 Korea clause with Foreign Minister Kimura's statement of July 1974, the essence of the "new Korea clause" was identical with that of 1969. It stated that the peace and security of the Republic of Korea were essential to the peace and security of East Asia, including Japan.[53]

The Miki-Ford meeting was followed by Secretary Schlesinger's visit to South Korea and Japan. He and his Japanese counterpart, Sakata Michita, agreed that the North Korean armed forces were a threat to peace. The United States pledged the continued stationing of its forces in South Korea and the Japanese side agreed to reinforce its effort for military buildup and to allow "stable use" of Japanese bases by U.S. forces in case of an emergency in Korea. Schlesinger also noted the close link between Japanese and South Korean defense. On August 29, he stated that "Japan already is playing a role in South Korea's defense. The capacity of the Japanese air-defense force is exerting influence on the defense of Korea."[54] At his meeting with Foreign Minister Miyazawa, Schlesinger stressed the need for Japanese-American support for South Korea. The United States clearly sought to build a triangular defense network in East Asia, in which South Korea would be the advance defense zone and Japan would be the rear base.[55]

South Korean president Park clearly supported this network. He told Richard Halloran of the New York Times on August 20, 1975, that Japan and the Republic of Korea should have a special security relationship, inasmuch as the two countries were linked by a respective security treaty with the United States. Park also told the senior editors of Mainichi Shimbun in Tokyo that Korea, the United States, and Japan must "consolidate triangular cooperative relations to maintain peace," and that Japan should provide economic assistance from the "perspective of maintaining peace in Asia and the world."[56]

The Japanese government was not willing to articulate its strategic concept involving South Korea, but it was willing to permit the American use of Japanese bases in case of need. The shift in the Japanese attitude was also reflected in its policy on economic aid for South Korea. The eighth Japanese-Korean ministerial talks in September contrasted sharply with the atmosphere of the previous talks, held in December 1973. Although the Japanese declined to commit themselves to a specific amount of aid, they reversed their 1973 position and promised to provide public loans for various projects contained in South Korea's third economic developmental plan (1972–1976) and the fourth five-year plan (1977–1981).[57]

CARTER'S WITHDRAWAL PLAN

Having normalized relations, the Japanese and South Korean governments proceeded to tackle other matters of mutual concern, the most serious of which was President Carter's decision to withdraw all U.S. combat troops from South Korea.

Carter had announced his Korean policy on January 16, 1975, two weeks after leaving the governorship of the state of Georgia and only a month after declaring his candidacy for the presidency. The decision to withdraw U.S. troops was a product of Carter's humanitarian ideology and a domestic political environment inclined to the neoisolationist mood reflected by Richard Nixon's slogan, "Asia for Asians." President Park Chung Hee, once acclaimed for producing the miracle of the Han River and for rapidly developing South Korea's economy, had been widely denounced in the United States after he adopted the 1972 constitution, assumed absolute control over South Korea, and imposed draconian measures against his opponents. The kidnapping of Kim Dae-jung and his subsequent persecution, along with the incarceration of the popular poet, Kim Chi-ha, aggravated the situation. Many aroused activists—including a goodly number of vocal Korean-Americans—called for the United States to reduce aid and withdraw its troops from South Korea. In the post-Vietnam era, the American public also found congenial Nixon's opposition to fighting Asian land wars. Rather than depend on U.S. troops, Asians should fend for themselves with whatever materiél, air, and naval support the United States might provide. The United States needed more troops in Europe, where the bulk of the troops withdrawn from Korea were to be transferred.

Unlike other American political leaders, Carter considered his campaign pledge a sacred commitment that he was determined to carry through in spite of strong opposition from the Pentagon and congressional leaders. Thus, barely a week after Carter took office in January 1977, Vice President Mondale announced in Tokyo that American ground forces would be withdrawn from the Korean peninsula within five years.[58] This situation aroused deep concern in South Korea, but the Park government found its hands tied because of the so-called Koreagate scandal. Between 1976 and 1978, the South Korean government had become embroiled in the Koreagate affair, in the course of which various South Korean officials and agents were accused of bribing American congressmen in an effort to (1) mobilize congressional support for a $1.5 billion aid package to compensate for the 20,000 U.S. troops withdrawn in 1970, (2) prevent further U.S. troop withdrawals, and (3) counter the criticism advanced against the dictatorial regime.[59]

The Japanese had their own reasons for concern about the Carter plan. I have already alluded to Japanese fears immediately after the Vietnam debacle. In spite of repeated U.S. assurances that it would maintain "an active Asian role" and abide by its security commitments to Japan and South Korea, the Japanese—and many other Asian nations—regarded Carter's insistence on troop withdrawal as a sign of an overall retreat from the Pacific. Following the so-called Nixon shocks of 1971 and the scurry of U.S. withdrawal from Vietnam, Carter's unilateral decision caused a profound uneasiness about U.S. reliability.[60] The situation looked more ominous as the Soviet Union continued its military and naval buildup in the region.

Japanese leaders, including Premier Miki, his successor Fukuda Takeo (after December 1976), and Foreign Minister Kosaka Zentarō, publicly expressed their apprehension; others, such as former vice minister of defense Kubo Takuya, urged the postponement of withdrawal. When Vice President Mondale visited Japan in January 1977, a number of LDP Diet members, including two members of the Fukuda cabinet, submitted an anti-pullout petition to him.[61] These efforts and the opposition of the Joint Chiefs of Staff at the Pentagon were to no avail. President Carter announced at a press conference in early October that he would abide by his campaign pledge and withdraw the combat troops by 1981.

In March 1977, when Premier Fukuda visited Washington for a summit meeting with Carter, Fukuda proposed that the joint communiqué use the word "reduction" instead of "withdrawal" in referring to the "intended withdrawal of U.S. ground forces in the Republic of Korea," but Carter was adamant. The Carter administration's position was that (1) the risk involved in U.S. troop withdrawal was of an acceptable degree; (2) South Korea's economic and defense capabilities were substantial; (3) neither the Soviet Union nor China would encourage or support a North Korean armed invasion; (4) the United States would supply equipment to South Korea "to offset the fighting power of the ground forces withdrawn"; and (5) the United States would leave air squadrons and key support and naval units in South Korea.[62]

Japanese supporters of South Korea stressed, however, that U.S. ground troops in South Korea symbolized the U.S. security commitment in East Asia and that their withdrawal would have an undesirable social and psychological impact on Asian nations, possibly destabilizing the security and political balance of the region. Clearly the twain could not meet. President Carter's concern was global and Europe-centered; Japan and South Korea were preoccupied with East Asian regional security. A Japanese cabinet member vented his anger by denouncing Carter's strategic orientation as "antiyellow."[63] U.S. credibility in East Asia was at a low ebb.

President Carter's withdrawal plan, however, was short-lived. Conservative senators mounted an attack in Congress, and in the Fiscal Year 1978 Foreign Relations Authorization Act, signed by President Carter in August 1977, he was instructed to implement the "gradual and phased *reduction*" of U.S. ground forces in South Korea in stages consistent with the security interests of South Korea and U.S. interests in Asia, notably Japan. The president was required to submit to Congress a written annual report treating implementation of this policy in Korea.[64] In his January 1978 State of the Union message, Carter used the word "reduction" rather than "withdrawal" with respect to U.S. troops in Korea. In April, he announced an "adjustment" in the troop pullout schedule; only one battalion (eight hundred people) was to be withdrawn in 1978.

With the leak of "new" intelligence data concerning North Korean military strength in January 1979, which allegedly ascertained that North Korea enjoyed "clear ground superiority" over South Korea, the Carter plan for withdrawing U.S. troops from South Korea was doomed. The signing of the Soviet-Vietnam treaty in November 1978 also gave reason to ponder the military balance in Asia. The Joint Chiefs of Staff recommended in April 1979 that the United States suspend further troop withdrawals. On July 20, 1979, Presidential Security Advisor Zbigniew Brzezinski announced the president's decision to suspend U.S. troop withdrawal from Korea until 1981.[65] Carter's term of office, however, ended in January 1981.

Thus the Carter plan to withdraw U.S. troops from South Korea brought the Japanese and South Koreans substantially closer to each other. For the South Koreans, the implementation of Carter's plan would have been a catastrophe. The South Korean armed forces might or might not have been able to withstand a frontal attack from North Korea by the time Carter had completed the implementation of his original plan, but one of the main psychological deterrents to such an attack would have been lost. Once U.S. ground troops were withdrawn, U.S. assurances of support for South Korea would have become less credible and fear of war would have heightened, adversely affecting the morale of the population as well as the attitude of foreign investors, creditors, and buyers.

A large portion of South Korean adults had experienced the Korean War. Having witnessed the bellicosity of North Korean forces in the 1960s and 1970s through such events as the commando raid on the Presidential Palace in 1968, the capture of the USS *Pueblo*, and the axing of U.S. army officers at Panmunjom, even the younger generation had come to harbor fears of and animosity toward North Korea. Continuous North Korean broadcast of shrill propaganda against "American imperialists" and their "lackeys" was clearly audible in South Korea and tended to reinforce such fears rather than to produce the results intended by North Korea. The South Korean government, thus, had every reason to oppose President Carter's decision and to strive for a change through every means at its disposal.

Japanese apprehension over the Carter plan has been noted earlier. Although Premier Fukuda was initially hesitant to press the Carter administration on the withdrawal issue, partly because he had been accused in the Japanese press of having established illicit ties with President Park and partly because he feared that the United States might counter his pressure by demanding that Japan share the cost of defending South Korea, there was no reason for the conservative and pro–South Korean wing of the LDP to be reticent.[66] The political and even economic cost for Japan would have been very high if President Carter had prevailed. But it cost absolutely nothing for Japanese politicians to lobby on behalf of South Korea and for themselves. Even if their efforts were unsuccessful, they gained the goodwill of the South Korean government, which could be transformed into economic and other advantages. It was only natural for Japanese politicians to make their views known to their American counterparts in Washington, and American politicians were more attentive to Japanese views on Korea than the self-serving views of the Koreans.

Although Japan and South Korea did have outstanding problems involving territorial questions (Tokto or Takeshima), trade imbalances, and fishery problems, the two countries maintained an amicable relationship in 1977 and 1978. As was the case between 1966 and 1973, joint ministerial meetings involving economic and foreign ministers from Tokyo and Seoul were held annually, on September 9, 1977, and September 10, 1978.

In April 1979, the two governments took an epochal step in Japanese-Korean relations. For the first time since August 1945, General Nagano Shigeto, chief of staff of the Japanese Land Self-Defense Forces (the army), visited South Korea in his official capacity. The same month also saw the emergence of the Japanese-Korean Parliamentary Council on Security Affairs, involving Japanese Diet members and representatives from the South Korean National Assembly. In July, Yamashita Ganri, the director-general of the Japanese Defense Agency (the minister of defense) paid an official visit to South Korea.[67] These were clear signs that the two countries were moving toward closer cooperation on security matters. Japanese–South Korean relations had come a long way since the days of the Korean War, when President Syngman Rhee had threatened to conclude a truce with the North Korean Communists to repel any Japanese troops that might set foot on Korean soil—even if they were sent to provide support for South Korea.

THE ASSASSINATION OF PRESIDENT PARK

While Japanese–South Korean relations improved, domestic conditions in South Korea deteriorated. In October 1979, President Park was killed by his trusted lieutenant, the incumbent director of the Central Intelligence Agency. President Park had alienated a large segment of the populace by his oppressive political measures, rationalized in the Yushin (Revitalization) constitution. The economic downturn experienced by South Korea in 1978 brought political grievances into a sharper focus and increased support for both organized and unorganized opposition forces, including those who took their grievances to the streets. The Yushin system had provided for neither a pressure-release valve nor an escape hatch. It could be maintained only through fine-tuning of all the political and economic mechanisms, but this proved impossible.[68]

The death of Park Chung Hee marked the end of an era in Japanese–South Korean relations. Park had normalized Japanese–South Korean relations in 1965 despite vociferous domestic opposition. Under his leadership Japanese–South Korean trade had blossomed and Japanese loans and investments multiplied. It was under his regime that South Korea began to build a security link with Japan. Had his government not been so unscrupulous and stringent in its suppression of opponents, at least not to the extent of kidnapping Kim Dae-jung from Tokyo, Japanese–South Korean relations would have been even closer.

Park Chung Hee, as president of the Republic of Korea, of course pursued the interests of his own regime, just as the Japanese followed their own imperatives. But in the person of Park Chung Hee the Japanese had much more than a Korean president seeking to enhance his own interests. Park was a Japanophile who had maintained close personal ties with many Japanese political and financial leaders. He understood the Japanese political process and the intricate nature of personal and group relations in Japan. Although he had to operate in the adverse environment created by the Kim Dae-jung affair after 1973, he proved on the whole to be an adroit strategist in negotiating with Japanese political, financial, and business leaders. Although vigorously denounced by liberal and left-wing elements in Japan for his dictatorship, he had the respect of many Japanese political and business leaders who admired his acumen, will, and ability to steer a tight ship.[69]

Japanese policy toward Korea, of course, was determined by factors that transcended individual Japanese views regarding Korean leadership. But, once the overall policy framework was established, Japanese politicians and businessmen found the Park regime congenial. They knew that President Park was in command of South Korea and they knew the proper ways to approach him. With the death of Park Chung Hee, the Japanese were forced to reassess the situation in South Korea and to open a new channel of communication.

DETERMINANTS OF JAPANESE POLICY TOWARD KOREA

Japan began to grapple with its Korea policy only after 1971, in the wake of the implementation of the Nixon Doctrine, which thrust Japan into the international arena for the first time since 1945. Japan did not draw up a Korea policy before then because it possessed neither options nor the need to deviate from the international structure established by the United States. It was only when U.S. policy toward the region became uncertain and trends more unpredictable that Japan began designing her new policy.

Between 1971 and 1975, Japanese politicians strove to improve their relations with North Korea. For the United States, détente meant an improvement of relations with China and the Soviet Union, but it meant more than that for Japan. Japanese leaders attempted to rid themselves of the responsibilities imposed by the Korea clause and to improve their relations with North Korea. The cold war seemed over insofar as Japan was concerned. Although South Korea was important to Japan, it was not important enough to sway Japan's policy toward the Korean peninsula as a whole. Once the United States removed itself—or appeared to do so—from the dominant role it had assumed in East Asia after World War II, Japan was obliged to accommodate the interests and perspectives of China and the Soviet Union, the two communist powers that maintained alliance with the DPRK. Objections from South Korea had to be ignored.

The situation changed drastically in 1975 when the euphoria of détente died and Japan faced the prospect of another war on the Korean peninsula. President Carter's pronouncements and actions with respect to Korea heightened Japanese apprehensions. Realizing the limits of their relations with the Soviet Union and the fragility of peace in the region, the Japanese rediscovered the importance of South Korea for their security.[70] A sober Japanese leadership moved to repair badly damaged relations with South Korea.

Thus it was Japan's concern with its position in East Asia as a whole that determined Japanese policy toward the Korean peninsula. Although specific issues and problems did affect Japanese–South Korean relations at various times, they were overshadowed in importance by Japan's overall concern with its position in international politics. Notwithstanding the strong desire among the Japanese for an autonomous foreign policy posture, Japan's position in the region was determined more by the policies and actions of the two superpowers than by what the Japanese were able to do on their own. Japan's Korea policy, thus, was reactive rather than active.[71] This was so because Japan has never been able to control or regulate the political atmosphere of the region or the degree of bellicosity and cordiality among China, the Soviet Union, and the United States on the one hand and between the two Koreas on the other. Japan, perforce, was obliged to react to the vicissitude of events rather than charting a course based on domestic consensus.

Even though the emergence of a multipolar world was thought to grant such intermediate powers as Japan more opportunities for autonomous decisionmaking, Japan has had a very limited range of choices. Japan could have exercised more autonomy and exerted more influence over the outcome of international politics only if the atmosphere of the region had been more peaceful or had it possessed more military might; neither of these conditions was present in the 1970s. Japan, therefore, found it necessary to accommodate to the environment and to exert whatever influence it could on the United States. The shift in Japan's Korea policy after 1975 was the result of these factors.

The frequent changes in Japanese political leadership during this era also demonstrate the meager impact that personal and factional political differences had on Japanese policy toward Korea. In contrast to the long reign of Premier Satō, a number of politicians, including Tanaka, Fukuda, Miki, and Ōhira, occupied the office of premier during the turbulent era. Yet these turnovers made no visible difference in Japanese policy toward Korea. Ironically, Premiers Fukuda and Tanaka, known to be among the more conservative of LDP politicians, moved the government in the direction of an equidistance policy, and Miki, who was known as a liberal, took measures to improve Japan's ties with South Korea. I have also mentioned the activities of Yatsugi Kazuo, a close lieutenant of Kishi Nobusuke, vis-à-vis North Korean trade. Clearly, situational, factors rather than political leadership determined Japanese foreign policy.

5

The Limits of Japanese–
South Korean Security Ties:
The Loan Negotiations

I noted in the previous chapter that Japanese policy toward Korea closely reflected the vicissitudes of the international political climate and that, since 1975, Japan has restored its close ties with South Korea. Japan and South Korea again normalized their relations, Japan reaffirmed the Korea clause, and Japanese leaders actively lobbied for the cancellation of President Carter's plan to withdraw combat troops from Korea. Moreover, the two governments opened a new chapter in Japanese-Korean relations through the visit of Japanese defense officials to Seoul and the establishment of an interparliamentary group on security matters. These events gave the impression that the two governments were moving toward the establishment of close defense ties, a proposition the United States had been urging for some years.

THE BACKGROUND

The loan negotiations between 1981 and 1983, however, clearly revealed the limits of Japanese–South Korean security ties and the gap between the perspectives of the United States and South Korea on the one hand and Japan on the other. The loan negotiations and the events surrounding them also revealed the limits of U.S. ability to influence Japanese decisionmaking. A U.S. president may extract a promise from a Japanese premier, but the promise will remain hollow as long as Japanese politicians and bureaucrats are unwilling to implement it. Japan in the end did promise South Korea a significant sum of loans in 1983, but only after the Japanese had satisfied their own requirements. The prolonged negotiations, therefore, merit a detailed analysis.

Quite apart from the Korea clause in the Nixon-Satō communiqué, the interrelated nature of the two countries' security has long been a subject of comment and discussion among Japanese and Korean leaders. Kishi Nobusuke stressed the point in the early 1960s; the joint ministerial meetings of 1968, 1969, and 1970 reaffirmed the point; and after Japanese vacillation during the détente era, President Park busied himself in 1975 attempting to persuade Japanese politicians and journalists of the importance of maintaining the close link between Japanese and South Korean security.

Two reasons led decisionmakers in Washington and Seoul to dwell on the linkage between Japanese and South Korean security. The first was the necessity for the use of U.S. bases in Japan, including Okinawa, in the event of a war in Korea, as I discussed earlier. This point did not constitute a particular problem because the Korea clause in the Nixon-Satō joint communiqué was tied to the reversion of Okinawa to Japan. The second reason was the U.S. desire to have Japan share the financial burden of buttressing South Korea's security. As I have noted, Secretary Schlesinger told the Japanese in 1975 that the United States and Japan should jointly provide support for South Korea's defense. President Park also told the *Mainichi* editors in the same year that Japan should provide economic assistance from the "perspective of maintaining peace in Asia and the world."

The U.S. objective did not change even under the Carter administration. Thus, in November 1980, two defense officials in the Carter administration, Secretary of Defense Harold Brown and Deputy Secretary Robert Komer, told three former directors of the Japanese Self-Defense Agency (ministers of defense) who were visiting Washington that the United States hoped Japan would provide loans for South Korea's military modernization efforts. In view of the increased U.S. burden in protecting southwest Asia and the Indian Ocean, a region vital to both the United States and Japan, the United States had to rely on intensified Japanese efforts for the defense of the northwest Pacific. The United States regarded Korea as essential for Japan's defense; the American commitment to Korea provided security for Japan. Hence the U.S. government hoped that Japan would provide South Korea with capital loans on easy terms for the modernization of its armed forces.[1]

Although the Japanese government had acknowledged the importance of South Korea to Japanese security (as in the Nixon-Satō joint communiqué of 1969 and the joint communiqués of Japanese–South Korean ministerial conferences in 1968, 1969, and 1970), it resisted U.S. and South Korean pressures to translate the principle into action. Providing capital loans for South Korea's military modernization would have raised thorny political issues, if not constitutional questions, since Article 9 of the Japanese constitution outlaws war. Such an action would have provided the opposition parties with a convenient target for attack and would have jeopardized the LDP, which had been suffering from a steady decline in popular support. And, in spite of the improving ties between the two governments since the Vietnam debacle, Japanese sentiment toward South Korea was not at all favorable. Perhaps most important, U.S. pressure on the subject of South Korea was not as intense as on such other issues as increasing Japanese military spending or restraining Japanese exports to the United States. In short, Japan was aware of American and South Korean desires, but it was not a matter that called for immediate attention.

Between 1981 and 1983, however, Japan was forced to grapple with the question because the South Korean government under President Chun Doo Hwan requested a $6 billion long-term public loan and linked it with security ties between Japan and South Korea. Just as the Japanese search for a Korea policy during the détente era had revealed many facets of Japan's Korea policy, the interactions between the Suzuki and Chun regimes on the loan issue brought into the open many factors that underlay Japanese foreign policy making in general and Japanese-Korean relations in particular. I shall analyze the loan negotiations after describing some of the events that affected Japanese-Korean negotiations.

Emergence of the Reagan Administration

The most important factor affecting Japanese foreign policy after 1980 was the election of Ronald Reagan as president of the United States. Jimmy Carter was resoundingly defeated in November 1980 by Reagan, a strong advocate of a military buildup against the Soviet Union who favored the creation of a U.S.–Japanese–South Korean united front in East Asia.

The International Political Climate

Japan was also affected by the heightened tension between the two superpowers and developments in the Middle East and Indochina. The sudden demise of the Pahlavi regime in Iran in January 1979 ushered in a reign of chaos that threatened the fuel supply of a resource-poor Japan heavily dependent on oil from the Middle East. The crisis compelled the United States to transfer some of its Seventh Fleet contingents from the Pacific and to reduce the strength of U.S. forces in East Asia.

In this context, some of the actions taken by the Soviet Union appeared very alarming. In November 1978 the USSR signed a treaty with Vietnam that enabled it to use the naval facilities at Cam Ranh Bay facing the South China Sea, a vital sea lane for Japan, and Soviet naval contingents in the Pacific continued to be reinforced. Moscow also established a military base on Shikotan Island at the southern edge of the Kurile Islands, only miles away from Japan's northern island. The eruption of the Sino-Vietnamese War in February 1979 threatened to escalate the Sino-Soviet conflict and destabilize the peace in East Asia. All these developments were climaxed by the Soviet invasion of Afghanistan in December 1979. The aggressive nature of the Soviet Union disturbed Japanese policymakers because the Soviet Union had engaged in such a massive military buildup so close to Japanese territory.

Political Transition in Japan

Japanese politics also went through significant changes. Japan had been rocked by the Diet's unprecedented vote of no confidence in the Ōhira cabinet in May 1980, but the outcome of the elections on June 22 strengthened rather than weakened the hand of the LDP. The sudden death of Ōhira on June 12 won the LDP a large number of sympathy votes. Favorable weather on election day produced a huge turnout of conservative voters, and the double elections for both houses of the parliament worked in favor of the LDP. The party reversed its past losses by winning 44.6 percent of the vote and 289 (or 57 percent) of the seats in the House of Representatives. In the post-election scramble for the top position, LDP leaders chose Suzuki Zenkō, a consensus-oriented politician with no experience in foreign affairs, as premier. Suzuki in turn selected as his chief cabinet secretary and chief advisor Miyazawa Kiichi, who as foreign minister had negotiated the settlement of the Kim Dae-jung affair with South Korea in 1975 and who had held such key cabinet portfolios as minister of international trade and industry (MITI) and minister for economic planning. Itō Masayoshi, a close associate of former premier Ōhira, was chosen as foreign minister.[2]

Political Changes in South Korea

Meanwhile, General Chun Doo Hwan took control of South Korea. After President Park's death in October 1979, many parties wanted a new and more democratic constitution to replace the Yushin constitution of 1972. The National Assembly, still dominated by Park appointees and supporters, created a special committee on November 26, exactly a month after President Park's assassination, to draft a new constitution. But the government under President Choy Kyu-hah (inaugurated on December 21) was in no hurry to lift martial law and adopt a new constitution. The military's role in politics steadily grew and opposition forces became more vociferous about the government's "delaying tactics." Students held massive street demonstrations in early May supporting the immediate restoration of democracy, and, on May 16, 1980, Premier Shin Hyon Hwack promised in a televised speech that the government would attempt to speed up the process of adopting a new constitution.

On the following day, however, the Martial Law Command took over, dissolving the National Assembly and all political parties, closing down colleges and universities, outlawing all forms of political gatherings, and imposing strict censorship on the press. The Martial Law Command also arrested a number of prominent politicians of the Park era, including former premier Kim Jong-pil and opposition leader Kim Dae-jung, who had been released from prison only five months earlier, on December 9. Major General Chun, who had carried out a coup against the chief of staff of the army on December 12 and had effectively placed the entire armed forces under his control, promoted himself to four-star general, retired from the army, and had himself elected president by the rubber-stamp electoral college on June 27. A new constitution was promulgated in October.[3]

The Japanese were confronted by a total stranger in Chun, a graduate of the Korean Military Academy without any experience in government, business, or foreign affairs. In addition, a totally new slate of young men entered virtually every sector of South Korea's leadership. General Chun Doo Hwan was determined to bring about a thorough cultural revolution in South Korea. The generation that had been trained under Japanese colonialism and had played the leading role in the 1960s and 1970s was regarded as corrupt and corrupting. It was time for the pure *Han'gŭl* (Korean alphabet) generation to take over.

Chun was also very critical of the way in which President Park had conducted Korean-Japanese relations through personal ties and informal contacts that often blurred the line between the legitimate and illegitimate and thus compromised Korea's integrity. One of General Chun's first acts after assuming power in May 1980 (before being elected president in June and inaugurated in September) was to arrest and confiscate the properties of Kim Jong-pil, Lee Hu-rak, and Park Chong-gyu, the closest lieutenants of President Park. These men had been directly involved in Japanese-Korean political and financial relations as heads of the cabinet, the Korean Central Intelligence Agency, the presidential secretariat, and the presidential security forces. President Chun wanted them out of power. He insisted on dealing with the Japanese in a very different manner.

Japan had little alternative but to deal with the new South Korean leader. Kanemaru Shin, former defense minister and an outspoken proponent of close ties with South Korea, visited Seoul in August and promised his support to General Chun. Former premier Fukuda paid a three-day visit in September to engage in private conversations with the new president.[4] Stability in South Korea was of major concern to the Japanese, who had just won the struggle to rescind President Carter's plan to withdraw U.S. combat troops from South Korea and who had huge investments and trade relations to protect. But Japan was soon engulfed in a dispute with the Chun Doo Hwan regime over Kim Dae-jung, which strained relations to an extreme degree.

Rekindling of the Kim Dae-jung Affair

The Kim Dae-jung incident of 1980 began purely as a domestic affair. The Martial Law Command charged on May 22 that Kim Dae-jung had planned "mass agitation, and a popular uprising, and attempted to turn campus unrest into a popular revolt to overthrow the government by strengthening his ties with the universities."[5] The military held Kim responsible for the Kwangju incident of May 18–27, when students in Kwangju, a city of 800,000 people 170 miles southwest of Seoul, had demonstrated in defiance of martial law. The enraged army had dispatched a contingent of special forces (paratroopers) to suppress the demonstrators. The paratroopers were withdrawn three days later, but they left a large number of demonstrators and bystanders dead. Enraged citizens held mass rallies to denounce the military dictatorship, and some took the law into their own hands with arms seized from raids on police and militia posts. The army then sent a division of regular troops to squash the protests. A total of 167 persons was killed, according to official accounts, but antigovernmental sources often referred to 2,000 or more deaths.[6] Kim was to be punished for these events.

The Japanese public was agitated by the Kwangju incident, which was broadcast on Japanese television, and by the charges against Kim Dae-jung, whose name had been a household word since his 1973 kidnapping from Tokyo. The Japanese government was concerned about an additional charge lodged against Kim, that is, his alleged violation of the National Security Law while in exile in Tokyo. His violation consisted of organizing and heading (in 1973) the National Conference for the Acceleration of the Restoration of Democracy and Unification. The ROK government had decided that the organization was a creation of the Federation of the Korean Residents in Japan (Chō-sō-ren), an organization actively supported by North Korea. Kim was put on trial in July 1980, found guilty, and sentenced to death by the martial law court on September 17.

Although Premier Suzuki had publicly declared on September 25 that he would not interfere in "Korea's domestic problems," the fate of Kim Dae-jung was obviously a matter of grave concern for the LDP government. As noted previously, the political settlement of the Kim Dae-jung incident, reached in November 1973 and July 1975 (by Japanese Foreign Minister Miyazawa Kiichi) had been subjected to sharp criticism from liberal opinion leaders and the opposition parties. Concerns about Kim were a domestic problem for Japan. The charges against him clearly violated the terms of the 1973 agreement, since the Park government had pledged not to prosecute Kim for any actions he may have taken in Japan, in return for which Japan had dropped the issue. On the evening of September 17, 1980, the day the death sentence was imposed on Kim, more than ten thousand people demonstrated against the conviction in Tokyo's Hibiya Park.[7] Execution of Kim Dae-jung was sure to cause political embarrassment to the LDP.

On the same day, therefore, the Japanese government officially notified the Korean ambassador in Tokyo that the court decision would have a gravely adverse influence on Japanese policy toward South Korea. And when Kim's appeal was denied by the appellate martial law court, Premier Suzuki confronted the Korean ambassador on November 21 to express his concern. He reportedly told the ambassador that Kim's execution might prevent the Japanese government from providing further assistance to South Korea and strengthen sentiment in Japan for improving ties with North Korea.[8]

Although Suzuki's comments were made in private, the South Korean goverment chose to release his November 21 remarks through the government-controlled press, and a massive anti-Japanese campaign was launched throughout the country. Countless rallies were held, and numerous newspaper articles were printed to denounce Japan's "blatant interference in Korea's domestic legal process" and "the ignoring of rudimentary international law." The demonstrators and the government-controlled press went beyond the immediate issue at hand and laid bare all their frustrations and anger with Japan. They attacked Japan for its discrimination against Korean residents in Japan; they also denounced "new Japanese imperialism." In response to a November 27 announcement by the Japanese General Council of Trade Unions (*Sōhyō*) that it would launch a boycott of South Korean goods and might refuse to handle cargo to and from Korea in the event of Kim Dae-jung's execution, the Federation of Korean Trade Unions announced on November 29 that it would retaliate by boycotting Japanese goods.[9] Japanese–South Korean confrontation reached a new height.

The release of Premier Suzuki's comments by the South Korean government and the strong language used by the South Korean press clearly indicated the vindictive mood of the new generation of leaders. These true believers had removed a whole generation of senior generals in December 1979 for alleged corruption. They had sent special forces to Kwangju to suppress student defiance of martial law. They viewed the country's elites as unpatriotic and corrupt and dismissed thousands from public and private offices. These angry young men intended to build a "new and just society."

The counsel of caution voiced by the Japanese premier was most intolerable to these vindictive men. They were already angry at the way Japanese–South Korean relations had been normalized in 1965 by those they had just purged. The Japanese offer and South Korean acceptance of $300 million in reparations for 36 years of colonial rule was humiliating to them. Since that time South Korea had continued to suffer trade deficits vis-à-vis Japan (the total deficit reaching $20 billion by 1981), and no relief was in sight. South Korea was clearly turning into a dependency of "neo-Japanese imperialism," a matter that required urgent attention. At such a juncture, the last thing the Koreans wanted from Japan was interference in a South

Korean political affair involving Kim, the nemesis of both President Park and the new leaders. Japanese interference must be repulsed, whatever the consequences.

THE UNITED STATES AND
JAPANESE–SOUTH KOREAN RELATIONS

Kim Dae-jung was spared, for the new U.S. president intervened even before his inauguration. Kim's death sentence was commuted and President Chun was invited to the White House in February 1981, one of the first foreign heads of state to be invited by President Reagan. His invitation had great ramifications, both domestic and foreign, for the Chun regime. Reagan's gesture had the effect of legitimizing General Chun's rule in spite of the deep abhorrence created within Korea by Chun's brutal trampling of the democratic process. The visit also dispelled uncertainties about U.S. commitment not only to South Korea but also to East Asia as a whole. By inviting Chun Doo Hwan to the White House, President Reagan signaled that his commitment to East Asia transcended the popularity of a regime in power. Reagan assured Chun that the security of South Korea was vital to the United States and that the United States would reinforce its commitment to South Korea as a part of an overall anti-Soviet strategy. In other words, South Korea was to serve as a U.S. outpost in its confrontation with the Soviet Union and constituted an important element in the anti-Soviet united front of all the countries in East Asia that were threatened by the USSR.[10]

President Reagan's overall strategy also required close cooperation between Japan and South Korea. A key element in Reagan's anti-Soviet strategy in East Asia was Japan's assumption of a greater role in regional security. Reagan had inherited this policy from previous administrations, but the turbulence in the Middle East and increased Soviet military might in the Pacific region, coupled with continuing economic difficulties in the United States, rendered the task more urgent. Not only should Japan share more of the burden of defending itself against the Soviet threat, but also the United States hoped that Japan would take responsibility for shoring up South Korea's defenses.

President Reagan pressed Japan on this policy. Details of the Reagan-Chun talks of February 1981 and the Reagan-Suzuki talks of May 1981 (to be discussed presently) have not been made public. Nevertheless, the argument presented by the Chun Doo Hwan government in its subsequent request for a large loan from Japan and the content of the Reagan-Suzuki joint communiqué leave no doubt that President Reagan emphasized the need for Japan to aid South Korea. The Reagan-Suzuki joint communiqué stated, for example, that the two leaders agreed to "promote the maintenance of peace on the Korean peninsula as [it is] important for peace and security in East Asia, including Japan," and that they "acknowledged the desirability of an appropriate division of roles between Japan and the United States to insure peace and stability in the region and the defense of Japan."[11]

It appeared from the communiqué that Premier Suzuki was willing to meet head-on the persistent U.S. criticism that Japan had not borne its responsibility as a major ally. His acknowledgment of the "desirability of division of roles" was interpreted to mean that Japan was ready to support President Reagan's strategy to stabilize the situation in East Asia by cooperating with the United States and South Korea. Hitherto, Japanese loans to South Korea had been treated as a bilateral problem, but it was agreed at the Reagan-Suzuki talks that henceforth the Japanese would provide economic aid to South Korea from the perspective of anti-Soviet strategy and that this aid would be considered an important element of overall strategy.[12]

The validity of Suzuki's promises in the joint communiqué was quickly subjected to question, however. The premier disowned portions of the statement, saying they did not reflect his own opinion. He let it be known after his return to Tokyo that the communiqué had been drafted before he had his second meeting with Reagan on May 8, when he had frankly presented the Japanese perspective on defense.[13] Suzuki was referring to a statement in the joint communiqué that said "Japan, on its own initiative and in accordance with its Constitution and basic defense policy, will seek to make even greater efforts for improving its defense capabilities in Japanese territories and in its surrounding sea and airspace." Strangely enough, the press had reported that the premier had reaffirmed this position during his question-and-answer session at the National Press Club.[14] The internal dispute in Japan was settled through Foreign Minister Itō's resignation, but the meaning of the joint communiqué was left unclear. It should be noted, however, that the Korea clause in the joint communiqué was not at issue.

To clear up this confusion, Premier Suzuki requested a talk with President Reagan on the occasion of the summit meeting held in Ottawa in July 1981. There was strong concern within the ruling Liberal Democratic Party that unless Japan made a maximum effort to meet the U.S. request for increased armaments, the U.S.-Japan security treaty might be seriously jeopardized and the conflict might eventually bring down the Suzuki government. Clarification of the Japanese position was urgently needed in any event, and the Ottawa summit provided a fortuitous opportunity. On July 10, the Japanese cabinet had decided on closer cooperation with the United States and a hardened posture toward the Soviet Union.[15] The Reagan-Suzuki breakfast meeting took place at Chateau Montebello on July 21.

As one might expect under the circumstances, Premier Suzuki reaffirmed the agreements reached in May and the two leaders easily established a "mutual understanding." Their talks were broad in scope and very general in character, but Suzuki did make some specific remarks on Korea. He informed Reagan that Japan had received a request for a huge loan from South Korea and that he would decide the matter in consultation with President Chun Doo Hwan.[16] In the opinion of a Japanese reporter, Suzuki promised Reagan that Japan would provide a "huge loan" to South Korea. Reagan could not have been happier: Suzuki had requested the meeting, he was apologetic for what happened after their May meeting, and he voluntarily pledged to keep the promises he had made. In addition, Suzuki offered to look after South Korea. There was no doubt about Suzuki's determination to settle the Korean matter. On July 23, at his stopover in San Francisco, he referred to the undesirable delay in normalizing Japanese–South Korean relations and promised to resolve the situation as soon as possible.[17] The stage was set for loan negotiations— or so it seemed. A Japanese–South Korean foreign ministers' meeting was set for August 20–21 in Tokyo; on August 2, President Chun expressed his desire to invite Premier Suzuki to Seoul for talks. The Japanese side, through Chief Cabinet Secretary Miyazawa, accepted the invitation on the following day, the date for the visit to be determined later.

THE FIRST ROUND OF LOAN NEGOTIATIONS

The Chun Doo Hwan government understandably stressed the "special relationship" between Japan and South Korea. It invited leading Japanese journalists to South Korea in early August and expounded its views before them; a week later, five Japanese parliamentary vice ministers were accorded similar treatment. The message was clear: South Korea was facing the threat of a massive North Korean army; the South Korean military buildup was contributing to regional security; Japanese stability would be jeopardized if South Korea fell to communism; and a country such as Japan could not be secure without regional security, and hence should play a larger role by providing aid to South Korea.[18]

President Chun evidently worked under the assumption that the principles embodied in the Reagan-Suzuki communiqué and Suzuki's pledges to Reagan would continue in force during the loan negotiations. Suzuki had been in accord with Reagan on the need for a united anti-Soviet strategy. Suzuki also had agreed to share responsibilities with the United States, the United States assuming military and Japan assuming economic burdens. Although President Chun had yet to cement Japanese–South Korean ties through a personal meeting with Premier Suzuki, both had supported the same principles when they met President Reagan. Under the united front concept stressed by the American president, Japan and South Korea were to be partners in their common struggle against the Soviet Union. Suzuki had repeatedly asserted that South Korean security was essential to Japan.

President Reagan's united front strategy, however, underwent a severe test on the Japanese–South Korean front. The strain caused by the Kim Dae-jung affair obviously did not help the cause of united action. President Chun Doo Hwan also was bereft of Japanese supporters for his cause, since he had purged numerous politicians in Korea who had established close personal ties with their Japanese counterparts. The tension was aggravated further when a member of President Chun's staff made a direct and vengeful remark to a Japanese diplomat regarding the forthcoming loan request. The unnamed secretary, widely regarded in Seoul as a member of Chun's brain trust, reportedly told the Japanese diplomat in May that "Ours is a pro-American and anti-Japanese regime. The $6 billion loan request is made in the spirit of conducting the second round of the reparation talks of 1965. We will not hesitate to expose the details of collusion between the Japanese and Koreans during the Park Chung Hee era."[19] The specter of the 1965 treaty haunted Japanese–South Korean relations in 1981 and threatened the Reagan strategy of the united front. The reaction of Japanese leaders to this remark can be easily surmised.

Premier Suzuki was aware of the prevailing sentiment in Japan when he made his promises to President Reagan, but his foreign minister, Sonoda Sunao, was determined that Suzuki's promises would not be translated into action. Sonoda was a close political ally and intimate of Premier Suzuki who had two years of experience (1977–

1979) as foreign minister under Premiers Fukuda and Ōhira. He was a veteran of the Sino-Japanese treaty of 1978 and had traveled widely. Above all, he supposedly had been chosen to succeed Minister Itō because he was experienced in dealing with the United States.[20] The premier had no experience in diplomacy and evidently chose to let his foreign minister handle the Korean affair.

Sonoda had made his mark as a blunt diplomat during his previous tenure as foreign minister. The logic behind his refusal to involve Japan in the anti-Soviet united front can be garnered from remarks he had made in 1978 concerning Japan's position in the Sino-Soviet dispute. In an interview with a *Christian Science Monitor* reporter just prior to his trip to China to conclude the Sino-Japanese treaty, which had been stalled by the so-called hegemony clause, Sonoda said:

> When thinking of the world's future, China operates on the premise that some day war is inevitable. We in Japan believe that we must do everything possible to avert war.
>
> As for China, she talks of Soviet hegemony now because the Soviets are strong and China is weak. But when China becomes strong, will she commit hegemony-seeking acts against those weaker than herself? That is the most important question I shall be going to discuss with the Chinese. Looking at China's attitude toward the Vietnam-Cambodia dispute, I shall not be able to refrain from asking the Chinese how they really feel.[21]

He was equally direct in expressing his opinion concerning "U.S. manipulation" of the Sino-Soviet dispute. According to Sonoda's own account, he told presidential advisor Zbigniew Brzezinski that "it might seem advantageous for the West to manipulate the Chinese-Soviet dispute because it tied down Soviet troops in Asia, but to try to take diplomatic advantage of the Sino-Soviet dispute . . . is an adventure, and full of a thousand risks." Sonoda viewed his role as a peacemaker. He said "I didn't learn my pacifism from a book. Whether people call me a coward, whether they call me un-Japanese, I shall never tire of my search for peace, nor give up my feeling that war must be prevented at all costs, by whatever means."[22]

Although the foreign minister did not reveal his philosophical and strategic thoughts about President Reagan's united front concept, he made it abundantly clear between July 25, when Premier Suzuki returned from Chateau Montebello, and August 20, when the foreign ministers' conference was held in Tokyo, that the accord reached between Reagan and Suzuki would not be translated into action, at least vis-à-vis South Korea. Sonoda stated on July 28 that though he had no difficulty understanding South Korea's argument about being the bulwark of the United States and Japan, he could not agree with South Korea's position that it had a right to massive aid or that Japan had a duty to provide aid. On August 8, while visiting Buenos Aires, he again told the press that he would absolutely reject South Korea's request for aid if it insisted on being paid for shouldering Japan's defense.[23]

This view was affirmed by Suzuki in spite of his promises to Reagan and his public statements. On August 14, 1981, Suzuki, Sonoda, and Cabinet Secretary Miyazawa decided that though Japan should assist South Korea as much as possible, it should not provide aid from a strategic and military standpoint. The chief of the Asia Bureau in the Foreign Ministry, Kiuchi Akitane, told a Diet committee on August 18, two days before the arrival of the ROK foreign minister in Tokyo for the foreign ministers' conference, that (1) the Japanese government did not share President Chun's view that South Korea served as a bulwark of the United States and Japan; (2) there was no likelihood of a massive North Korean attack on South Korea; and (3) economic assistance could not be provided from a security point of view.[24]

The atmosphere chilled even further on the eve of the foreign ministers' conference due to a blunt statement by the Japanese foreign minister. Sonoda's remarks of August 19, reported widely in the Japanese press, contained the following points: (1) South Korea was using the notion that it was the bulwark of Japan because it could not admit that its economy was in a shambles; South Korea should acknowledge its economic problems; the Ping-Pong game of rights and duties would lead nowhere; and South Korean use of the security argument was like tying Japanese hands and demanding money; (2) if South Korea was Japan's bulwark, Japan was South Korea's rear fortress; the Japanese-American security treaty provided protection for South Korea; and South Korea had no reason to flaunt its good deeds for Japan; (3) Korea had attacked Japan before Empress Jingū; and the Japanese conquest of Korea was canceled out by what Korea had done before.[25] The South Korean press minced no words in denouncing Sonoda's statement. It would have taken a miracle for the foreign ministers' conference to produce any significant achievement.

The two-day talks produced no positive results. In fact, when Japanese television reported on the evening of the first day that the two sides were far apart on their security perspectives (that is, on their views about the threat posed by North Korea), the Korean side was ready to terminate further discussion.[26] A Japan that did not perceive a North Korean threat was obviously not going to provide support for South Korea's security. On the second day, Foreign Minister Lho Shin-young officially presented a request for a $6 billion government loan to finance South Korea's five-year economic development plan, but all the Japanese were willing to do was "to make every effort to assist South Korea's civilian economy."[27] The South Korean government was also reported to be seeking $4 billion in nongovernmental funds.

Although Minister Lho did not directly link the loan request with the security question at the two-day meeting, he insisted later, when he met a Japanese visitor in Seoul, Chairman Takeiri Yoshikatsu of Kōmeitō, that the loan request could not be separated from the security link. According to Lho, South Korea's loan request was "larger than the previous year, but it should not be so compared. The premises are different. What had taken place before was economic cooperation, not security cooperation."[28]

The Suzuki administration, in any event, did not wish to conclude the kind of "special relationship" the Chun regime demanded. The Foreign Ministry announced on August 24 that the loan request must follow established Japanese procedure and be examined project by project. Since the Japanese budget was drawn up on an annual basis, the government could not predetermine the amount for an extended period.

The outspoken foreign minister vented his frustration again on September 2, this time before the Foreign Affairs Committee of the House of Representatives, where Sonoda charged that South Korea was unwilling to take "even a penny less" and it was highly unusual for a borrower to take such a stance. As for assistance with security implications, the minister declared that it was "not a question of difficulty but impossibility." He also made it clear that the territorial question involving Takeshima (or Tokto) would be raised.[29] The Japanese and South Korean governments had argued over possession of the island between 1951 and 1965 when they were engaged in intermittent negotiations. In 1965, the two sides had decided not to attempt to resolve the problem but to shelve it for future resolution.

The Foreign Ministry also forecast that the Chun-Suzuki summit meeting was not likely to take place in 1981, a signal that the two sides were too far apart for the top leaders to negotiate fruitfully. The press also reported the Finance Ministry's request to postpone the Japanese-ROK joint ministerial conference scheduled for September

10, 1981, because no progress on the loan issue was anticipated before then. The Foreign Ministry decided to hold the conference as scheduled, if only to facilitate South Korea's explanation of the five-year plan.[30] The ministry probably did not wish others, particularly the United States, to blame Japan for the strained relations. (It was perhaps symbolic that the ROK government lodged a protest with Japan on August 29 concerning an intrusion by Japanese patrol boats into Korean waters near Tokto or Takeshima on the previous day.[31] Neither the Japanese nor the South Korean government refers to Tokto or Takeshima when their relations are cordial.)

Six Japanese cabinet members did go to Seoul to attend the eleventh joint ministerial conference, held on September 10 and 11, but the only agreement reached was not to issue a joint communiqué at the end of the conference, thus breaking the pattern of the past ten meetings. Instead, the two sides issued a "joint news release," which announced that Japanese–South Korean consultation would continue. An unnamed Japanese minister, most likely the finance minister, did intimate at the conference that Japan could provide a $1 billion government loan in five years.[32]

This conference was followed by the sixth session of the Japanese–South Korean Parliamentary Federation on September 16 and 17, when some sixty "pro–South Korean" Diet members traveled to Seoul. Even that meeting did not encourage the South Korean government. The principal Japanese speakers mostly repeated the official Japanese position.[33] The first round of talks between President Chun and Premier Suzuki was moribund. Negotiations had to be postponed as Japan and South Korea engaged in an emotional confrontation surrounding the so-called textbook controversy, discussed in Chapter 6.

THE SECOND ROUND OF NEGOTIATIONS

The breakup of the first round of negotiations, however, put Japan and South Korea in a quandary. In spite of all that both sides had said and done during 1980 and 1981, neither Japan nor South Korea could afford to prolong the emotional uproar that accompanied the Kim Dae-jung affair and the first round of loan negotiations. Economic reasons alone required that the two sides mend their ways: Japan had been one of the two largest trading partners of South Korea since the 1950s and South Korea had been one of the largest export markets for Japan. Japan also had invested $3.1 billion in South Korea's economy as of the end of 1981.[34]

In spite of its unwillingness to establish an official security link with South Korea, there was no question that South Korea's political and economic stability was important to Japan. Instability in South Korea would reduce Japanese exports and render Japanese investment there precarious. It also would heighten the chances of conflict on the Korean peninsula and raise the level of regional tension.

The Japanese also worried about the United States. Both Democrats and Republicans wanted Japan to play a more active role and assume more responsibility in East Asia. Even if Japanese leaders had misgivings about joining Reagan's crusade against the Soviet Union, the time had come for Japan to assume the role of a regional economic leader. World public opinion was increasingly turning against a Japan that continued to reap benefits from her rising exports without supporting less fortunate countries.

South Korea badly needed Japanese funds. In 1981, the ROK's economy had just begun to climb out of the worst slump in twenty years, and the government was able to control the rampant inflation. Yet certain sectors still suffered from the adverse effects of past policies and the general slump in the international economy. There was a large trade deficit, nearly 50 percent of it with Japan, and Korea needed injections of money from overseas to offset its current account deficit, to permit debt servicing and repayment of loans, and to enhance its foreign exchange holdings. By the end of 1982, South Korea had accumulated $37 billion in foreign debts, equal to the amount owed by Argentina and exceeded only by Brazil's $87 billion and Mexico's $85 billion. The interest paid to foreign lenders in 1982 alone reached $3.75 billion. Although the debt service ratio was still well below 20 percent and therefore the possibility of default was slight, the debts nevertheless began to arouse concern in the international financial community. Exports were not rising as fast as had been hoped, the country had lost much of its advantage because of rising wages, and tax collection was sluggish.[35]

Above all, President Chun Doo Hwan needed an economic stimulus in the form of Japanese loans to stabilize his political regime. Even though his strong-arm tactics kept the opposition disorganized and disillusioned, he was far from winning popular support. University students at various campuses encountered the police almost daily between September and November 1982, demanding freedom of the press, a free labor union movement, and even the resignation of the president.

The impasse in the loan negotiations offered Premier Suzuki an opportunity and a challenge. It was clearly time for him to act. He also needed to define the practical meaning of the Reagan-Suzuki joint communiqué, in which Japan had promised to share "responsibility" with the United States. Premier Suzuki, however, was not the man who met the challenge or seized the opportunity. It would have been out of character for him to articulate Japan's long-range strategy: to do so would have aroused too much controversy within his party and Japan as a whole, which in turn would have conflicted with his principal goal of creating harmony (*wa*). Suzuki evidently hoped that the two countries' foreign and finance ministries could resolve the impasse. He would then ratify the agreement at an appropriate moment.

Some intense behind-the-scene negotiations took place after the breakup of the foreign ministers' talks of late August (with the United States probably playing the role of mediator). The linkage of security with the loan was clearly unacceptable to Japan; South Korea, however, badly needed the loan. If Japan agreed to continue the negotiations in exchange for South Korea's relinquishment of the security linkage, the interests of both parties as well as those of the United States would be served.

None of the parties involved have yet divulged any information on what happened behind the scenes, but the atmosphere changed drastically in October, when South Korea dropped the security linkage from the loan talks. The negotiators, by simple obfuscation, also resolved the impasse on the loan formula, that is, the conflict between the South Korean formula for a lump sum for five years and the Japanese formula of annual loans for approved projects.

The Security Connection

It is not clear who wrote the scenario or when, but Premier Suzuki made the first compromise gesture during the loan negotiations. In answer to an interpellation by the Diet on October 1, 1981, he commented on the linkage of the security of Japan and South Korea. Although he denied that Japanese aid to South Korea constituted a Japanese takeover of responsibility for South Korea's security from the United States (*kata kawari*), he said that the "political, economic, and social stability of the Republic of Korea is essential to peace and stability on the Korean peninsula, which have deep implications for the peace and security of Japan."[36] The concept of security used on this occasion was that of "comprehensive security" (*sōgō anzen hoshō*) rather than military security: this same concept, introduced by Suzuki in 1980, included food, energy, industry, and economic cooperation, as well as military preparedness. His argument lacked clarity, but, for the first time, the premier expressed a willingness to relate the security issue to the loan negotiations.

Suzuki's statement was followed by the South Korean government's turnaround. Testifying before the National Assembly on October 19, after his three-week visit to the United States in late September and early October, Foreign Minister Lho Shin-young stated that Japan could not engage in military cooperation because of constitutional constraints. Furthermore, he said, he was willing to "study the wisdom of accepting Japan's possible offer to render a $6 billion loan untied to security."[37] As it turned out, this was the last time the South Korean government official mentioned security links.

Perhaps the Japanese government requested a clearer statement from Seoul on the security issue: Foreign Minister Lho told the *Korea Times*, an English daily published in Seoul, that the public loan from Japan would not be used for military purposes but solely for the fulfillment of the fifth five-year economic development plan. The significance of the statement was obvious to all. Even though the *Korea Times* interview was wide-ranging, Japanese newspapers spotlighted the sentence dealing with the use of the loan fund. In contrast, South Korean dailies reporting on the same interview gave only passing reference to it.[38] The South Korean government evidently hoped to retreat from its previous position without appearing to do so.

The Negotiators

The most controversial issue having been settled, the two sides proceeded to negotiate the amount of the loan. Three parties were involved in the negotiations: the Korean government, the Japanese Ministry of Finance (Ōkurashō), and the Japanese Foreign Ministry (Gaimushō). The first two parties presented their extreme positions; Gaimushō played the role of mediator. The negotiations were carried out virtually in the public eye, each party stating its position of the moment either through press leaks or official statements. The Japanese government was evidently attempting to apprise all concerned, both in Japan and Korea, about the negotiations, lest it be criticized later.

The atmosphere of the negotiations improved substantially

when, on December 1, 1981, the Suzuki cabinet replaced Foreign Minister Sonoda with Sakurauchi Yoshio, the incumbent vice president of the Japanese–[South] Korean Parliamentary Federation. Right-wing elements within the LDP, particularly those belonging to the Seirankai (Blue Storm Society), had been attacking Sonoda for his handling of Japan's relations with the United States and South Korea and for his frequent off-the-cuff remarks. The Japanese–[South] Korean Parliamentary Federation consisted of those Diet members most sympathetic to South Korea.

Sakurauchi spoke of the need for Japanese–South Korean friendship upon the announcement of his appointment and talked of deep historical links and the need to cultivate a better relationship "based on the feeling of brotherly ties." As for the loan negotiations, however, he hoped that the ROK government would present its request for individual projects.[39] His remark signaled that the substantive position of the Japanese government had not changed although the new foreign minister was more sensitive to South Korean feelings.

The Negotiation Procedure

On the evening of December 1, Premier Suzuki proposed that the two governments hold a working-level conference to determine the amount of the public loan to be provided in fiscal year 1981. The Japanese government needed to close the books for the year but, because of the stalemate in negotiations, the loan for 1981 had not been settled. For 1981 the Japanese were willing to raise the Overseas Development Aid (ODA) fund, the yen-denominated low-interest public loan fund, to 40 billion yen from the previous year's 19 billion yen.[40] In addition, Japan was willing to consider Export-Import Bank loans for large construction projects in South Korea (50 to 60 billion yen) and to confer on South Korea's needs for the fifth five-year economic development plan. On December 4, Sakurauchi invited the South Korean ambassador for a talk. The Japanese were understood to be ready to provide 40 billion yen in ODA funds (approximately $200 million) on an annual basis for five years, the five-year total (200 billion yen) amounting to $1 billion.[41]

The Chun government still insisted on high-level talks, which Suzuki had promised Reagan, to determine the total sum of the loan, and it rejected the Japanese proposal. But the South Koreans did agree to hold "higher" (bureau chiefs) working-level talks as a preliminary step toward another round of foreign ministers' talks. The answer, in short, was "No, but yes." Kiuchi Akitane, chief of the Asia Bureau in the Foreign Ministry, was dispatched to Seoul to hear South Korea's explanation for the five-year plan and its request for a $3.5 billion ODA fund and a $2.5 billion commodity loan.[42] The ODA fund was to be used to import materials necessary for approved development projects, such as steel mills and river works. The commodity loan, also yen-denominated, could be used to import commodities of whatever nature the borrower deemed necessary; South Korea could sell these commodities in the domestic market and use the proceeds at its own discretion.

The Koreans hoped to mix the Japanese formula of project-by-project loan application with a substantial amount of discretionary commodity funds. The Japanese could not agree to this, but Foreign Minister Sakurauchi announced on February 16, 1982, that the total amount of the loans would be decided by the two foreign ministers on political grounds, and the agreed amount would not necessarily correspond with the sum of the various projects to receive aid. A Foreign Ministry source reportedly said that officially the Japanese government would adhere to the annual allocation principle, but the gentlemen's agreement reached on the total figures would serve as a framework for future allocations.[43]

The Japanese press reported a flurry of negotiations between the Foreign and Finance ministries. Both easily agreed to provide $4 billion to South Korea, $2 billion less than requested, but they disagreed on the kinds of funds and their interest rates. On the one hand, the Foreign Ministry proposed that $1.5 billion should be from ODA funds (carrying a 4 percent annual interest rate) and $2.5 billion should be an Export-Import Bank loan (at a 7.5 percent interest rate). The average interest rate for the total sum would be 6 percent. The Finance Ministry, on the other hand, wished to provide $1 billion in ODA funds, $1.5 billion in Export-Import Bank loans at the prevailing interest rate of 9.25 percent (raised from 7.75 percent in November 1981), and $1 billion in private funds. Finally, on April 20, the two ministries agreed to a $4 billion package that would include $1.3 billion in ODA funds and $2.7 billion from the Export-Import Bank and private sources. The average interest rate for the package was to be kept at 6 percent. On April 29, the Japanese government dispatched Deputy Foreign Minister Yanagiya Kensuke to Seoul to convey officially the Japanese response to the Korean request. Yanagiya told the Koreans that Japan was willing to provide an additional $200 million in ODA funds for the seventh year of the loan program.[44]

The South Korean government found the Japanese proposal totally unacceptable. Foreign Minister Lho Shin-young reiterated to Yanagiya his government's position that it wished to receive a $6 billion ODA loan.[45] There was no room for compromise. The government-owned English-language paper, the *Korea Herald*, carried a headline on May 1 that read "Tokyo Loan Stance 'Unneighborly,' Bares Intent to Promote Sales." The South Korean government fumed in anger:

> The arithmetic jumble of the recent Japanese counterproposal to the Korean bid for $6 billion loans has failed to disguise Japan's intent to promote sales activities rather than economic cooperation with its "closest neighbor" . . . The offer is nothing but an amalgamation of a meager $1.3–1.5 billion from the Overseas Development Aid (ODA) fund with about $2.5 billion from the Japanese Export-Import Bank and some private sources. This is not a $4 billion proposal but actually a $1.5 billion reply to the $6 billion request.

The paper interpreted the Japanese action as having a twofold purpose: to make economic gains for Japan's cooperation with Korea and, should there be no solution to the issue, to project to the world an image of Japan doing its best.[46] Japanese reports on the stalemate were not as direct, but they indicated that there was nothing more the Japanese government could do and that the Japanese people shared the feeling of former foreign minister Sonoda, who said that "It is strange for the borrower to be overbearing."[47]

The Japanese undoubtedly considered their offer generous. In April 1982, the Korean Exchange Bank arranged a $500 million loan with a group of seven banks, including the Bank of Tokyo and the Chase Manhattan Bank, of which $300 million was based on an interbank interest rate of 15.5 percent per annum and $200 million was based on the U.S. prime rate, which was then 16.5 percent. Just before this transaction, the Korean Export-Import Bank had borrowed $300 million at half a point above the interbank rate of 15.5 percent.[48] The Japanese offer of $4 billion at an average annual interest rate of 6 percent would save South Korea millions of dollars in interest. The South Korean premise, however, was different, as Foreign Minister Lho's statement of August 1981 to the Kōmeitō leader had indicated: "What had taken place before [was] economic cooperation, not security cooperation." Although the security linkage had been dropped, the same premise applied in the loan negotiations.

Political Turbulence in South Korea

The Chun government, in the meantime, was undergoing a serious internal problem that attracted international attention. On March 18, 1982, a small group of university students set fire to the Pusan branch of the United States International Communications Agency (popularly known as Pusan USIS), killing one student and injuring three others who were using the library facility. Although Korean and U.S. officials dismissed the incident as an "aberration" perpetrated by a group of extremists, the action was interpreted by many Korean intellectuals, including religious leaders, as an expression of anti-U.S. sentiment created by the Reagan administration's uncritical support for Chun Doo Hwan, who had brutally suppressed the opposition, including the demonstrators in Kwangju.[49]

In May, the Chun regime was rocked by a domestic loan scandal that aroused questions about its ability to govern. The scandal centered on a curbside money-market operator who was related to the president's wife. The first lady was widely rumored to have directly aided the culprit; a close associate of President Chun and secretary general of the government party, known as the Democratic Justice Party, resigned in the aftermath of the scandal, suggesting the likelihood that the loan-shark operation was linked to the building of a political base for the regime. The total amount the money-market operator had handled was said to be equivalent to nearly $1 billion.[50]

The scandal was particularly damaging to President Chun because he had presented the elimination of corruption as the basic aim of his regime. In December 1979, as major general, he had arrested the incumbent army chief of staff on a charge of corruption and had subsequently purged virtually all the top-ranking generals on the same grounds. He then removed, for the same reason, a generation of bankers, journalists, and politicians, including many close associates of his mentor and predecessor, President Park Chung Hee. Now, as the news about his relatives hit the front pages day after day, Chun's credibility as a clean political leader and the rationale for his coup d'etat all but vanished. To make matters worse, that same month a disgruntled policeman in a remote village went on a shooting rampage, killing and wounding many villagers and tarnishing the image of the regime, which had projected itself as an upholder of law and order.

Suffering a loss of credibility and facing mass discontent with the sluggish economy, President Chun instituted a change in the cabinet in May and June, appointing Kim Sang-hyŏp, the president of Korea University, as premier. Thus the spotlight was focused on a man known for his integrity, raising hopes that some fundamental change would be instituted in the government, which still relied heavily on strong-arm tactics. Foreign Minister Lho, who had served as the government's chief negotiator, was replaced by Lee Bum-suk, a career diplomat who had earned public respect as the South Korean representative at the North and South Korean Red Cross talks held between 1971 and 1973.

The newly constituted Korean government broke the stalemate with the Japanese on June 22 by lowering its request to $4 billion with a different combination of loans. South Korea now wanted $2.3 billion in ODA funds plus a $1.7 billion commodity loan instead of the Japanese proposal of $1.3 billion in ODA funds and $2.5 billion from the Export-Import Bank and private funds. The U.S. had probably interceded again to facilitate a compromise. Ambassador Richard Walker had been to Washington for consultations on June 13, and he returned with an invitation for the ROK's new foreign minister, Lee Bum-suk, to visit Washington, a move characterized by South Korea's government newspaper, the *Korea Herald*, as "unusual."[51] The United States had ample reason to be concerned about the rising tide of anti-Americanism, which was directly related to President Reagan's uncritical support for the Chun regime. That regime was in disarray, and its negotiations with Japan were at a stalemate. It was in the interests of all concerned to resolve the loan question.

Lee's Washington visit coincided with Secretary Alexander Haig's resignation, and none of the details about Lee's consultations in Washington have been made public. But the ROK foreign minister stopped in Tokyo on his return journey and held marathon talks between July 5 and 6 with Japanese leaders. The proposal he presented to Foreign Minister Sakurauchi in Tokyo was identical with his proposal of June 22, which was unacceptable to the Japanese government.[52] The end, however, was in sight. Both sides hoped that a settlement could be reached by August. More than a year had passed since the Koreans had first approached the Japanese with a loan request, and the two sides were in accord on the total sum to be granted to South Korea. All that was required was a political decision on the differences about the content of the loan.

By the time Foreign Minister Lee arrived in Tokyo, however, the mass media in Japan was deeply engaged in the textbook controversy, which, as I shall discuss in Chapter 6, soon came to absorb the energy of the Japanese and Korean governments. Suzuki Zenkō resigned as premier, and Nakasone Yasuhiro eventually settled the affair.

Premier Nakasone and the Final Settlement

Nakasone Yasuhiro not only contrasted sharply with the stodgy Suzuki Zenkō in terms of personality and style, but also he was uncharacteristic of most postwar Japanese leaders. Nakasone was articulate and outspoken, and he had his own views about Japan's foreign and defense policies. He was an active man seeking a leadership role, not one who would wait for a consensus to emerge. Nakasone favored stronger Japanese armament, the cementing of an alliance with the United States, and removal of the no-war clause in the constitution. Although his articulateness had often worked against him in consensus-oriented Japanese politics, his time had arrived. He was now premier, and the Japanese were becoming wary of stolid and wavering leaders whose inaction and frequent shifts in position aggravated Japan's relations with many of its allies and neighbors, including the United States and China.

The improvement of relations with South Korea was one of Nakasone's priorities. The loan negotiations had been all but concluded when Suzuki resigned, and the relationship with South Korea needed to be put on a normal plane for economic reasons and for the stability of South Korea. Perhaps more important, Nakasone needed to pre-empt the Korean issue before his forthcoming meeting with Reagan. Not only would the settlement of the loan negotiations eliminate an embarrassing subject at the Japanese-American summit meeting, but also it would strengthen Nakasone's position in discussions with the American president on Japan's position on defense and trade issues. Nakasone could fend off American pressure for more military spending and increased assumption of other responsibilities by citing Japanese efforts on the Korean front. As for domestic opposition, he could count on the latitude normally granted to a new premier. For Suzuki Zenkō, the entire episode of Korean negotiations had been a liability; for Nakasone Yasuhiro, it was an opportunity. He had much to gain in both the domestic and international arenas by showing his leadership through a resolution of the Korean impasse. The onus of giving in to American and Korean pressure had been taken away by prolonged negotiations, compromises, and Suzuki's resignation.

The new premier showed initiative by taking the first step toward settling the Korean problem immediately after assuming office. On November 30, 1982, his fourth day in office and the day of his first cabinet meeting, Nakasone told his foreign and finance ministers and the cabinet secretary that he wanted to end the Korean negotiations as soon as possible and that he wished to visit Seoul to meet President Chun Doo Hwan, possibly on December 26 or 27. The cabinet selected Sejima Ryūzō, senior counselor of the Itō Chū Company, as emissary to conduct all preliminary negotiations on the loan issue and to arrange for Nakasone's visit. The Itō Chū Company had been deeply involved in Korean industries since 1963 through loans, construction projects, and joint enterprises; Sejima, a former officer in the Imperial (Military) Headquarters, was said to have gained the confidence of President Chun Doo Hwan, a former general. Sejima settled all matters by December 30 and went to Seoul on that day with Nakasone's personal letter to Chun. He returned the following day with Chun's reply, the details having been settled during his two-day talks with President Chun and Korean cabinet officers.[53]

Nakasone took other actions that bordered on the melodramatic. On the same day that he initiated the secret negotiations, he called President Chun Doo Hwan by telephone and told the Korean president that he would make every possible effort to build up bilateral relations "on a truly broad national basis."[54] Chun had reason to be receptive to this unprecedentedly warm gesture. The brief conversation was broadcast repeatedly on Korea's national TV and radio network. Nakasone also displayed his progressive attitude toward South Korea by appearing before a meeting of the Japanese-Korean Parliamentary Federation held at the end of the year in Tokyo. There he expressed his desire to do his best to build a friendly and cooperative relationship between Japan and South Korea.[55] Although such meetings had been held many times before, other Japanese premiers had found it inconvenient to attend them.

The Release of Kim Dae-jung

One of the matters Sejima is most likely to have negotiated with the South Koreans was the fate of Kim Dae-jung. Even though Kim's life had been spared by President Reagan's intervention, he was still incarcerated in prison and faced an uncertain future. The Japanese had requested Kim's release during previous loan negotiations, but the Korean government had not been receptive. Nakasone faced vociferous opposition in Japan, South Korea, and elsewhere, if he were to become a state guest of the Chun regime while Kim Dae-jung was still in confinement. Outright release of Kim, however, would pose problems for the Chun regime, since he might become a rallying point for opposition forces within Korea. Even if Kim's political rights were restricted, his very presence would serve as a reminder of the turbulent Tokyo-Seoul relations.

The obvious solution was to release Kim but to send him into exile abroad. The U.S. government must have been consulted. Kim, therefore, was "given permission" to go to the United States "for medical treatment." He was informed of the decision on December 12, 1982, transferred to a hospital on December 16, and sent to Washington, D.C., on December 23.[56] The road was clear for Premier Nakasone's Korea visit.

Nakasone to Seoul

The excitement felt by President Chun Doo Hwan can be easily imagined. The $4 billion loan, even when spread over seven years, promised to boost South Korea's credit rating and stimulate its economic recovery. Even though his impetuous request for a huge public loan did cause problems between the two countries temporarily, his strategy had succeeded. Japan had been allowed to reap profits from Korea for far too long. President Park's submissive posture had reduced public loans to South Korea to 19 billion yen ($95 million) a year. But now the situation had changed. A Japanese premier was willing to pay a state visit in a show of solidarity with South Korea. Premier Satō had visited Seoul in 1967 and 1971 to attend President Park's inaugurations, and Premier Tanaka had attended Mrs. Park's funeral in 1974, but there had not been any state visit by a Japanese premier since Korea's liberation in 1945. The occasion certainly called for a celebration from Chun's perspective. Premier Nakasone must receive a hearty welcome.

President Chun, accordingly, changed the rules of protocol so that Premier Nakasone received the treatment of a head of state rather than that of a ministerial head. On January 11, Nakasone was welcomed by an honor guard and a gun salute. Japanese flags and Nakasone's photograph lined the streets from the airport to the capitol building in Seoul. Schoolchildren were mobilized to line the route of the premier's motorcade. In short, South Korea accorded Premier Nakasone royal treatment. Above all, for the first time in more than 37 years, a huge Japanese flag adorned the dome above the central government building, the old structure where the Korean

Government-General had once been housed. South Korea was entering a new epoch.

Premier Nakasone responded in kind. He referred to the "need for a penitent attitude regarding the unfortunate past" of the two countries and allocated a considerable portion of his banquet speech to the "superb" Korean culture that had contributed to the formation of the early Japanese state. Some two hundred official guests warmly reacted to his speech, which began with a Korean sentence and ended with a toast in Korean.[57] The two national leaders later joined for an Oriental-style party sans neckties, during which Nakasone sang a Korean song. Through every gesture and every remark exchanged during Nakasone's 24-hour stay in Seoul, the two leaders strove to break down the thick barrier that had been built over many years.

As for the loan issue, the two sides met midway between their previous positions. The $4 billion loan, to be provided over seven years (retroactive to 1981), was divided into $1.85 billion from the ODA fund, $350 million in bank loans, and $1.8 billion from the Export-Import Bank. The ODA loan was a government loan in yen that carried a 4 percent annual interest rate and was to be used for various construction projects. The bank loan, also in yen, was from the Japanese Export-Import Bank to Korean banks and could be readily converted into cash, thus creating a form of discretionary funds. The third category, also known as "suppliers' credit," was dollar-denominated and carried a higher interest rate. It could be used to purchase Japanese products and labor. This formula was, of course, far below what the Korean government had requested most recently ($2.7 billion in ODA funds plus $1.3 billion in discretionary funds), but it was considerably more generous than what the Japanese had offered. The sum, to be repaid in 25 years, after a grace period of 7 years, was to carry an average 6.1 percent interest rate.[58] The long period of loan negotiations is summarized in Table 12.

By paying an unprecedented state visit to Korea, choosing to go to Seoul before his scheduled visit to Washington, and offering generous aid to South Korea, Premier Nakasone clearly demonstrated his goodwill toward South Korea. But there were limits to the Japanese premier's discretion. This was clearly reflected in the joint communiqué issued by the two leaders at the end of the visit. The South Korean side insisted on recognition of the threat posed by North Korea, but the joint communiqué repeated the same expression that had become standard during the détente era, that is, "peace and stability on the Korean peninsula are essential to those in all of East

TABLE 12   Synopsis of Loan Negotiations
(In billions of U.S. dollars)

Month	Year	Country	Ministry	ODA Fund[a]	Commodity or bank loans	Ex-Im Bank[b] and private loans	Total	Period
Aug.	1981	ROK		6		4	10	
Dec.		Japan	Foreign	1			1	
Dec.		ROK		3.5	2.5		6	
Dec.		Japan		1.25		2.75	4	1981–86
April	1982	Japan	Foreign	1.5		2.5	4	
			Finance	1		1.5 + 1	3.5?	
April		Japan		1.5		2.5	4	1981–87
April		ROK		6			6	
June		ROK		2.3	1.7		4	
Jan.	1983	ROK/Japan		1.85	0.35	1.8	4[c]	1981–87

[a]Overseas Development Aid Fund (ODA) is a yen-denominated government-to-government loan carrying 4% annual interest.
[b]Export-Import Bank (Ex-Im Bank) loan is dollar-denominated. Normal interest rate was 7.75% until November 1981, when it was raised to 9.25%.
[c]The $4 billion loan agreed upon in 1983 was to be provided in installments between 1983 and 1987. The loan is to be repaid in 25 years after a grace period of 7 years.

Asia including Japan."[59] The South Koreans would have preferred the expression used in the Nixon-Satō joint communiqué of 1969, which stated that the security of *South Korea* was "essential to Japan's own security." That phrase, however, would have created too heavy a burden on the new Japanese premier, often dubbed the "young samurai," particularly in the aftermath of the harsh confrontation over President Chun's claim that South Korea was Japan's bulwark. The Korean side also wished to specify the principles behind the loan and its terms in the joint communiqué, but the Japanese refused to incorporate those items even in the minutes of foreign ministers' meetings that followed the summit talks. The Japanese adhered to their formula of granting aid on an annual basis. The joint communiqué employed the most ambiguous language on the matter:

> The prime minister expressed the view that Japan is willing to render cooperation for Korea's socioeconomic development projects envisaged in the fifth five-year socioeconomic development plan *as long as Japan's basic economic cooperation plan permits it*, and that in order to facilitate the realization of the [five-year] plan, Japan would provide various cooperative funds, including long-term, low-interest government loans *on an annual basis.*[60] (Italics added.)

Any reader of the communiqué unfamiliar with its background will hardly know that more than two years of turbulent negotiations had preceded it or that Japan had pledged $4 billion in loans to South Korea.

The document was a result of a compromise in the true sense of the word. The Chun government had yielded on its basic principles, and the Japanese had substantially increased the amount of the loan. Most important for the Chun regime, however, was the forward-looking attitude of the Japanese premier.

Although some Korean newspapers noted the absence of comments in the joint communiqué about either the thorny past of Japanese-Korean relations or the textbook affair, Nakasone's decision to visit Seoul and his banquet speech mollified a significant number of Koreans. Of course, the complicated emotional conflict between the Japanese and Korean peoples could not be resolved by a single visit by any person or by one man's statements. The opposition within Korea also treated the Nakasone visit as a measure that solidified the Chun regime rather than as an event that improved the friendship between the two peoples. Much, therefore, still depends on how the Japanese handle their relationship with Korea in the future.

The final settlement of the loan issue and the content of the joint communiqué showed that although the disposition of Japanese leaders does make a difference in resolving interministry and international differences, their discretion is sharply delimited by the state apparatus. But given the cultural environment of the two peoples, in which gestures, innuendos, and unarticulated attitudes play such important roles, Nakasone's visit and his speech can be considered an important step toward a genuine improvement in Japanese–South Korean relations, particularly in light of what had transpired immediately before his trip.

CONCLUSIONS

The presentation of the Korean request for a Japanese government loan so soon after the Kim Dae-jung affair fanned antagonism between the Chun Doo Hwan regime and Japan. Although the formal request was presented at the foreign ministers' talks in August, the Japanese had been notified of South Korean intentions as early as March 1981, when Foreign Minister Itō visited Seoul on the occasion of President Chun's second inauguration as president. This was less than two months after the Chun government had orchestrated a massive anti-Japanese campaign.

Another outstanding aspect of the episode was that the amount of the request was extraordinarily large, even in the context of Japanese–South Korean relations. It is also noteworthy that the time span between the oral notification and the official request was relatively short. The Korean side completely ignored the normal practice of sending out feelers and cultivating support in Japanese political and financial circles—a practice known in Japan as *nemawashi,* or digging around the root of a plant. Thirdly, the Korean side justified its request purely on the grounds that Japan must pay its dues for South Korea's maintenance of peace and security on the peninsula. Finally, the South Korean government openly displayed its anti-Japanese sentiment even after presenting its request.

Thus the timing, manner, and the sum involved clearly revealed the South Korean leaders' frame of mind. They presented a demand, not a supplication, for aid. The young leaders conducted the loan negotiations in the same manner in which they pushed their cultural revolution in South Korea. Of course, their attempt was rebuffed by Foreign Minister Sonoda, who came just short of saying that the South Korean government was trying to extort funds from Japan with American backing. If President Chun and his lieutenants thought that President Reagan's backing would bend the Japanese to the extent of accepting South Korea's demand, they had clearly misunderstood the Japanese political process and the nature of U.S.-Japanese relations.

Obviously, President Reagan's backing was not sufficient to sway the Japanese on the loan request, and that is no surprise. The record since 1945 shows that the United States has always had considerable difficulty getting the Japanese government to follow its advice, recommendations, and military-government directives except in situations where Japanese leaders were in complete accord with what the Americans desired and the recommended policy was palatable in the Japanese political context. Japanese resistance to U.S. pressure for increased military spending is well known. But the following conversation with a Japanese official, recorded by American Colonel Frank Kowalski during the height of the Korean War, graphically reveals the problems encountered by the United States in pressuring the Japanese, even in the 1950s:

> "I can't understand," I began, "why the Prime Minister refuses to increase the defense forces of your country when we are willing to assume the costly burden of supplying weapons and equipment. Surely, this is all to the advantage of Japan. All you're asked to furnish is manpower and you have a lot of that."
>
> "Ah so," responded my friend. "We will strengthen our forces, but not until 1955."
>
> "Why 1955?" I asked.
>
> "By then the Korean War will be over."
>
> "But why must you wait until the war is ended?" I persisted.
>
> "Because Mr. Yoshida does not want Japan to become involved in the Korean War. If we organized 300,000 troops as your Mr. Dulles wanted us to do, your government will insist that we send some of these troops to Korea. That is why the Prime Minister agreed to expand our forces only to 110,000."
>
> "Mr. Yoshida shudders every time he recalls how the Japanese army was bogged down in China. In that the people share his fears. Should Japan have 300,000 ground troops, a strong argument would be made that we don't need that many to defend Japan from attack and the United Nations, under your influence, would ask us to cooperate by sending at least a hundred thousand to Korea. Once these troops are dispatched, there is no telling when they will be withdrawn."[61]

In short, while the Japanese were willing to follow U.S. policy when they perceived it as in their own interest, they would implement it only at their own pace, carefully weighing the costs and benefits at each stage. There is nothing strange in this practice, of course. Any student of U.S.–South Korean relations under President Syngman Rhee and President Park Chung Hee would have witnessed the same process. It may be superfluous to say so, but many Japanese did not consider the security linkage with South Korea or the grant of the $6 billion loan to be in their interests.

Moreover, in 1981 the United States was hardly in a good position to pressure Japan. Washington had too many bilateral defense and economic issues to resolve vis-à-vis Japan. In April, the Japanese public was in an uproar after the American nuclear-powered submarine USS *George Washington* accidentally rammed and sank a Japanese freighter and left the scene without rescuing the crewmen. Foreign Minister Itō's resignation in the wake of Suzuki's Washington visit also created a delicate situation. In May, the Japanese government was placed in an embarrassing situation after former Ambassador Edwin O. Reischauer mentioned an "oral agreement" which allowed American warships and planes carrying nuclear weapons to visit or pass through Japan. The mood of disenchantment with the United States was so high in June that Secretary of State Haig had to cancel his scheduled visit to Japan on his way to Peking. This situation clearly affected the U.S. position in Japanese–South Korean negotiations. One report had it that at their Manila meeting in June Foreign Minister Sonoda exacted a promise from Secretary Haig not to interfere in Japanese–South Korean negotiations.[62]

The Japanese refusal to link the loan to Japanese and South Korean security ties also reflected Japanese ambivalence toward Reagan's anti-Soviet strategy and the Japanese desire not to become embroiled in the North Korean–South Korean confrontation. There is no doubt that LDP leaders fear the increasing Soviet military presence in East Asia and that this fear propels the Japanese to increase their military strength. The Soviet Union is clearly regarded as a potential enemy. But Japanese leaders have assiduously avoided provoking the Soviet Union, as can be seen from the prolonged negotiations with China on the "hegemony clause" and the 1981 uproar in Japan about the meaning of the U.S.-Japan "alliance."[63] Given the volatility of the defense issue within Japan and the sensitivity of the Soviet Union, Japanese leaders were inclined to stay clear of international military confrontation as much as possible.

For Japan to emerge as a financial supporter of a South Korean military buildup would have nullified these past efforts. In spite of their increasing concern over Soviet strategy in the Far East and in spite of U.S. urging, the Japanese were not willing to take such a giant step. The Korean situation was all the more complicated because of the presence of North Korea. As our discussion in the previous chapter clearly showed, most Japanese leaders—including the so-called pro–South Korean elements—were eager to improve their relations with North Korea when the international environment appeared favorable.

Most Japanese leaders, with strong backing from opinion makers in the press, see a North Korean–South Korean détente as the only way to resolve tension on the Korean peninsula, and they are determined not to take any action that Pyongyang might regard as provocative. Foreign Minister Itō, for example, did not believe North Korea would attack the south. He urged a dialogue between the two Koreas and told a reporter on the eve of his departure for Seoul in March 1981 that, if asked by South Korea, Japan would send a mission to North Korea to serve as a bridge between the two Koreas.[64] A Japanese grant of aid to South Korea in the name of security linkage would preclude a mediatory role in the future, since Japan would be seen as South Korea's military ally.

Finally, South Korea's unmitigated anti-Japanese attitude obviously affected Japanese leaders. The Chun government's handling of the Kim Dae-jung affair and the presidential staff member's crude remarks left no room to doubt the Chun regime's attitude toward Japan. To give in to the South Korean demand for $6 billion under the circumstances—and to accept the South Korean rationale for it—would have been tantamount to Japanese capitulation to U.S.-Korean pressures, clearly an unacceptable alternative.

These factors still do not explain the enigma of Suzuki Zenkō. The statements he made on the American continent were so diametrically opposed to his actions in Tokyo that one cannot help but suspect the effect of his flights over the Pacific. Until Suzuki clarifies the reasons for his frequent reversals in policy, I can only speculate on his behavior. Perhaps he meant what he said but found domestic opposition—particularly from Foreign Minister Sonoda—too formidable to translate his words into deeds. His first foreign minister, Itō Masayoshi, had resigned over the content of the Reagan-Suzuki joint communiqué and Suzuki could not afford Sonoda's resignation over the Korean question. Or perhaps Suzuki is a person who is affected most by the last persuasive argument he has heard. Whichever is closer to the truth, Premier Suzuki's statements were clearly irresponsible.

The strident attitude displayed by the Chun Doo Hwan regime

throughout the period under study reflects the effect of normalizing Japanese–South Korean relations in 1965 without an adequate resolution of the emotional conflict between the two peoples. As noted in Chapter 3, the 1965 settlement was a marriage of convenience between the Park regime and the Japanese. Afterward, President Park concentrated on economic relations without making any serious effort to improve the attitudes between the two peoples. Except for the brief airport speech of Foreign Minister Shiina Etsusaburō in 1965, no Japanese leader showed any sign of understanding the deep-rooted feelings of the Koreans. To the contrary, the Japanese continued to hold prejudiced and sometimes erroneous views of their past relations with Korea.

As the Japanese economy made more inroads into South Korea, and as South Korea continued to pile up trade deficits, the generation of Koreans that had opposed the 1965 treaty, fearing that Korea would again be exploited by the Japanese, thought that their fears had been realized. Although the Japanese government did provide considerable capital to South Korea for numerous public projects and Japanese corporations invested large sums in South Korea, unremitting reports of scandals and the bankruptcies of loan-based Korean enterprises intensified the feeling of exploitation. This can be seen from the explosive popularity that the *dependencia* theory of Latin American economists won among Korean university students in the early 1980s. The theory gained considerable currency in spite of the government's attempt to suppress it. Clearly, a significant portion of the articulate population felt that Japanese–South Korean economic relations enriched the Japanese while transforming South Korea into a tool of neoimperialist Japan. The embers of resentment and suspicion of Japan continued to burn among Koreans 36 years after the Japanese colonialists had left Korea, and they could easily be fanned into flame.

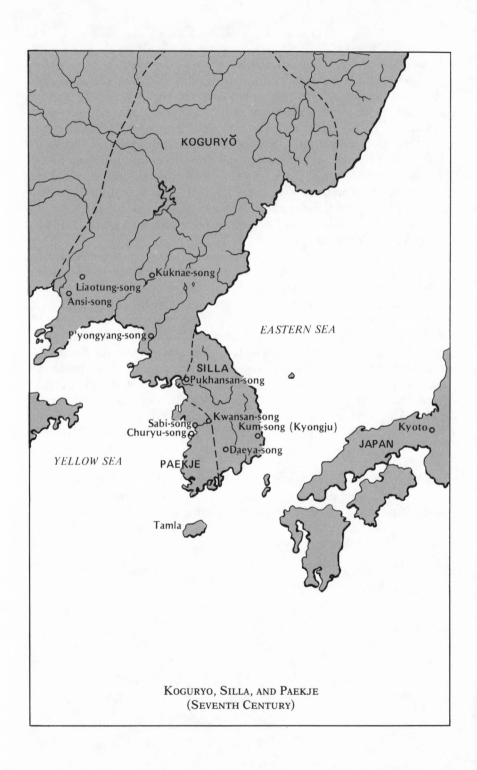

KOGURYŎ

EASTERN SEA

oKuknae-song

Liaotung-song
Ansi-song

P'yongyang-song

SILLA

Pukhansan-song

Kwansan-song
Sabi-song
Churyu-song
Kum-song (Kyongju)

Kyoto

JAPAN

Daeya-song

YELLOW SEA

PAEKJE

Tamla

KOGURYO, SILLA, AND PAEKJE
(SEVENTH CENTURY)

6

History and Politics:
The Textbook Controversy
and Beyond

The textbook controversy flared up in the summer of 1982, just as the Suzuki and Chun governments were beginning to narrow the gap in the loan negotiations. It highlighted once again the volatility of the relationship between the two nations. The controversy and the factors underlying it will be explored in this chapter because they allow us to analyze an important aspect of the unresolved emotional conflict.

The textbook controversy illuminated only a fragment of the misunderstandings that plague the relationship between the Japanese and Korean peoples. The whole range of questions involving historiography is very complicated and defies easy solution. As one might expect, discussions among specialists are highly technical. But one cannot understand the conflict between the two peoples without some awareness of the debates that have taken place among scholars. I shall, therefore, examine the textbook controversy of 1982 and provide also an account of the debate surging among Japanese intellectuals on the historical ties between Japan and Korea.

THE TEXTBOOK CONTROVERSY

The textbook controversy was a domestic squabble over the Japanese government's textbook certification system that expanded into an international incident. A brief account of the certification system, therefore, is in order.

The certification system was instituted by the U.S. Military Government in 1947 as a safeguard against militarist tendencies in Japanese textbooks. Between 1903 and 1945, the Ministry of Education (Monbushō) had published uniform national textbooks and hence had complete control over the content of education. Under the new system anyone could write and publish textbooks, but only those approved by the ministry could be used in schools. Monbushō could either withhold certification, require revision as a precondition for approval, or recommend revisions. As the system evolved, individual high schools were given the freedom to select any approved textbooks; the selection of textbooks for elementary and middle schools was entrusted to the officials of "Combined Textbook Areas," the size of whose jurisdiction varied from one region to another.[1]

The certification system had long been a subject of controversy within Japan, particularly between the left-oriented Japanese Teachers' Union and the establishment-oriented Monbushō. Most textbooks were written by college and university professors who naturally abhorred the certification system as a form of censorship. The two opposing camps differed greatly in their understanding of history, and they had debated a number of important questions: Should the teaching of history concentrate on the miseries of the nation's past or on its glories? Should it emphasize the doings of the rulers or of the ruled? Should it inculcate the values of patriotism and dedication to national progress or of resistance to authority and the establishment of individual rights? The controversy clearly had political implications. The Teachers' Union supported opposition parties and favored a type of education that would inculcate critical attitudes toward the established government; whereas Monbushō, like any other ministry, was subject to the political direction of the Liberal Democratic Party that had held power in Japan since 1948.[2]

The smoldering controversy heated up between 1980 and 1981 after the resurgence of the conservative LDP in the double elections of June 1980. The party reversed its recent downward trend in popular votes and won 289 (or 57 percent) of the seats in the House of Representatives, and, as a result, conservative politicians became more confident than ever before. In July, Minister of Justice Okuno Seisuke stated publicly that the avoidance of the term "patriotism" in textbooks constituted a serious problem that needed correction. In October, Diet member Mitsuzuka Hiroshi complained to the Diet's

Education Committee that civics textbooks were biased toward the left. In December, the Education Department of the LDP established a committee on textbooks and subsequently published a white paper, *Ureerubeki kyōkasho no mondai* (The Deplorable Textbook Problem).[3] Obviously the conservatives wanted some action. The mass media also began to publish articles and books on the meaning of patriotism, a word that had long been equated with prewar militarism. The textbook censors were clearly under pressure.[4]

In 1981, Monbushō became more assertive. Textbooks on contemporary society, it felt, should better reflect the government's position on the pacifist constitution, self-defense forces, the northern territory, military ties with the United States, and so on. Less emphasis should be placed on people's rights and more on people's welfare. Criticism of capitalism ought to be balanced by criticism of socialism. History writers were advised to moderate their account of Japan's responsibility for expansionist wars in the past and were told to substitute the term "advance" for "aggression."[5] It was improper, in the opinion of the conservative leaders, for the young to be inculcated with guilt feelings about their country.

The controversy broke into the open on June 26, 1982, when the mass media reported that government censors were requiring all publishers of 1983 high school textbooks to designate the Japanese movement into north China between 1935 and 1937 as "advance" (*shinshutsu*) rather than "aggression" (*shinryaku*). Relentless denunciation of the attitude and ideology of the censors and of the certification system followed. The uproar in the mass media was characterized by one commentator as "kyōsōkyoku," a parody of the word for rhapsody, with a Chinese character changed to alter the meaning to "frenzied clamor."[6] Editorials, commentaries, and interviews with textbook writers filled the airwaves and the press.

The clamor in Japan naturally drew the attention of the Chinese and Korean mass media, which published editorials and commentaries denouncing the Japanese educational officials' attempt to embellish and distort history. In China, *Renmin Ribao*, the official organ of the Communist Party, published its first editorial on the subject on July 20. In Korea, major Seoul newspapers began to publish commentaries and editorials in early July. The South Korean Ministry of Education reported to the press on July 22 that it had examined copies of five Japanese textbooks and had found them to contain distortions. It was planning to obtain ten more textbooks for examination before lodging a protest.[7] The Japanese alteration of the word "aggression" was a serious matter for the Korean government, since it had been seeking a "penitent" attitude from the Japanese for so long.

The controversy could have been contained at this stage had the Japanese government acknowledged the gravity of the problem and promised a thorough review. But the cabinet, at a meeting on July 23, decided to take a hard line. It determined that the certification process had been fairly and justly conducted and that there was no need for change. Not only that, but the minister of land administration, Matsuno Yasuyuki, told the press after the meeting that there were inaccuracies in Korean history books as well. "For example," he was quoted as saying, "Korea describes the annexation [of 1910] as an act of aggression. But in view of the Korean domestic situation of that time, I don't know which is the accurate description. Japan should thoroughly study the situation." Matsuno also said that "making an issue of the contents of the new Japanese textbooks by Korea could constitute an interference in internal Japanese affairs."[8] Korean newspapers on the following day carried banner headlines stating that "Reckless Remarks by Japanese Cabinet Member Anger People."[9] Matsuno's remarks again accentuated how differently Japan and Korea perceive each other. The textbook controversy escalated.

Although the Korean government expressed deep concern about Matsuno's remarks and requested clarification from the Japanese Foreign Ministry, it was more cautious than the Chinese government, which lodged an official protest on July 26.[10] The July 30 issue of South Korea's English-language government newspaper, the *Korea Herald*, expressed optimism that a satisfactory resolution could be reached, citing a high-level Japanese Foreign Ministry official's alleged admission of "erroneous descriptions of history facts." On the same day, a spokesman for the ROK Foreign Ministry spoke in the same vein.[11] The South Korean government was obviously concerned about the effect of the controversy on the loan negotiations. Its Foreign Ministry official reportedly said on July 27 that his government would not link the textbook issue to the loan negotiations. The *Korea Herald* of July 30 also quoted Miyazawa Kiichi, the Japanese chief cabinet secretary, as saying that Japan hoped to conclude the loan negotiations by September.[12]

But when Monbushō announced on July 30 that no change would be forthcoming in its textbook policy, and the Chinese government on August 1 canceled its July invitation to Education Minister Ogawa Heiji, the ROK government had little alternative.[13] The Chun government in Seoul had to do something to meet Japanese intransigence and the Chinese hard-line reaction. On August 3, the ROK foreign minister handed the Japanese ambassador an aide-mémoire "strongly demanding" swift and concrete measures on the textbook issue.[14] South Korea's complaints can be summarized as follows:

1. Previous textbooks had correctly stated that the "Japanese side induced a collision [with Korea in 1875], and using it as a pretext, forced the opening of Korea." This was revised to say that the "collision took place because the Korean side launched a bombardment on the Japanese ships," and so on.
2. The word "aggression" in the previous textbooks was changed to "advance" to describe the Japanese movement into Korea after 1905.
3. The March First uprising of the Korean people in 1919 was revised and depicted as a riot, rationalizing harsh Japanese suppression.
4. Previous expressions about Japanese imperialists' exploiting the lands belonging to Koreans were rephrased as "Koreans lost their rights to lands."
5. "Koreans were forced to worship at Shinto shrines" was changed to "Koreans were encouraged to worship at Shinto shrines."
6. Previous accounts of the banning of the Korean language in Korea were changed to a statement that "the Korean and Japanese languages were used simultaneously."
7. Many Koreans were "forcibly drafted" into the Japanese army or work force, but the new textbooks made the Japanese actions more innocuous by eliminating the expression "forcibly drafted."[15]

The overall effect of the revision, as depicted in the Japanese press, was to gloss over Japan's guilt for its past actions. Although most authors of high school textbooks—as was shown later—effectively resisted the censors' pressures and retained their original language, it was clear from the few examples of those who had given in and from authors' complaints published in the previous year that government censors were intent on modifying the language of the textbooks to mitigate Japan's responsibility. The Japanese press also discovered that the word "aggression" had been expunged from all middle school textbooks in use since 1981. The censors had also caused authors to avoid the same offensive word in describing Hide-yoshi's invasion of Korea in the late sixteenth century.[16] The South Korean government, enjoying the solid backing of the Japanese and Chinese media for the first time in history, naturally pressed its case.

The Suzuki regime was placed in a quandary. Monbushō officials and LDP leaders met on April 4 and resolved that the Japanese government must not yield. LDP leaders, including Mitsuzuka Hiroshi, the chairman of the Diet's subcommittee on textbooks, insisted that any immediate revision would deny the legitimacy of the entire educational administration, since Monbushō had been instructing the expurgation of the term "aggression" for more than ten years. The LDP also feared that once Monbushō gave in to foreign pressure, a flood of demands from the Teachers' Union and others would overwhelm the ministry.

The premier also could not accept the Foreign Ministry's advice to accommodate the strong emotions abroad, for to do so could very well have an adverse effect on his political future. Suzuki had been hinting at the possibility of re-election in the fall, and he had hoped to cap his governmental record with a visit to China in late September to commemorate the tenth anniversary of the establishment of diplomatic relations. Yielding to Chinese and Korean demands would bring charges that he was a weak-kneed politician and would reduce his prospects for re-election.[17] Only an early settlement of the controversy would have saved the premier from his predicament, but time was clearly running out. Monbushō attempted on July 29 and 30 to placate the Chinese and Koreans with explanations of the certification system, but to no avail. On August 6, the LDP and the government also sought to send a high-level explanation team to Seoul, but the offer was rebuffed.

In the meantime, anti-Japanese feelings began to mount in China and Korea. In Korea the mass media launched a massive campaign during which the press serialized long articles on past Japanese atrocities and carried reports of rallies and statements denouncing Japan. Taxis, restaurants, and other establishments normally catering to Japanese tourists posted signs refusing them service. Campaigns against Japanese goods were launched in some localities. The Korean government sent its second protest to Japan on August 12. The Japanese press reported on the same day that the Korean government was considering the recall of its ambassador from Tokyo. (The Chinese had sent their second protest demanding immediate correction on August 6, and their ambassador returned to Beijing on August

19 for a three-week consultation.) Also on August 12, the Korean Athletic Association informed its Japanese counterpart of its decision to postpone the tenth Korea-Japan Junior Games scheduled for August 21–23.[18]

Anti-Japanese feeling in Korea was at its zenith as the thirty-seventh anniversary of Korean liberation approached. On August 15, in his speech commemorating the liberation, President Chun Doo Hwan dwelled on the effects of Japanese colonial rule in Korea, including the division of Korea in the aftermath of the Japanese defeat.[19] Not even a dictatorial government could contain the strong emotions aroused among the Korean people. Minister Matsuno's second statement on August 9, referring to the "nervous" or "oversensitive" Korean reaction, did not help matters.[20]

Unrelenting pressure from China and South Korea as well as harsh criticism from North Korea, Taiwan, and the Southeast Asian countries produced a tug of war between Japanese officials in charge of foreign affairs and educational affairs. In a classic case of bureaucratic politics, the officials brought their respective bureaucratic perspectives to the decisionmaking arena. On August 12, Foreign Minister Sakurauchi issued a public statement that stressed the need to accommodate the emotions of foreign countries by revising textbooks.[21] Although he had conferred with the premier and Chief Cabinet Secretary Miyazawa just before issuing the statement, the latter immediately disassociated himself from the foreign minister—an indication of the delicacy of the political situation. Monbushō insisted that there had been no change in its policy. Premier Suzuki was unwilling to make an intellectual or moral choice. He was bound to lose no matter what his decision. He chose instead to sit on the sidelines until the two sides had hammered out their differences and reached a compromise.

The Foreign Ministry proposed on August 14 that the government should enunciate its penitence or self-reproach (*hansei*) to the countries that had been wronged and should promise to revise textbooks within the year. Monbushō and LDP leaders were unmoved, and evidently hard bargaining continued. On August 17, the government (presumably the chief cabinet secretary) and the LDP arrived at a compromise. The three-year cycle of certification would be accelerated to two years so that the revision could be implemented two years hence. Monbushō and LDP educational leaders in turn retreated from their earlier position of absolute objection to any revision.[22]

Japanese and South Korean leaders were concerned about the

effect of the controversy not only on bilateral relations but also on South Korea's domestic politics. The Japanese press reported that Suzuki feared that strong anti-Japanese emotions in South Korea could turn into an anti–Chun Doo Hwan movement, thereby destabilizing South Korea's political system once more. If the stalemate continued, Korean students returning to campuses in September could ignite an uncontrollable anti-Japanese and antigovernment movement. Since conflict within Japan had not been resolved, therefore, the premier decided to dispatch to Seoul Mitsuzuka Hiroshi and Mori Yoshirō, the LDP's chairman of the Subcommittee on Textbooks and the vice chairman of the Committee on Education, respectively. Monbushō, however, was still adamant about the three-year certification cycle as of August 21.[23]

Finally, on August 23, 1982, Premier Suzuki held his first press conference on the controversy. He acknowledged Japan's responsibility to various nations for damages done in the past and pledged the best possible effort to reflect Japan's penitent attitude in the textbooks. The outstanding issues, he stressed, must be corrected before his impending trip to China. Although the changes had to be implemented within the framework of the existing system of certification, the textbooks should not become a subject of criticism from abroad again. The premier, however, hedged on the crucial question of whether the Japanese had "aggressed against" or "advanced into" China. In response to a request for the premier's opinion, Suzuki replied: "Evaluation of our country's actions in the past needs to *await the judgment of future historians.* But it is a fact that there are severe judgment, criticisms, and understanding about them on the part of the world including China. The government must recognize them."[24] (Italics added.)

The premier's statements were supplemented by those of the chief cabinet secretary, Miyazawa, on August 26. The next round of certification, Miyazawa stated, would take place two years hence, starting with textbooks to be used in 1985. As for the 1983 and 1984 textbooks, Monbushō would instruct education committees at local levels to reflect the government's new attitude on the controversial issues.[25] The content of Miyazawa's statement was transmitted to China and South Korea along with aides-mémoire.

The South Korean government was obviously eager to settle the controversy as soon as possible. Although the government spokesman noted that the timing of the revisions fell "far short of expectations," he stated that "we consider that this promise by the Japanese government is an affirmative response to repeated demands for corrections by the government and the Korean public opinion."[26] The South Korean mass media, however, were outraged. The Chinese issued no immediate response.

The Chinese government informed Japan on August 28 that it found the Japanese formula of August 26 objectionable. The Chinese could not accede to an ambiguous judgment on Japanese aggression against China. They were not satisfied that the premier wished to leave the judgment on Japan's past actions to future historians. Fearing the cancellation of Suzuki's visit to China, the task of explaining the Japanese position was entrusted to the ambassador in Beijing. Having made their point, the Chinese finally accepted the Japanese formula on September 9, and Premier Suzuki made his China visit in late September. Obviously stung by the Chinese turnabout, the ROK government submitted on August 31 a new demand that Japan correct the textbooks immediately, but no one anticipated a change in the Japanese position.[27]

THE TEXTBOOK CONTROVERSY: THE AFTERMATH

The textbook controversy rocked Japan, China, Korea, and the surrounding Asian nations during the summer of 1982. Although Premier Suzuki was spared the long lecture from his Chinese hosts that Tanaka had received from Premier Zhou Enlai in 1972, Suzuki did have to start his talks with the Chinese leaders on the textbook issue and heard sharp-edged criticisms of "militarist tendencies in Japan" and "the wanton revision of history by a small number of people." The premier received no welcoming editorial from *Renmin Ribao*, the organ of the Chinese Communist Party, as his predecessor Ōhira had three years before, nor was he able to issue a joint press release with Chinese leaders.[28] The Chinese were clearly not in a mood to show enthusiasm for the stoic and stodgy Japanese leader. Although he had had numerous other problems as Japan's top political leader, the textbook controversy must have weighed heavily on Suzuki. It was only twelve days after his return from China, on October 12, that he made the unanticipated announcement of his resignation.

Postmortem debates in Japan focused on whether, in fact, any revisions of the term "aggression" to "advance" had actually occurred in high school textbooks. Textbook writers had a meeting on September 4 to present a request for errata slips in the 1983 edition of the textbooks, but on September 17 Monbushō announced a policy of refusing such requests. The Publication Labor Union Federation announced on September 27 that "forced revision" of the word "aggression" had taken place in textbooks on contemporary society as well as in history books.[29] Thus everyone assumed that the Monbushō censors' pressure had resulted in wholesale expurgation of the word "aggression."

As it turned out, however, none of the twenty history books had changed the original word "aggression" to "advance" (*shinshutsu*); rather, four had altered the word to *shinnyū* (invade or make inroads) or *shinkō* (invade). The Japanese public was bewildered by a recantation in *Sankei Shimbun* on October 18, which stated that the reporters' club at Monbushō had not closely examined the actual textbooks and that in no case had "aggression" been changed to "advance" at the censors' insistence.[30] Prominent and popular magazines such as *Chū-ō Kōron* (Central Review), *Shūkan Bunshun* (Weekly *Bungei Shunjū*), and *Shokun!* (Everyone!) carried articles that attacked the "left-leaning" press for erroneous reporting and for not correcting the error once it was discovered.[31] The ethics of journalists and publishers were questioned. The exposé carried in *Shokun!* was entitled "Ten Thousand Dogs Barked in False Alarm: The Textbook Case," an allusion to a Han dynasty proverb best remembered in Japan as "If one dog barks in false alarm, a thousand others take up the cry."[32] Had the Japanese press stirred up an international storm over nothing, as some of the critics charged?

The original reports alleging the revision from "aggression" to "advance" evidently were in error, and had the error not been compounded by provocative headlines and captions, the storm would not have erupted and the Japanese government would have been spared considerable embarrassment. But the actual examples cited in the press left no doubt that the Monbushō censors had tried to mitigate Japanese responsibility for such events as the Nanjing massacre of December 1937, the massacre of Koreans during the March First movement in 1919, and the conscription of Korean laborers during the early 1940s.[33] Japanese atrocities were often treated as reactions to provocations, and descriptions of harsh treatments of victims were modified or deleted. The number of victims was often deleted for reasons of "uncertainty of reports." These were certainly matters that deserved correction as much as the use of such terms as "aggression" and "advance." As Korean scholars resident in Japan had repeatedly pointed out well before the controversy, many other historical entries were biased in Japan's favor.

It is unfortunate that the establishment-oriented historical perspective in Japan was challenged in the context of highly heated domestic and international political strife. But, seen in the context of Japanese-Korean relations since 1945, the uproar—even though it was triggered by careless and erroneous reporting—was badly needed. For the first time, Japanese leaders and the public were fully exposed to the deep-seated anti-Japanese emotions of neighboring peoples. Despite the massive anti-Japanese demonstrations in Korea since 1965, Premier Zhou Enlai's celebrated lecture to Premier Tanaka in 1972, and student riots in Indonesia and Thailand in 1974 on the occasion of Tanaka's visit, the Japanese press had never before engaged in such massive soul-searching about Japan's past.

The textbook controversy probably did not change the outlook and values of the older-generation conservatives. The revelations concerning the initial errors in reporting probably erased any effect the controversy might have had on them. Most probably agreed with Premier Suzuki's statement of August 23, which implied that history might yet judge Japan's past actions favorably. Although the conservative Japanese might have conceded that the militarists had committed occasional excesses, they would probably have insisted that the basic ideas behind Japan's continental expansion and the "Great East Asian Coprosperity Sphere" were sound ones that required no apologies.

But the Japanese public was deeply affected by the furor from China, Korea, and other countries. *Yomiuri Shimbun*'s national opinion survey of 3,000 voters in 250 localities conducted between September 18 and 19, just after the Chinese had formally accepted the Japanese formula, indicated that 50.2 percent of those responding thought the government should have made corrections before the problem expanded into an international issue and 69.4 percent felt corrections were needed in the textbooks.[34] For a time at least, a large number of people agreed with the press that the Japanese historical perspective should be altered. Although it is regrettable that the controversy heightened anti-Japanese feelings among the neighboring peoples, it did have a positive effect in Japan. A new understanding was necessary before Japan could assume a more active role in the regional arena.

THE DEBATE ON ANCIENT JAPANESE AND KOREAN HISTORY

The textbook controversy of 1982 narrowly focused on the term "aggression." Both Korean and Japanese political leaders chose to ignore, however, a long list of other distortions in Japanese textbooks that a Korean government agency (the Committee for the Compilation of National History, an agency within the Ministry of Education) had submitted. The list contained 167 items in sixteen 1983 high school textbooks on Japanese history, world history, and contemporary society. The list covered topics ranging from ancient to contemporary history.[35]

It will not serve a useful purpose here, nor will it be possible, to examine all the points raised. Fortunately, Japanese historians have been concerned with many of the points raised by the Korean side and have engaged in a heated debate among themselves. I shall trace their debate because it illuminates not only the nature of the Korean complaints but also the evolution of Japanese thought on them. A substantial number of Japanese historians have found that traditional Japanese accounts of ancient history contain distortions and create a prejudice against Korea, but these scholars have met strong resistance from some of their more conservative colleagues, whose point of view receives the support of the political leadership.

What relevance does the historians' debate on Japanese-Korean relations in antiquity have for contemporary international relations? How does the traditional account of ancient history, distorted or not, prejudice the Japanese against Korea? To a Westerner accustomed to the principle of equality among nations, the relevance of the debate is not obvious.

The Asian peoples have been highly conscious of status, as the statement of Fukuzawa Yukichi quoted in Chapter 1 vividly illustrates. Even today, both Japanese and Koreans are said to be obsequious to superiors but contemptuous and haughty to inferiors.[36] These norms and rules are germane to the relations between Japan and Korea because, for centuries, the same pattern had been applied to relationships among nations in East Asia. A superior nation not only had the right but also the moral obligation to act the part. The inferior had to know its place and fulfill its duties. This tradition is deeply implanted in the minds of the Japanese and Korean peoples even today. "At any given time," a Japanese scholar noted, "there is a definable rank order between two nations, whereby one is higher, the other lower."[37] Edwin Reischauer also noted that "to speak of a country as number one or as a third or fifth rate power is not just vaguely figurative, as in the American mind, but is a much more precise and meaningful statement to the Japanese."[38] It is in this context that the historians' debate becomes important.

The matter is made additionally sensitive and difficult because the ancient relations between Japan and Korea are intricately related to the founding myth of Japan. One cannot be changed without affecting the other. This is also why the Japanese public pays so much attention to some of the highly specialized intellectual discourses on ancient history that appear to the outsider to be esoteric at best. Another reason for the difficulty is the ingrained prejudice of the conservative intellectual and political leaders. To alter the founding myth of Japan is a serious enough matter; to alter it for the sake of a "correct" history of Japanese-Korean relations is simply too humiliating for them to contemplate. The result is a veritable Catch-22 situation, that is, the alteration of one factor depends upon another factor, but the change in the second factor requires a change in the first factor. How did such a situation come into being?

The Founding Myth of Japan and Early Japanese-Korean Relations

The source of the problem was the *Nihon Shoki* (Chronicles of Japan), compiled between A.D. 681 and A.D. 720, which traced the founding emperor of Japan, Emperor Jimmu, back to 660 B.C. Japan had emerged as a unified nation-state by the seventh century, and the ruling elites decided that an account should be made of its founding.[39] Naturally, the rulers of that era wished to embellish their ancestors; they created mythology, adapted legends, and interpolated historical works of China and Korea. Korean historical sources of Paekche origin were incorporated into *Nihon Shoki* in such a way as to support the existence of Mimana Nihonfu. The chronicle alleged that the gods of Yamato had ruled Korea, and it narrated the supposed conquest of the southern part of the Korean peninsula by Empress Jingū in A.D. 200. The Japanese rule of Korea was allegedly located in a principality called Mimana, located at the southern end of the peninsula. It served as the colonial outpost of Yamato, similar to the Korean Government-General established by Japan in 1910.[40]

Japanese elites of successive generations knew about this account, but, for centuries, no attempt was made to use it for political purposes. Since there was a considerable infusion of Korean culture into the Japanese archipelago in the ancient period, the Japanese royalties and other elites honored and respected the Korean kingdoms not only during the formative period of the Japanese nation but also during later periods. Products of Korean civilization were highly treasured. For example, between the fourteenth and fifteenth centuries, over a time span of 140 years, monks from Japan beseeched the

Koryŏ (918–1382) and Chosŏn (Yi dynasty, 1392–1910) kingdoms more than twenty times for a printed copy of the Tripikata Koreana woodblocks, which contained the complete Buddhist scriptures.[41] Koryŏ's great bronze bells and Buddhist paintings were also treasured, sought, and obtained.

After Tokugawa Ieyasu unified Japan in 1603, following centuries of feudal disorder, the new regime actively sought to promote amicable relations with Korea. To some of the new elites, Korea under the Yi dynasty was a source of new knowledge. The Tokugawa regime (1603–1868) adopted the neo-Confucianism of the Chu Hsi school as its official philosophy in its early period. Neo-Confucian learning had made much progress in Korea, where the Yi dynasty had adopted it as the Korean official philosophy. Such leading Japanese philosophers as Fujiwara Seika (1561–1619) and Hayashi Razan (1593–1657) based their neo-Confucian learning on Korean writings, particularly those of Yi Hwang (1501–1570), better known by his nom de plume, T'oe-ge.[42] Fujiwara had introduced neo-Confucianism to Ieyasu in 1593; Hayashi, who was Fujiwara's disciple, became Ieyasu's Confucian tutor.[43]

The Tokugawa regime also had an important political reason for cultivating amicable relations with Korea. The new regime had unified Japan by force, but it needed to win legitimacy both in domestic Japanese society and in international society. Within Japan, Toyotomi Hideyoshi's seven-year-old son had the mantle of legitimacy. In international society, Japan had become an outlaw as a result of Hideyoshi's seven-year war (1592–1598) in Korea. The Tokugawa regime in Edo (present-day Tokyo), therefore, actively sought diplomatic missions from Korea, which were accorded lavish treatments and put on ostentatious display. The travels of Korean embassies produced the "illusion that the Shogun's grace extended beyond the seas," and served to demonstrate the power and majority of the Edo regime. Between 1607 and 1811, the Yi dynasty dispatched twelve missions to Japan. Hayashi Razan, the Tokugawa regime's chief ideologue, used Korean recognition as evidence of Tokugawa legitimacy in his attempts to win direct recognition from the Ming.[44]

The Koreans, however, were understandably suspicious of Japan in view of the recent memory of Hideyoshi's invasion. They did not permit Japanese delegations to proceed to Seoul, the capital, but required them to conduct diplomacy and trade in Tongnae, near Pusan at the southern tip of the peninsula.

The surge of nationalism within Japan precipitated a change in the Japanese perception of Korea. As Japan prospered under the peace fostered by the Tokugawa regime, nationalism began to manifest itself, and more and more scholars began to delve into the classic works, including *Nihon Shoki*. They attached increasing significance to passages asserting Japan's superiority over Korea. As the Yi dynasty declined, the scholars of "national learning" (*kokugaku*) in Japan began to hold Korea in contempt. Until the end of the Tokugawa era, however, most others continued to be respectful toward Korea.[45]

In the late eighteenth century, when Japan was menaced by the West, the Japanese perception of Korea changed further. Some Japanese argued that Japan would not be strong enough to deter Western aggression if it did not conquer Korea. Yoshida Shōin (1831–1860) of Chōshū, that "fiery imperial patriot," advocated the restoration of the ancient imperial system, expansion abroad, and hatred of the Western barbarians. This argument gained momentum after the Meiji Restoration (1868) and strengthened until the Japanese takeover of Korea in 1910.[46]

The Colonialist Perspective

This was the atmosphere in which the accounts in *Nihon Shoki* and *Kojiki* (Account of Ancient Affairs) were given prominence.[47] In a book entitled *Kokushigan* (A View [literally, an eye] of National History), written under government auspices in 1877 and first published in 1889, three prominent historians at Tokyo Imperial University argued that the Japanese gods had ruled Korea in antiquity; some of them had gone to Korea and become Korean gods. After the imperial system or system of emperors was instituted, Japan conquered Korea and incorporated it into the Japanese domain. Thus, according to this view, the Koreans had the same ancestors as the Japanese. Therefore, it was the legitimate right and duty of Japan to integrate the two peoples as before.[48] This theory came to be known as *Nissen dōsoron*, or the theory of the identical ancestry of Japan and Korea. Implicit in it was the presumption of Japanese superiority.

Supporters of this theory had other alleged evidence. In 1884, an army captain, Sakawa Kagenobu, who had been dispatched to China by the Army General Staff to collect intelligence information, discovered north of the Yalu River a giant stone stele (6.2 meters high) erected in honor of the Koguryŏ king, Kwang-gae-t'o (A.D. 375–413). Even though most of the inscriptions were devoted to the wide-ranging exploits of the king and were unrelated to Japan, several lines did touch on the country of Wa, the predecessor of Yamato. The General Staff translated the lines as follows: "Paekche and Silla had

long been the subject peoples of Koguryŏ and had originally presented tribute to Koguryŏ, but in 391 the Wa came, crossing the sea,
and made subjects of Paekche . . . and Silla."[49]

The General Staff and scholars made good use of such evidence.
The fact that the inscription was found not on a Japanese historical
document but on a Koguryŏ stele in Manchuria strengthened their
convictions, proving to them that "Japan was the truly rich and
strong head family and that the three kingdoms in Korea, i.e. Koguryŏ [37 B.C.–A.D. 668], Silla [57 B.C.–A.D. 668] and Paekche [18 B.C.–
A.D. 660], were the feeble branch families" that required Japanese
protection.[50] On this basis, they celebrated the annexation of Korea
in 1910 as the restoration of the legitimate arrangement of antiquity.
Their evidence also seemed to prove that the country of Wa had become a strong state by the fourth century. How else could Japan have
subjugated Paekche and Silla and even challenged the giant state of
Koguryŏ in the north?

The Japanese imperial government soon adopted this theory as
orthodoxy, and publications buttressing it multiplied. The theory
was incorporated into textbooks used in Japan as well as in Korea,
and it was assimilated into Japanese culture. Although a few Japanese scholars disagreed with the translation of the stele inscription
and opposed the theory, their views were suppressed by the government as heresy. The orthodox view prevailed, and several generations
of Japanese grew up with it.

Japanese historians not only rationalized Japan's conquest of Korea by using these dubious sources but also undertook the task of
negating Korea's traditions and its integrity as a nation-state. In the
Taishō era (1912–1925), a group of scholars were brought together in
the Research Department of the South Manchurian Railway Company, the Japanese counterpart of the British East India Company.
The scholars' mission was to rationalize Japanese expansion into
Manchuria. When these scholars saw the Korean nationalist resurgence after 1919, the year of a nationwide uprising, they promulgated the theory of "the inseparability of Manchuria and Korea." The
argument of Inaba Iwakichi, a representative of this group, was that
most of the royal families in Korean history had originated in Manchuria rather than Korea; these rulers of Korea were, furthermore,
defeated Manchurian and Chinese elements who deserved no
respect.[51]

Implicit in Inaba's argument was the notion that there was no
true Korean dynasty that merited respect, and hence Korean demands for independence were not founded in history or tradition.

The argument also justified the Japanese policy of displacing a large number of impoverished Korean farmers to Manchuria; Koreans were returning to their original home, not being pushed out by the unscrupulous Japanese colonial regime in Korea. The theory also rationalized the Japanese conquest of Manchuria; since Koreans were now Japanese subjects, Japan had a legitimate claim over the original Korean homeland.

Debunking of the Myth

After Japan's defeat in 1945, the legends and myths used to justify Korea's subordination were quickly debunked. Some historians soon discovered that the principal sources for the myth of Japan's foundation, the *Nihon Shoki* and *Kojiki*, were based more on fiction than fact. Empress Jingū, along with the earlier emperors, was a mere creation of eighth-century historians intent on legitimizing the new regime that had come into being. Empress Jingū's supposed subjugation of Korea is now believed to be a story interpolated from the Wa's dispatch of forces (between A.D. 661 and 663) to assist Paekche, which was under a massive attack from allied T'ang and Silla forces.[52] The Wa forces, in this instance, were routed, and Silla soon unified the peninsula south of the Taedong River.

Most Japanese historians, however, continued to believe that "Japan extended its influence over the Korean peninsula in the latter half of the fourth century, turned Mimana into its domain, conquered Paekche and Silla, and even threatened the giant Koguryŏ in the north."[53] Their convictions about the inscription on King Kwang-gaet'o's stele remained undiminished. Textbooks, reference works, and history books continued to convey the same message that prewar historians had preached. The stele's inscription occupied a more important role than ever, because it was the only evidence to buttress the theory that the state of Yamato, the successor of Wa, was consolidated around the middle of the fourth century.[54]

In the 1960s, however, Japanese historians were jolted by a challenge from North Korean historians, particularly Kim Sŏk-hyŏng. In an article and book, *Ch'ogi Cho-Il kwan'gye yŏn'gu* (A Study of Early Korean-Japanese Relations), published in 1963, Kim denounced Japanese historians for uncritically perpetuating the "imperialistic" historiography of Korean-Japanese relations in antiquity.[55] He advanced a bold thesis, claiming that (1) the Mimana Nihonfu (the Japanese agency in Mimana) was a fiction, (2) Korea had never been a Japanese colony in antiquity, and (3) branches of Korean states or Korean

colonies in various parts of ancient Japan had exerted a strong influence on Japanese politics and culture. Another North Korean historian, Pak Shi-hyŏng, published a book on the Kwang-gae-t'o stele in
1966 that advanced an alternate reading of the stele inscription.[56]
Japanese historians had ignored a similar view advanced earlier by
a South Korean historian, Chŏng In-bo, but North Korean arguments
were too powerful to ignore.

Japanese historians' initial reaction to these challenges was negative. They dismissed North Korean scholars for their "nationalistic
predisposition" and accused them of being ignorant about the advances made in Japanese historiography since the end of the Second
World War.[57] Tōma Shodai, in his long review of Kim's work, published in 1970, did admit that the stele, erected more than fifteen
hundred years ago, had been badly damaged by the elements.[58] Some
of the words were no longer legible, and the inscription, written in
Chinese, did not contain sentence demarcations. Hence there were
grounds for re-examination.

Shisō [Thought], a widely read intellectual magazine, carried an
article in March 1971 by Nakatsuka Akira. Nakatsuka pointed out
that the text of the stele inscription was first introduced to Japan by
an army intelligence officer in 1884, when the Japanese military had
begun preparing for the war against China; that the text with its
missing words was interpreted by the General Staff of the Army to
suit its political purposes; and that scholars and other writers since
then had uncritically and willingly accepted the interpretation. Nakatsuka also discovered that the few "facsimiles" of the inscription
published in various publications, including high school textbooks,
tampered with the text and that, in 1922, "a book of antiquity," *Minabuchi no sho* (The Book of Minabuchi), had been manufactured to
buttress the General Staff's interpretation.[59]

The implications of Nakatsuka's arguments and evidence were
far-reaching. Many progressive historians abandoned the idea that
Japan had consolidated its state system by the fourth century. They
came to believe that only after the Wa's expeditionary fleet suffered a
disastrous defeat at the hands of Silla and T'ang forces in A.D. 663 did
Japan consolidate itself as a strong state.[60] More doubts were cast on
the previous interpretation of the stele inscription when Yi Chin-Hŭi,
a Korean scholar in Japan, followed up Nakatsuka's study and advanced the argument that Japanese military officers had tampered
with the stele and had altered some characters on it to suit their
purpose.[61]

Thus, Japanese historiography has been undergoing a dynamic change in recent years. But not all Japanese historians were converted to the new interpretations, and, indeed, many in the conservative wing persist in the old views of history.[62] School textbooks and reference works continue to say what has been said before.[63] A large portion of the Japanese public, of course, will not relearn history.

The Horseback-Rider Origin of Japan

The theory of identical ancestry took an interesting turn in the postwar era, particularly in the 1960s and 1970s. Although such prewar historians as Kita Sadakichi had recognized as early as 1916 that immigrants from the continent had "conquered, assimilated, and amalgamated the original inhabitants," they had overshadowed such recognition with the colonialist argument that ancient Japan had been Korea's overlord.[64] Kita was one of the leading exponents of the latter view. But, in the postwar context, the theory of the "horseback-rider origin of the Japanese state" came to receive more attention.

This theory said, in essence, that the horseback-riding people of the Tungustic line, either of the Koguryŏ kingdom or of the Puyŏ tribe (Fuyü in Chinese) in Manchuria and northern Korea, crossed from the Korean peninsula to present-day northern Kyūshū in Japan around the fourth century A.D. They conquered the Wa people in the vicinity and subsequently established the first Japanese state of Yamato. The theory is based on an ethnological study by Oka Masao, who believed that the "imperial race" (*tennō zoku*), the dominant force of the Tomb or *Kofun* period (ca. A.D. 300–710), were latecomers to Japan who had close links with societies historians knew had existed in Korea and Manchuria. Oka believed that this group had originated in eastern Manchuria as a mixed herding and farming people and that around the second and third century A.D. they moved through the Korean peninsula and into the Japanese archipelago. They would have conquered the peoples of the earlier Japanese culture, in the process absorbing many of their traits and beliefs.

Oka did not specifically identify these conquering people, but he suggested that they were in close relationship, culturally and ethnically, with the ancient Puyŏ and Koguryŏ states. The Koguryŏ, whose state included southern Manchuria and most of Korea and lasted from its traditional founding in 37 B.C. to A.D. 668, were one of the major constituents of the Korean people. The Puyŏ state in Manchuria lasted from the first through the third centuries; after its destruction in A.D. 286, its people continued to play an important role in Manchuria. One of its branches founded the southern Korean state of Paekche during the fourth century.[65]

Egami Namio, with whom the horseback-rider theory came to be more popularly associated, extended the argument further. He emphasized the different characteristics of Japanese ancient tombs and the artifacts buried in them. Whereas tombs of the earlier period (generally the fourth century) were smaller and showed many characteristics of an agrarian economy, the tombs of the later period (after the latter part of the fourth century) were much larger and the artifacts in them included weapons, armor, horse trappings, and gold and silver ornaments characteristic of continental royalties and horseback-riding peoples. Egami concluded that massive conquests by horseback-riding people took place around the fourth century. He also hypothesized that Emperor Sūjin, who allegedly founded the first strong kingdom in Japan between the end of the fourth century and the beginning of the fifth century, came from the Korean peninsula and was a descendant of the ruling class in the Pyŏnhan tribal state.[66]

This theory, first expounded in 1948 at the Symposium on the Origins of the Japanese People and Culture and the Formation of the Japanese State, was not taken seriously at first. But, as more and more evidence accumulated, historians began to pay more attention to it. A strong impetus for this theory was provided by the excavation of an ancient tomb, Takamatsuzuka, in Nara Prefecture in March 1972.[67] The mural paintings in the tomb and the artifacts buried in it bore striking similarity to those excavated in Korea and China; the continental origin of Japanese elites of the ancient period was beyond doubt.[68]

The horseback-rider theory aroused an intense and emotional controversy. Some scholars rejected it outright, and others accepted it with reservations.[69] Such prominent scholars as Inoue Mitsusada conceded the possibility of such events taking place in the second century B.C., but they found it difficult to accept the idea that the conquests took place so late in Japanese history.[70] Inoue, at the same time, insisted that Emperor Ōjin (A.D. 201–310), the fourth son of Empress Jingū, had managed Mimana at the southern tip of Korea during the fourth century and had imported technology and resources from Korea to Japan by receiving tributes and recruiting persons. This, of course, is a variation of the legend of Empress Jingū's conquest of Silla. Inoue also accepted the traditional interpretation of King Kwang-gae-t'o's stele inscription.[71] Such scholars as Okada Hidehiro, in contrast, argued that it was not a corps of horseback-riding soldiers who conquered Japan but rather the Chinese-speaking, lowest-class elements in Korea who migrated to Japan and introduced new technology. It was, in Okada's view, the "overseas Chinese" (*kakyō*) who built Japanese civilization.[72]

Much remains to be done by Japanese archaeologists and historians studying the origins of the Japanese state and the early relations between Japan and Korea. The hypotheses advanced by Egami Namio and Kim Sŏk-hyŏng deserve to be pursued further.[73]

The Conservative Reaction

It should be noted, however, that the critics of the horseback-rider theory show a distinct bias toward the prewar interpretation of Japanese-Korean relations. They are reminiscent of Inaba Iwakichi who, as noted earlier, had rejected the Korean tradition and Korea's integrity as a civilization. Inoue Mitsusada's view, for instance, is a continuation of the prewar interpretation. Okada Hidehiro attempted to purge all Korean elements from the horseback-riding newcomers. He was willing to admit Chinese riders but not Korean ones. Referring to the mural paintings in the Takamatsuzuka, he declared that "it was clearly a product of Chinese civilization, and it is difficult to comprehend the propaganda that it was a product influenced by Korean civilization." He argued that only after the Silla kingdom had unified Korea in the second half of the seventh century had "something that could be called Korean civilization" emerged; hence it is nothing short of an "anachronism" to argue that Korean civilization is the wellspring of its Japanese counterpart or that the immigrants from the peninsula were Koreans.[74] Anything introduced into Japan from the continent before the late seventh century, therefore, must be labeled Chinese, not Korean.

Such an argument raises important questions. If the Koguryŏ, Paekche, and preunification Silla were declared non-Korean, how should historians treat these kingdoms on the Korean peninsula? Are the Koreans mistaken in regarding these three kingdoms as their predecessors? If Korean civilization did not exist before Korea was unified in A.D. 668, should one also say that Japanese civilization did not exist before A.D. 760, when the unified state used the title of Nihon or Nippon for the first time?[75] If it was the overseas Chinese who built Japanese culture, as Okada argued, should Japan before A.D. 670 be called an extension of China? Why should the Puyŏ tribe be considered Chinese, since it was not of the Han race?

One should not belabor the obvious. If Japan received a massive infusion of people and culture from the continent through the Korean peninsula, the Koreans—or their ancestors—whether they were of the Koguryŏ, Paekche, or Silla kingdoms, must have made some contributions. As the stele of King Kwang-gae-t'o and countless Koguryŏ wall paintings clearly show, the Koguryŏ people were a horseback-riding people. During the 22 years of his reign (A.D. 391–413), Kwang-gae-t'o conquered a vast territory in the Manchurian plain. In A.D. 400, the same king dispatched fifty thousand troops to aid Silla's battle against the invading Wa, who had landed at the southern tip of the peninsula.[76]

The emotional conflict about ancient history unfortunately does not stop here. As Inoue Mitsusada's explanation of the importation of technology from the continent indicates, Japanese historians on the whole recognize the important contributions made by Korean immigrants to various aspects of Japanese civilization in its formative stage, including agriculture, the arts, architecture, the calendar, literature, medicine, philosophy, religion, and the written language.[77] Japanese classics, such as *Nihon Shoki* and *Kojiki*, are liberally sprinkled with references to naturalized Koreans. Many Japanese historians, however, find it more comfortable to depict the bearers of the new civilization as prisoners, political refugees, or personnel recruited by Japanese generals who had been dispatched to the peninsula by the well-established Japanese state. This is a corollary to the assumption that Japan or Yamato was superior to contemporary Korean kingdoms. Some scholars would rather ignore, conceal, or deny the influence exerted by Korean immigrants. Describing the immigrants as Chinese, as Okada Hidehiro has done, is one form of denial. Others took different tactics, which require brief consideration.

In more recent years, many Japanese scholars have identified the seminal contributions Korean immigrants made to the formative stages of early Japanese art. *Manyōshū* (Compendium of Ten Thousand Leaves), one of the most important anthologies of poems of the early period, is attributed by these scholars to Yamanoue Okura (A.D. 660–733), who has been identified as a man of Paekche origin. But some of the most influential Japanese scholars either gloss over his origin with silence or say that "nothing is known of his origins." This behavior led Roy A. Miller, an American student of Japanese literature, to conclude that some prominent Japanese scholars do not "hesitate to subject [their] proof-texts to every possible violence of interpretation, until they can be made to yield up the desired results." In the words of Professor Miller, to overlook the "towering milestones in the postwar studies of Japanese literature, which include the discovery of the Korean influence on the formative stages of Japanese writings, would be equivalent to an Egyptologist accidently overlooking the pyramids."[78]

Why then do these scholars choose to overlook these discoveries? According to Miller, it is because postwar discoveries "directly contradict the entire theoretical framework, as well as the dialectic, of the *kokutai no hongi* [Cardinal principles of the national entity of Japan], which defined the essence of imperial Japan." Such scholars as Katō Shuichi substituted "cardinal principles of the national entity" with "indigenous world view," but the content was the same. By the very definition of kokutai, Korean immigrants could not possibly have had a significant role in the formation of early Japanese literary culture. For these ultranationalists, according to Miller, "There was something mystical but palpably latent in every historical state of Japanese culture, something that resisted change and something against which waves of innovation and foreign borrowing broke themselves in vain, except on those rare occasions when they were allowed to leave behind something that would 'profit our country.'" Even Buddhism, according to this view, had no significant influence on Japanese culture, simply because it was a foreign religion.[79] It should be remembered that Miller was commenting on *A History of Japanese Literature: The First Thousand Years*, a book published in 1979, not in the 1930s or 1940s.

CONCLUSIONS

The textbook controversy of 1982 must be seen in this context. The whole controversy involving King Kwang-gae-t'o's stele and the Mimana municipality would have remained an esoteric topic for academic discussion had not Japanese historians since the seventh century attempted to use history as a political tool. Too often historiography has been used as a means to justify expansionist political action. In attempting to embellish Japanese history, scholars created among the Japanese population a prejudice against Korea that, in turn, perpetuated Korean resentment of Japan and made it difficult for the two peoples to establish a genuine sense of friendship. This is why the Koreans do not regard the revision of Japanese textbooks as a domestic matter.

There cannot be any pure or absolutely objective history, notwithstanding the attempt at "scientific history" by some contemporary historians. Prominent Korean politicians, including the late President Park, have called for history "with Korean nationality," and, indeed, Japanese historians find South Korean historiography on Japanese-Korean relations too nationalistic. There is a need for both sides to detach history from the politics of the past and present. History is complicated enough without injecting politics into it.

Separation of history from politics, however, is a very difficult task. Clearly the histories of the northeast Asian countries, including China, Japan, and Korea, were closely intertwined. Sometimes it is difficult to see where China and Korea ended and Korea and Japan began. Attempts to force a clear answer when no such answer is possible has led to distortions, misunderstandings, and conflicts. Myths and legends should remain such, not be transformed into historical facts.

7

Looking Ahead: Perspectives on Japanese-Korean Relations

Premier Nakasone's Seoul visit was an epochal event in Japanese-South Korean relations. So was President Chun's state visit to Tokyo in September 1984. But will future relations between the two nations be substantially different from those of the past, which have been marred by frequent emotional outbursts? What lies ahead for Japanese-Korean relations?

Since the Nakasone visit, both sides have striven to maintain the atmosphere of cordiality and have de-emphasized outstanding issues that could have aroused intense emotions. The Koreans, for example, were clearly dissatisfied with Japanese handling of the textbook revision and the the press was highly critical of Monbushō (the Japanese Ministry of Education), but its tone was much milder than before.[1] The conciliatory tone of the Koreans also surprised the Japanese at the sixteenth meeting of the Japanese–South Korean Conference on Economy, held in April 1984. The head of the Korean delegation told the Japanese that the Koreans were not asking the Japanese to transfer all the high technology they had developed. Nor did the South Korean side press for immediate solutions to the problem of the trade deficit, although South Korea had incurred a $1.2 billion trade deficit with Japan in 1982 and $2.6 billion in 1983. The Koreans asked only for the establishment of a basic policy that would reduce future deficits. The attitude of the Koreans contrasted sharply with that of the previous year. The meeting of Japanese and Korean scholars, politicians, and diplomats held in April discussed existing problems "frankly and without raising voices."[2] The Japanese provided 5.1 billion yen ($196 million) in 1983 and 9.5 billion yen ($365 million) in 1984 from the $4 billion loan agreement.[3]

President Chun was invited to Tokyo in September 1984 for a return visit and was accorded royal treatment. Premier Nakasone left no doubt that he was intent on improving his country's relations with South Korea. The press carried banner headlines, and TV newscasts repeatedly broadcast South Korea's national anthem. Japanese and South Korean flags adorned the streets, buses, and taxis of Tokyo. At a state banquet for President Chun, Emperor Hirohito referred to the Korean contribution to Japanese culture in the sixth and seventh centuries and expressed his regret for the unfortunate events of modern history, which "should not be repeated again." At a luncheon honoring President Chun, Premier Nakasone went a step further and said "the fact remains that there was a period in this century when Japan brought to bear great sufferings upon your country and its people. I would like to state here that the Government and people of Japan feel a deep regret for this error and are determined to firmly warn ourselves for the future."[4] President Chun repeatedly referred to his Tokyo visit as the beginning of a "new era of partnership" between the two countries.

Even before the Chun visit, the Japanese mass media had made a major effort to reorient Japanese attitudes toward South Korea. A nationwide newspaper, *Yomiuri Shimbun*, allocated large spaces on its front page to carry a best-selling novelist's serialized articles on Korean culture and the relationship between the Japanese and Korean civilizations.[5] Televised reports on South Korea became more frequent and less sensational. The government-owned NHK (Japan Broadcasting Corporation) launched an instruction program in the Korean language. The number of Japanese studying in South Korea also began to rise.[6]

There is no doubt that policies and attitudes of individual leaders play an important role in international relations, and the friendship forged between President Chun and Premier Nakasone began to have some effect on Japanese–South Korean relations. It should not be forgotten, however, that the personal friendship between the two leaders was formed in an environment, both domestic and international, that required it. Both leaders needed the amicable relationship for their own reasons. It should be noted also that the opposition forces in South Korea sharply denounced President Chun's state visit as a repetition of "submissive and humiliating" diplomacy and pointed out that the visit itself failed to produce positive solutions to any of the outstanding issues. The Japanese side had worked intensely to establish a government-level Japanese–South Korean cultural committee as one of the major items on the agenda for the Chun-Nakasone summit, but the Koreans rejected the offer for fear of Japanese "cultural invasion."[7] Japanese and South Korean officials also held a two-day meeting in Tokyo on trade, during which the Korean side requested the lowering of the tariff and expansion of the generalized system of preference for Korean products. But the meeting ended on August 24, two weeks before the Chun visit, without result.[8] This is why the joint communiqué issued by the two leaders at the end of President Chun's journey, on September 8, was limited to generalities. Chun's visit once again proved the limits of personal diplomacy. Prognoses of the future relationship, therefore, require an analysis of the factors that will continue to shape the environment.

GENERAL CHARACTERISTICS OF JAPAN'S KOREA POLICY

It deserves to be reiterated that Japan's foreign policy makers pursue their perception of Japan's national interest and its domestic and international requirements. The same thing, of course, can be said about North and South Korea's policymakers. Interactions among the three sets of policymakers will determine the future relationship between Japan and the two Korean states.

Japan's domestic environment has remained stable during the past three decades, and it will remain so in the foreseeable future. Even if the LDP fails to win majority seats in the parliament and is forced to form coalitions with other parties, there will be no major changes in Japan's foreign policy because, since the mid-1970s, such opposition parties as Kōmeitō, the Democratic Socialist Party, and the New Liberal Club have begun to seek a larger electoral base and have moved toward a middle-of-the-road position on many issues. The Korea policy of these parties is not substantially different from that of the LDP. The public's attitude toward foreign policy, particularly toward the Korea policy, has not changed significantly.

Japan's foreign policy, however, has been constrained by the international environment imposed on Japan after World War II. Partly because of circumstances and partly by choice, Japan placed itself under an American umbrella of protection, and its foreign policy has since been largely reactive and reflective of U.S. foreign policy, particularly when policies had security implications. Japan, thus, was obliged to delay the opening of diplomatic relations with China until President Nixon's Peking visit of 1971. With respect to the Korean peninsula, this meant Japan tilted toward South Korea. The strongly anticommunist conservative elements in Japan, including the business community, did not find this situation intolerable.

North Korea, in the meantime, has had a small but very vocal constituency in Japan in the form of socialist and communist parties and the left-wing intellectuals who had led the opposition to the Japanese–South Korean negotiations that led to the normalization treaty of 1965. Those advocating a more independent foreign policy and removal of Japan from the cold war structure also began to question the wisdom of closing Japan's doors to North Korea. The clamor for an equidistance policy on the Korean peninsula heightened during the détente era, and even the "pro–South Korean" Kishi faction moved in that direction.

Although the call for an equidistance policy has weakened as a result of the resurgence of the cold war atmosphere in the beginning of the 1980s, and chances are remote that the Japanese government will adopt such a policy as long as North and South Korea confront each other with large armies, it is quite likely that Japan will seek an improvement of unofficial ties with North Korea while it seeks to improve ties with South Korea. Such a policy agrees with a perspective most Japanese share and the international environment will be favorable for it. In spite of divergent views, most Japanese share a certain perspective toward the Korean peninsula and a certain unity of purpose and direction. Japan's policy toward the DPRK is most likely to follow the pattern of diplomacy Japan had practiced with the People's Republic of China before the conclusion of official diplomatic ties in 1975.[9]

The Japanese Perspective on Korea

Korea was of primary importance to the prewar Japanese government, which was intent on continental expansion, but, as Japan's environment changed, so did its perspective. Japan's security now depends on the support of the United States and its economic health depends on the flow of worldwide trade. Japan's orientation not only shifted away from the Asian continent for which Korea had served as the essential land bridge, but, because of the advance in technology, Japan no longer needs a land bridge even to be involved in continental affairs. Hence, Korea's value to Japan is primarily economic, and it is of value to Japan's security only insofar as it functions as a buffer against communism.

Japan's economic interest and its perception of South Korea as a buffer have led the Japanese to place a premium on stability and peace on the Korean peninsula. In the abstract, both North and South Korea, as well as China, the Soviet Union, and the United States, agree on the same need, but there is a sharp disagreement on the cause of the tension and the means to alleviate it. It was in part this discrepancy that rocked Japanese–South Korean ties in the early 1970s; the problem will remain between them as long as the two regimes on the peninsula face each other with unmitigated hostility. South Korea holds North Korea solely responsible for the tension and opposes any form of Japanese–North Korean contact prior to North Korean–South Korean rapprochement. The Japanese, on the whole, disagree with such a view.

The image of North Korea broadly shared in Japan is that of a fiercely nationalistic regime under a firm and dogmatic dictator who is intent on building a puritanical and orderly society. Even those who share South Korean views regarding North Korea's intentions consider the U.S. presence on the Korean peninsula adequate to prevent another North Korean assault on the south. Although the Japanese recognize the tension between North and South Korea, they do not hold North Korea solely responsible for it. A significant portion of Japan's elite, particularly in the "progressive" community, believe that tension on the Korean peninsula could be alleviated if more earnest attempts were made by South Korea to bring about reconciliation. South Koreans find this perception unrealistic and oppose Japanese policies based on such an assumption.

For two reasons, however, Japan and South Korea are not likely to repeat the trauma of the 1970s, even if the relationship between the superpowers begins to thaw and Japanese foreign policy is again removed from the cold war structure. First, Japanese politicians learned a valuable lesson from their experiences in the first half of the 1970s. Second, a changing international environment will make increased contact between Japan and North Korea less objectionable to South Korea.

The Impact of the Early 1970s on Japanese Diplomacy

The turbulent era of the early 1970s provided a valuable lesson to Japanese politicians and the public not only with respect to Japan's Korea policy but also to foreign affairs in general. Although the Japanese had been discussing the need for an autonomous foreign policy throughout the 1960s, they had been complacent until 1971. They were totally unprepared to face the new era of détente ushered in by the Nixon-Kissinger team or to play the autonomous role envisaged by U.S. leaders. As a result, Japanese leaders scrambled to design a new foreign policy without much deliberation. The new Korea policy they adopted was a stopgap measure arrived at in a crisis atmosphere. The Japanese were carried away by the euphoria of détente and acted more out of hopes, fears, and idealism than on the basis of a clear assessment of reality. Although they knew a great deal about South Korea, they knew very little about North Korea or inter-Korean relations. The Japanese placed implicit trust in the Nixon-Kissinger formula for relaxing tension on the Korean peninsula through détente among the great powers. They rushed to improve relations with North Korea lest they be left behind. This, one might note, is an aberration from the normal pattern of decisionmaking in Japan.

The failure of the détente policy and the subsequent events in Iran, Afghanistan, and Indochina, as well as the doubts cast on U.S.-Japanese relations, led many Japanese politicians and intellectuals to reassess Japan's position in the world and particularly in Asia. The troubled relations with South Korea also caused many to ponder the nature of Japan's relations with the two Koreas. Although many Japanese believe that Japan will benefit more by dealing with both Koreas on equal terms, since this would increase trade opportunities and might even contribute to stability on the Korean peninsula, they realize the importance of South Korea to Japan and the cost of moving too far ahead of South Korea in approaching North Korea. Such Japanese moves not only have not contributed to the stabilization of North Korean–South Korean relations but also have jeopardized Japan's profitable relations with South Korea.

Clearly, Japan's ability to affect the course of events on the Korean peninsula was limited. Japanese leaders all but stopped their favorite refrain of the past, the notion that Japan could serve as an intermediary between North and South Korea. One could say that in the 1970s the Japanese matured as far as foreign affairs were concerned. Their future actions are most likely to be more deliberate and realistic, particularly with respect to Korean affairs. Such a tendency undoubtedly will have a salutary effect on the future of Japanese–South Korean relations although the North Korean regime will find such a tendency unsatisfactory.

It is interesting to note in this connection that even the Japanese Socialist Party, which has steadfastly refused to recognize the existence of the Republic of Korea, began in April 1984 to deliberate the merit of establishing contacts with South Korea.[10] Abstract ideologies and idealism cannot serve as the basis of foreign policy.

Although the gap between Japanese and South Korean perceptions of North Korea will remain substantially wide, and Japanese moves to increase contacts with North Korea will continue to irritate South Korea, changes in the international environment are likely to reduce the magnitude of the problem. China and the Soviet Union, the two allies of the Democratic People's Republic of Korea, will no doubt continue the trend toward recognizing the status quo on the Korean peninsula, and the U.S. commitment to South Korea's defense will remain stable. This assertion calls for a brief discussion of the foreign policies of the various powers.

THE INTERNATIONAL ENVIRONMENT

Ironically, the strengthening of Soviet naval and military strength in East Asia and the aggravation of Soviet-American relations after the Soviet "advance" into Afghanistan in 1979 contributed significantly to a more stable environment for Japanese-Korean relations. These Soviet actions (1) strengthened U.S. resolve to support South Korea's defense system, (2) made it easier for the United States to encourage closer Japanese–South Korean cooperation, and (3) reduced the importance of North Korea to the Soviet Union. The situation is likely to continue at least in the remainder of the 1980s.

The Impact of the Soviet Policy

Although the Soviet Union justifies its military buildup in the Pacific region as a counterbalance to a U.S. attempt to encircle the USSR by alliances, the buildup has increased apprehensions on the part of China, Japan, and the United States. In the wake of the Soviet invasion of Afghanistan and the conclusion of a Soviet-Vietnamese treaty in November 1978, even President Carter, an advocate of a conciliatory approach to the Soviet Union, had to abandon his plan to withdraw U.S. ground troops from Korea. Even if Soviet-American relations improve in the latter part of the 1980s, as they should, the United States is not likely to diminish its support for South Korea, simply because of its strategic location. The Korea Strait, one of the major traffic routes for the Soviet Far Eastern Navy, is located at the southern end of the Korean peninsula.

The Soviet buildup, and particularly the strengthening of military installations close to Japan's northern island, have intensified Japanese apprehension. Although Japan is reluctant to be drawn into military ties with South Korea, the U.S. call for a "sharing of responsibility" in the region has become increasingly more persuasive. Japan, therefore, is likely to play an increasingly important security role in and around Japan, although it will continue to shun direct military ties with South Korea.

The Soviet buildup has also had the effect of freeing the Soviet Union from rigid adherence to North Korea's position toward South Korea. As the Soviet Union has increased its military strength in the Far East, the value of North Korea for Soviet strategy has diminished. In a war against the United States, North Korea will be of little value, since the theater of war will be the Pacific rather than the Korean peninsula. The Soviet Union will also gain little by involvement in a war over the Korean peninsula.

North Korea occupied an important position in Soviet Far Eastern policy during the 1960s and 1970s when Sino-Soviet confrontation was at its peak. At the time, North Korea was the only ruling communist party in Asia that had taken a neutral stand in the Sino-Soviet dispute. But, as the two communist giants shifted their engagements from the battleground to negotiating tables in the early 1980s, the significance of North Korea in Soviet—and Chinese—defense policy diminished. The Soviet Union and China will, of course, try to maintain amicable relations with the DPRK and provide it with a limited amount of economic aid, but their efforts will be within the normal range of diplomacy among socialist countries. The Soviet Union, therefore, is likely to become more open-minded about inter-Korean relations.

Indeed, South Korea has sought to establish informal contacts with both China and the Soviet Union since the early 1970s. Despite the slow pace of response, the subtlety of moves, and the occasional reversals, both powers have indicated their favorable inclinations. Beginning in 1973, the Soviet Union permitted South Korean officials and scholars to attend international conferences; then, in 1978, South Korea began to engage in indirect trade through third parties. Although the downing of Korean Airline flight 007 in September 1983 temporarily hardened bilateral relations, the trend of the past decade is likely to be maintained.

China and the Korean Question

The same pattern of transactions and exchanges was adopted by China in the early 1980s, and the pattern is likely to remain stable. China's relations with North Korea have proved more durable and amicable than Soviet–North Korean ties, in spite of the numerous frictions the two countries experienced in the early 1960s and late 1970s. But China has turned inward since the demise of Chairman Mao, and its foreign and military policies have centered on its goal of modernization. In the 1980s China needs a stable international and domestic environment; escalation of tension on the Korean peninsula is not in the Chinese interest. Indeed, in Janury 1984, Chinese premier Zhao Ziyang, in an effort to reduce tension on the Korean peninsula, officially assumed the role of intermediary between North Korea on the one hand and the United States and South Korea on the other. Although the tripartite talks proposed by North Korea—a proposal conveyed to the United States by the Chinese premier— were unacceptable to the Americans and South Koreans, Premier Zhao's action did indicate the direction of China's Korea policy.

It is interesting to note in this connection that the Chinese included Sichuan Province in President Kim Il-sŏng's itinerary when he visited China in September 1982. Sichuan, of course, is where Premier Zhao Ziyang made his mark by freeing the economy from tight state control and setting China on the road to recovery. The Chinese also showed the Shenzhen Special Economic Zone in Kwangtung Province to Foreign Minister Kim Yŏng-nam in February 1984, and to Premier Kang Sŏng-san in August. Perhaps the Chinese wished to influence the outlook and perspective of North Korean leaders through these visits. Or perhaps the North Korean leaders were exploring the prospect of change in North Korea. In any event, Premier Kang Sŏng-san of the DPRK openly praised the PRC's new economic policy that he said brought about an "unprecedented great prosperity" while visiting that country in August 1984, and on September 8, the DPRK's Standing Committee of the Supreme People's Assembly passed the joint-venture law to induce foreign investment. It is obvious that the North Koreans are emulating a part of China's economic policy. There is a distinct possibility that the DPRK will also follow the pragmatic orientation of China's foreign policy.

The United States and North Korea

The United States has also indicated from time to time since the early 1970s that it would not be averse to informal contacts with North Korea. Once North and South Korea reduce the level of hostility and begin to negotiate on the many issues that separate them, the United States would not oppose direct talks with the DPRK. Although there is a considerable distance between these minute moves and official diplomatic ties, the trend is unmistakable. All the major powers are inching toward the recognition of the status quo.

These moves by major powers are favorable for the future of Japanese–South Korean relations because the new international environment favors intensified political ties between the two. The new atmosphere should also render informal Japanese contacts with North Korea less conspicuous and hence less offensive to South Korea. As long as Japanese contacts with North Korea are synchronized with Chinese and Soviet overtures to South Korea, the latter has no reason to be aroused.

North Korean–South Korean Relations and Japan

The most effective way to remove the political irritation between Japan and South Korea, of course, is to bring about unification or, short of that, to improve the relationship between North and South Korea. Given the dim prospects for Korean unification in the near future, it may be more useful here to analyze the prospect of improved North-South relations. As noted previously, the inter-Korean relationship has remained tense since bilateral talks ended in 1973, and North Korea became much more belligerent after President Carter abandoned his original plan to withdraw U.S. combat troops from South Korea in 1979. The ascendance of General Chun in South Korea has not helped the situation, even though one of his first acts as president was to call for a dialogue with North Korea. North Korean leaders vowed never to deal with the government of Chun Doo Hwan because, according to official pronouncements, they could not shake the "bloodstained hands" of the man who masterminded the "Kwangju massacre" of May 1980. The warlike atmosphere was exacerbated by the Rangoon explosion of October 1983. Bombs detonated by North Korean agents killed numerous South Korean officials, including six cabinet members, and narrowly missed President Chun Doo Hwan, who was on a state visit.

It is difficult to predict when the stalemate can be resolved and tension reduced. Since the end of the Korean War in 1953, the DPRK leadership has consistently rejected the idea of peaceful coexistence of the two Koreas as a ruse designed to legitimize and perpetuate the division of Korea. For President Kim Il-sŏng of the DPRK, the only reason for North and South Korea to hold talks was to achieve unification, and the only possible way of reducing tension was to let the United States withdraw its troops from South Korea. The North Koreans would not accept the South Korean proposal to reduce tension and build trust through trade, personal visits, and de-escalation of hostile propaganda. Such an approach might have created a condition in which South Korea would find the U.S. troop presence unnecessary, and Koreans on both sides could have moved a step closer to unification.

The possibility of change in North Korea's policy toward South Korea does exist, however. In fact, economic and social needs in North Korea dictate such a change if the DPRK wishes to reduce its heavy burden of military spending and improve its chances of obtaining foreign capital and technology. President Kim Il-sŏng had stated in March 1975 that "[w]ith the economy developing rapidly and new economic branches emerging, we cannot satisfy our needs if we confine ourselves to the socialist market. Therefore, while relying on the socialist market, we must actively move into the capitalist market to purchase the materials, machines and equipment we need."[11] But the DPRK's belligerent attitude toward South Korea, and toward the United States and its economic policies, have prevented North Korea from expanding its contacts with Japan and Western countries. Domestically, ideological exhortations also had their limits. South Korea's economy, in the meantime, expanded rapidly, leaving North Korea far behind. The DPRK leadership, therefore, may moderate its stance toward South Korea and seek a modus vivendi.[12]

Indeed, much has happened since the autumn of 1984 in this respect. In September, the South Korean Red Cross accepted a North Korean offer to send rice and fabric to aid flood victims in South Korea. As a result, North Korea shipped 7,200 tons of rice, 500,000 meters of textile fabrics, and some 2,700 boxes of medicine to the ROK. In November the two sides opened talks to facilitate trade and the reunion of divided families, but the North Korean side chose to suspend further talks in January 1985. Nonetheless, President Kim Il-sŏng, in his new year's address, suggested the possibility of "high-level political talks" should negotiations at lower levels prove fruitful. (President Chun has called for high-level talks since he assumed power.) Only time will tell where these moves will lead, but there is a strong possibility for improved North Korean–South Korean relations in the near future. Such a change would also have a salutary effect on North Korea's relations with Japan.

THE PROSPECTS FOR JAPANESE –NORTH KOREAN RELATIONS

Japan's relations with North Korea, however, are likely to be limited for the foreseeable future even if North and South Korea begin to improve their relations. The tension-reduction process between the two states will be arduous even under the best of circumstances, and too bold a move on the part of Japan will jeopardize the very process it seeks to encourage, as the experience of the early 1970s too clearly showed. North Korea's economic structure is not conducive to a rapid expansion in foreign trade (unless, of course, Japan is willing to extend large amounts of credit), and its political system is not amenable to open exchange of personnel and information. Not only do the North Korean people feel the same primordial emotions for Japan as their South Korean counterparts have exhibited, but also the DPRK's ideology is diametrically opposed to that of Japan. It is possible that North Korea's political and economic systems will change, but such a change will come about only slowly, and the improvement in Japanese–North Korean relations cannot outpace the development within North Korea.

JAPANESE–SOUTH KOREAN ECONOMIC RELATIONS

Until the North Korean–South Korean relationship does improve, Japan's relations with the Korean peninsula will center on Japanese trade with South Korea. It will be useful to note some of the salient issues.

There is no doubt that South Korea has proved a lucrative market for Japanese industries, and the ROK has benefited as well from its economic ties with Japan. For ten of the seventeen years between 1966 and 1982, South Korea occupied the number two position in the world among importers of Japanese products. The volume of trade has continued to rise in spite of all the political problems Japan has had with South Korea.

Exports to Korea have been lucrative for Japan beyond the realm of statistics. Initially, the Japanese were able to dispose of many outdated facilities; they then sold Korea intermediate goods (crucial parts for assembled products). As South Korea acquired more sophistication and expanded its exports, Japan was able to sell new facilities and more intermediate goods.

South Korea, in turn, has acquired new technology and capital loans to expand its own exports. Growing industries have offered opportunities for employment and valuable training to a vast number of people. Fortuitously, Japanese–South Korean normalization took place when the world economy was expanding, and South Korea has had little difficulty in enlarging its export market. The fast pace of growth in exports has imbued confidence in a generation of Koreans who have scoured the world for new markets.

The rapidly growing trade relations, however, have produced problems of a serious nature. One has been the large trade deficit suffered by South Korea. A second has been the problem of competition in the export market. These are problems the two nations must attempt to resolve.

Given the framework of President Park's developmental strategy, it was inevitable that South Korea would accumulate huge trade deficits with Japan. The more South Korea's exports have expanded, the more it has needed Japanese plants, equipment, and intermediate goods. Japan has sold Korea capital-intensive and advanced technological goods whereas South Korea's exports to Japan have been either labor-intensive industrial products or agricultural and fishery products. Hence, price differentials were inevitable.

As long as the world economy was expanding and South Korea could increase exports, trade deficits with Japan did not constitute a major problem. South Korea was able to meet its obligations not only from exports to other countries but also from the sizable earnings from invisible trade, that is, remittances from numerous overseas construction projects that have brought in billions of dollars a year since the mid–1970s. (Between 1974 and 1978, South Korean construction firms won contracts worth $15 billion for construction projects in the Middle East.) But the worldwide recession after 1979 not only constricted the world market but also reduced income from invisible trade. The plummeting of demand for oil and its lowered price forced the OPEC nations to scale down and cancel many of their construction projects. South Korean trade also suffered from intensified competition from other developing countries, the rising tide of protectionism in advanced countries, and the rising cost of labor in South Korea. Clearly the expanded Korean economy became very susceptible to the vicissitudes of the world economy.

The competition for export markets resulted from the similarity of Japanese and South Korean developmental strategies. President Park was a noted Japanophile, and he chose to model South Korea's development after the successful experience of Japan since the Meiji era. Both countries lack natural resources to export, and hence it was logical for them to adopt an export-oriented industrial strategy. Japan was ready to provide the funds and technology necessary for President Park's plan. South Korea possessed an educated but underemployed labor force ready to operate Japanese machines. A symbiotic relationship was established.

As South Korea's technological level advanced and its economy expanded, it had little alternative but to move toward more advanced technological industries. This, of course, pitted South Korea directly against some sectors of Japanese industry that were competing for the same market. Inevitably conflict developed in some sectors and the Japanese began to talk of the "boomerang effect"; that is, South Korean industries that had been developed with Japanese capital and technology were driving out Japanese industries. Steel, cement, shipbuilding and overseas construction have been affected.[13] Naturally, Japanese industrialists began to cast a wary eye on Korean competition. Many Japanese who had taken pride in South Korea's copying of their own developmental model in the 1960s were caught by surprise and began to develop a different perspective on the Japanese–South Korean economic relationship. The more South Korean industries successfully challenged the Japanese, the more intense Japanese concern became. This was particularly so when the slump in the world market hit both countries' export markets.

The trend toward competition is likely to continue during the 1980s and beyond. Although South Korea is still far behind Japan in most areas, more sectors of Japanese industries will be challenged. South Korea must strive to expand exports by controlling inflation and improving productivity, technology, and management in its existing industries. Sustained growth will require exploration of new markets and require more advanced technology. As South Korea's technological level advances and its industrialists broaden their experience, Japanese industries at lower technological levels are likely to feel more intensified competition.

An anomaly of the situation is that further development of South Korea's technology will require further additions of Japanese capital and technology. Should Japan continue its support for South Korea's industrial and technological development when it is obvious that some sectors of Japanese industries will be adversely affected? The question is obviously an important one for the current and future leaders of Japan. Many industrialists understandably are not sanguine about such assistance. For example, all but one Japanese electronics company refused to send delegates to the Fifteenth Joint Japanese–South Korean Businessmen's Conference held in Seoul in April 1983, convened in the wake of Premier Nakasone's visit. They feared they might be asked to pledge assistance to South Korean industries.[14] Many Japanese entrepreneurs are also finding South Korea far less attractive than previously as a place for investment. Many Japanese companies began to withdraw their capital in 1979 when South Korea suffered economic stagnation and political instability. The rising cost of labor has also substantially reduced South Korea's attractiveness.

If Japan's concern is the "boomerang effect," Korea's is economic dependency and the trade imbalance. Past Japanese–South Korean economic relations precipitated fears that South Korean industry had become a foreign branch of Japanese capital and that South Korea as a whole had become a Japanese colony whose surpluses or profits were appropriated for the needs of Japanese capitalism. Within South Korea the gap between the loan-dependent capitalists on the one hand and labor on the other continued to expand. The export-oriented strategy has led to the growth of mammoth enterprises, which have benefited from preferential loans and other protective measures to the detriment of small and medium industries. For this reason not all Koreans welcomed the hoisting of the Japanese flag atop the government building in Seoul on the occasion of Premier Nakasone's visit. Since that building once housed the Japanese colonial government, many Koreans greeted the Japanese flag with uneasiness and misgivings. Even though it was President Chun Doo Hwan who welcomed Premier Nakasone, only a year before the Chun regime had unleashed Koreans' primordial antagonism toward Japan and one of the main charges against the Japanese had been economic exploitation. Chun's opponents charged in September 1984 that his Tokyo visit did nothing but solidify the exploitive and dependent system.

One may dismiss the neoimperialist argument as too simplistic in view of the benefits South Korea has reaped from Japanese–South Korean economic ties. One could cite the rising proportion of domestic savings in total investments, the heightened living standards of the population as a whole, and the competitiveness of Korean industries abroad. But, unless the trade imbalance is substantially reduced, Japanese industries are perceived to be fair in their dealings with Korea, and the benefits of economic development are more evenly spread among the Koreans, the neoimperialist thesis will remain potent.

The uproar that followed President Chun's request for a $6 billion loan manifested the political effect of problems that arise from the trade structure. Given this background, the future economic relationship with Japan will require a high degree of enlightened self-interest among Japanese and South Korean business and political leaders. Businessmen concerned with immediate interest are, however, not likely to take a broader or long-range perspective. A cooperative relationship will not emerge of its own accord. Considerable political leadership on both sides will be necessary to keep economic problems from escalating into political issues, domestically and internationally.

EMOTIONS AND ATTITUDES

Japan's desire for a cooperative relationship—not only in the economic but also in other fields—depends on its political and business leaders' assessment of the value of South Korea, both for Japanese security and the Japanese economy. Altruism for the sake of friendship in international relations is too rare to be observed. One could pursue this logic and conclude that cultural, emotional, and attitudinal relations among nations are of little significance in understanding political and economic relations—and hence students of international politics should ignore them.

It is beyond doubt, however, that individuals' perceptions and actions are affected by belief systems based on images of the past, present, and future. Belief systems become lenses through which information concerning the physical and social environment is received.[15] In this sense, attitudinal differences between the Japanese and Korean peoples merit close attention. Although public opinion seldom plays a direct role in foreign policy decisionmaking in Japan, it does affect leaders' perceptions and behavior. Also, in spite of the elitist nature of Japanese society, Japanese political, intellectual, bureaucratic, and economic elites are not markedly different from the masses in terms of their values and outlook on foreign countries.

In discussing the attitudes of Japanese and South Korean leaders, it is important to note that the ascendance of General Chun Doo Hwan in South Korea precipitated a massive turnover in the elites who dealt with bilateral affairs. As noted in Chapter 5, General Chun and his cohorts charged that the older generation (those in their late fifties or older) had been contaminated by Japanese education and that its members were corrupt and corrupting.

The generational change in South Korea had a very significant impact on Japanese-Korean relations. When President Park was in office, Japanese-Korean diplomacy had been conducted mostly in Japanese, since most South Korean politicians and high-ranking diplomats spoke the language. But the new generation's understanding of Japanese was minimal, and hence it was necessary to use English. The implicit understanding built by the ease of communication was thus removed. The situation contrasted sharply with the days when a Japanese politician had attended President Park's inauguration "with the joy of a father attending his son's inaugural." What the Japanese call *sengo*, the postwar era, effectively ended with the ascendance of General Chun.

General (later President) Chun's charges against older Koreans implied that their Japanese counterparts were equally guilty. (One might recall the presidential secretary's threat to expose illicit Japanese–South Korean dealings during the Park regime shortly after the Chun regime had requested a $6 billion public loan.) The new regime's charges were not aimed at any specific group of individuals but were wholesale in nature, just as the purge in South Korea was aimed at a large portion of the elites. The reaction of the Japanese elites was predictable. At least one prominent Japanese observer noted that "those who had been sympathetic to the Republic of Korea simultaneously withdrew from the scene."[16]

The textbook controversy compounded the situation. "Pro–South Korean" elements in Japan were conservative and overwhelmingly supported the position of the Ministry of Education, which was adamantly opposed to any changes in the textbooks. The progressive elements, who had traditionally been staunch opponents of South Korea, supported the Chinese and South Korean positions. These elements had consistently attacked the "Japanese economic invasion of South Korea," which was also the battle cry of the new regime in Seoul. Naturally, the ranks of the "pro–South Korean" elements dwindled.

Progressive elements in Japan, however, are likely to be fleeting allies for the Chun regime. For ideological reasons, they are predisposed against South Korea and its dictatorial regime. They shudder at the thought of supporting a government that sentenced Kim Dae-jung to death and harshly suppressed students and intellectuals demanding the restoration of democracy. Even if they did support Chun, they are in no position to influence the foreign and economic policies of the ruling conservative party or the business leaders.

Thus, the Chun regime is bereft of an elite constituency in Japan. Although new efforts will be made to cultivate support, and Japanese businessmen will seek to improve ties with those in power in Seoul, it is unlikely that President Chun will be able to establish the kind of friendship and understanding that President Park Chung Hee had built among the Japanese. The volatility of the situation on the Korean peninsula—both internally and in terms of North-South relations—does not incline new supporters to take a long-range view. Whatever support Chun receives will be linked to the short-range tactical interests of Japanese business and political leaders.

Premier Nakasone's historic visit in January 1983 must be seen in this context. He did act decisively on loan negotiations and displayed his progressive attitude by volunteering to visit Seoul. The Chun regime, in turn, treated Nakasone royally and labeled the visit the dawn of a new era in Japanese–South Korean relations. Possibly the premier genuinely aspired to improved relations between the two nations. One could, however, interpret the premier's gesture as a step taken to mollify Washington's pressure for increased military spending and the assumption of increased responsibility in East Asian politics and economics. As for the conclusion of loan negotiations, Nakasone's personal outlook did influence the amount of funds added in the final stage, but negotiations had been virtually completed when Premier Suzuki stepped down.

Even if Nakasone hopes to provide more support to South Korea, however, he will find himself much constrained. A Japanese premier can enforce his will only if his position within the Liberal Democratic Party and the polity as a whole is overwhelming. He must also be able to muster broad support among relevant constituents. When Nakasone visited Seoul, however, neither of these conditions existed. The Chun government, therefore, had to yield on many key points in drafting the joint communiqué. The fact that Premier Nakasone dared to visit Seoul and to invite Chun to Japan, in the Japanese political context of the day, shows that the LDP leadership as a whole favored a continuation of the general pattern of relationship established since the mid-1960s. That is, even after Nakasone Yashuhiro steps down from his current position, the basic framework will continue with only minor variations. The situation is not likely to change, at least in the 1980s, even if the LDP loses its majority position within the Diet and is forced to establish a coalition government.

Japanese public opinion regarding South Korea, however, has been fluctuating. The adverse impressions the Japanese have had of Korea and the Korean people as a whole have been slowly changing thanks, in part, to the efforts of progressive intellectuals who have been chipping away at the stereotypes created by the colonialists. The slow but steady improvement of the status of the Korean minority in Japan has had its effect. North Korea's economic achievements during the 1950s and 1960s and its strong nationalistic stand during the height of the Sino-Soviet conflict earned it some respect. South Korea's phenomenal economic growth during the past two decades has also led many Japanese to alter their views. Above all, a new generation of Japanese is growing up with less bias against Korea than its forefathers had.

The character of and actions taken by the South Korean government, however, damaged much of the favorable impression Koreans had gained in Japan. The student revolt of April 1960 improved the adverse image created by the Syngman Rhee regime through the long period of intermittent negotiations, but the imposition of a military regime after the coup d'etat of 1961 blackened Korea's image. Subsequently, the Park regime's economic performance earned the admiration of many Japanese, but the Kim Dae-jung affair of 1973 decisively reversed this trend. South Korea became synonymous with barbarity and cruelty as the confrontation over Kim Dae-jung dragged on. The Chun regime's persecution of the former presidential candidate aggravated the situation further. The North Korean regime effectively utilized the hostile atmosphere to improve its image in Japan by using its supporters among left-wing intellectual and political groups.

I have frequently noted the Korean resentment of the condescending attitude the Japanese have adopted toward Korea and Koreans. Historical and contemporary events contributed to the formation of this attitude. Since embarking on Westernization after encountering the Black Ships in 1854, the Japanese have considered themselves the most civilized nation in the Orient, and they have been contemptuous of all who failed to emulate Japan. This attitude hardened after Japan defeated the Middle Kingdom in 1895: Japan became not only the most civilized but also the strongest nation. Japanese pride knew no bounds when Japan defeated Russia in 1905. In the meantime, the Korean kingdom meandered along, having suppressed all the progressive elements who advocated reform. The Japanese perforce regarded Korea as a backward, feeble, and decadent country. This notion was reinforced during the colonial era when the Japanese were the masters in Korea. The Japanese attitude toward Korea today reflects this legacy. When Japan re-emerged as a leading economic power in the postwar world, its people had all the more reason to be proud.

The Japanese are highly status-conscious, as are the Koreans. Even though the Meiji Restoration of 1867 eliminated class distinctions in Japan, centuries-old traditions remained intact insofar as the hierarchical orientation of the people was concerned. The system used to rank individuals was extended to nations. Just as two persons could not be equal in status—either in terms of age or other attributes—no two nations could be equal. And, in the eyes of most Japanese, Korea was and is less civilized and inferior to Japan. The Japanese are not the only people with condescending views toward others, and normally such an attitude does not become a source of diplomatic friction. But, in the case of Japan and Korea, the inability of the two peoples to resolve their conflicting views about the past thrust the psychological dimension into the diplomatic arena, marring political relations.

The ideological and political division on the Korean peninsula also hampers the development of any affinity between the Japanese and Korean peoples. Japanese intellectuals and political parties are sharply divided among themselves on perspectives toward the Korean peninsula. Although most of them accept the division of Korea as a reality and see Japan's proper role as stabilizing the relationship between the two states on the peninsula, they do not agree on the proper outlook toward the two regimes there or on the means to stabilize the situation in Korea. In the progressive camp, opinions range from those who regard it as evil for Japan to continue political and economic ties with South Korea to those who advocate a balanced relationship between Japan and the two Koreas. The conservative camp ranges from those who advocate the strict separation of politics and economics in Japan's dealings with the two Koreas to those who favor no contact at all with North Korea.

The actions of the South Korean regime have had a significant effect in shaping the Japanese image of Korea because most of the younger Japanese have no other basis for judgment. Although they may be less biased in their views of Korea than the older generation, they are equally poorly informed, and, for the most part, they are indifferent to Korea. Although an increasing number of books about Korea are being published in Japan, they constitute a minuscule portion of Japanese publications and seldom attract the attention of the mass media. If the younger Japanese are attentive at all to foreign affairs, it is to the developments in the West. Perforce, the younger generation's knowledge about Korea is limited to the unsavory news disseminated by the mass media. Leaders in the mass media are clearly intent on changing the situation, but much work lies ahead.

The situation is not helped by the prevailing ignorance of Japan among younger Koreans. Although the Koreans are much more interested in Japan than the Japanese are in Korea, their knowledge about Japan is severely limited or distorted because, until the late 1970s, the Korean educational system made no serious effort to develop curricula about Japan even at the university level. Korean knowledge of Japan, therefore, is strongly colored by the anti-Japanese content of curricula dealing with the colonial period of Korean history, frequent anti-Japanese outbursts in the mass media, and the widely shared image of the exploitive nature of economic relations between the two countries. All these factors explain the listing of Japan among the least-liked nations in various Korean opinion polls.

Building an affinity between Japan and South Korea under such conditions will require Herculean efforts. Intellectual exchanges will improve mutual understanding, but this will be a time-consuming process. South Korea's continuing economic development and resolution of underlying problems in Japanese–South Korean economic relations will undoubtedly affect the attitudes of both peoples, but, as I have noted, many problems lie ahead in the economic sector. Until South Korea is able to adopt a more democratic government, the Japanese will continue to regard it as an underdeveloped country deserving little respect.

The South Korean image of Japan will likely be affected by changes in the Japanese attitude toward Korea. But the litmus test for the Koreans will be in the economic arena and in the Japanese treatment of the Korean minority in Japan. The Koreans will come to feel an affinity for the Japanese only if they feel that the Japanese are interested in building a genuine partnership with South Korea. Increased assistance alone, even if it is provided, will not automatically improve the Korean image of Japan. Given the sharp division within Korea between a government headed by former military officers and the suppressed opposition forces, perspectives on Japanese assistance to the Korean economy will surely differ. Such assistance will be regarded by the opposition as Japan's effort to buttress the South Korean dictatorship for the sake of maximizing selfish Japanese interests. In short, improved understanding between the Japanese and South Korean peoples cannot be established until the wide disparity between the Japanese and Korean economies is narrowed and South Korea institutes a more open political system.

The Koreans will also closely watch the Japanese treatment of the Korean minority in Japan. Of all the millions of Koreans abroad—including residents of China, the Soviet Union, and the United States—the Koreans in Japan suffer the most from discrimination. Until this situation is corrected, all the talk of friendship and cooperation, and the expression of "regrets," will sound hollow to the Koreans.

Numerous and complex problems thus lie ahead for Japan and the two Koreas. One bright spot, paradoxically, is that the two peoples have weathered the four turbulent decades and, in the process, have learned the limits of their relations and the problems involved in dealing with each other. Contacts among the three states have been intensive, particularly between Japan and South Korea, who have confronted virtually every kind of problem one could anticipate. Given this experience, Japan and Korea may face each other with more sophistication in the future and attempt to resolve their problems more deliberately and amicably.

Appendix A

Japanese Premiers, 1945–1983

Name	From	To	Duration
Higashikuni Naruhiko	Aug. 17, 1945	Oct. 9, 1945	7 weeks
Shidehara Kijūrō	Oct. 9, 1945	May 22, 1946	7 months
Yoshida Shigeru	May 22, 1946	May 20, 1947	12 months
Katayama Tetsu	May 24, 1947	Feb. 10, 1948	9 months
Ashida Hitoshi	Mar. 10, 1948	Oct. 7, 1948	7 months
Yoshida Shigeru	Oct. 15, 1948	Dec. 10, 1954	74 months
Hatoyama Ichirō	Dec. 10, 1954	Dec. 23, 1956	24 months
Ishibashi Tanzan	Dec. 23, 1956	Feb. 25, 1957	6 weeks
Kishi Nobusuke	Feb. 25, 1957	July 19, 1960	40 months
Ikeda Hayato	July 19, 1960	Nov. 11, 1964	52 months
Satō Eisaku	Nov. 11, 1964	July 6, 1972	92 months
Tanaka Kakuei	July 6, 1972	Dec. 9, 1974	29 months
Miki Takeo	Dec. 9, 1974	Dec. 24, 1976	25 months
Fukuda Takeo	Dec. 24, 1976	Dec. 7, 1978	23 months
Ōhira Masayoshi	Dec. 7, 1978	June 12, 1980	18 months
Itō Masayoshi (acting premier)	June 12, 1980	July 17, 1980	1 month
Suzuki Zenkō	July 17, 1980	Nov. 26, 1982	28 months
Nakasone Yasuhiro	Nov. 26, 1982		

Appendix B ═══════

Chun-Nakasone Joint Communiqué, January 12, 1983

1. Prime Minister and Mrs. Yashuhiro Nakasone of Japan paid an official visit to the Republic of Korea (ROK) from Jan. 11 to Jan. 12, 1983, at the invitation of the Republic of Korea's Government.

The Prime Minister and Mrs. Nakasone were accompanied by Minister of Foreign Affairs Shintaro Abe, Minister of Finance Noboru Takeshita, Deputy Cabinet Secretary Takao Fujinami, Ken Yasui, chairman of the Japan-Korean Parliamentarians' League, and some Diet members and senior government officials.

2. The president and the prime minister held summit meetings in a very respectful and friendly atmosphere, exchanging frank views on holding constructive debates on international affairs, bilateral relations and matter of mutual interest.

3. The president and the prime minister shared the view that Korea and Japan, as neighbors pursuing the common ideals of freedom and democracy, can serve their national interests by maintaining and developing relations of close cooperation.

The two leaders agreed that the prime minister's visit, the first official visit by a Japanese prime minister, will prove an important milestone in further promoting friendly and cooperative relations following the diplomatic normalization in 1965.

SOURCE: *Korea Herald*, January 13, 1983, p. 5.

4. The president and the prime minister exchanged frank views on the recent developments in the world in general, shared the view that peace and stability on the Korean Peninsula are essential to those in all of East Asia including Japan, and pledged to make concerted efforts to promote peace, stability and prosperity in the region.

While discussing the dialogue efforts of the Republic of Korea including the South-North Korean leaders' talks and the formula for national reconciliation and democratic unification advocated by President Chun, the prime minister noted that the Republic of Korea's defense efforts and dialogue efforts are contributing to maintaining peace on the Korean Peninsula despite the harsh international situation surrounding the peninsula.

5. Prime Minister Nakasone commended the steady developments made in political, economic, social and other fields under the excellent leadership of President Chun since the inauguration of the Fifth Republic.

He manifested that Japan will play a role commensurate with its national power for world peace and prosperity and will emphasize its relations with Asian countries. The president highly evaluated the prime minister's position and expressed expectations for Japan's international role in the future.

6. The president explained to the prime minister the concept of a Pacific summit revealed in a Chinhae news conference July 31, 1982, and the prime minister expressed his appreciation over the explanation.

The two leaders, noting a growing inter-dependence among Pacific-rim countries and rapid economic and social developments in the region, agreed on the need and importance of promoting cooperative relations among Pacific-rim countries.

7. The president and the prime minister exchanged candid views on relations between the two countries, and shared the view that the two countries should develop good neighborly relations on a new plane on the basis of a spirit of mutual trust and reciprocity.

The two leaders agreed to make joint efforts to ensure smooth cooperation in various fields by promoting dialogue and exchanges between the governments, parliamentary and private levels. They had a significant exchange of views on finding a reasonable solution to the Korea-Japan trade issue, the treatment of Korean residents in Japan and fishing problems in a spirit of friendship and cooperation.

8. The president and the prime minister conducted sincere dis-

cussions on the economic cooperation issue, the negotiations of which have been under way between the two countries at the request of the Korean Government.

The president explained about Korea's economic and social development programs including the fifth five-year socioeconomic development plan.

The prime minister expressed the view that Japan is willing to render cooperation for Korea's socioeconomic development projects envisaged in the fifth five-year socioeconomic development plan as long as Japan's basic economic cooperation policy permits, and that as a substantive means to materialize the plan, Japan would provide various cooperative funds, including long-term, low-interest government loans on an annual basis.

The two leaders agreed that the two governments will start negotiations at an early date to embody the supply of yen loan for this year.

9. The president and the prime minister shared the view that it is desirable for the two countries to expand the industrial and technological cooperation.

10. The president and the prime minister held the common view that increasing exchanges, based on a national basis, is very important on a long-term perspective for the development of relations between the two countries, and agreed that the two countries should gradually expand academic, educational, athletic and cultural exchanges.

11. On the occasion of the prime minister's visit to Korea, the president and the prime minister agreed to open, at the earliest possible date, telephone or other appropriate lines that will facilitate direct and prompt dialogue between the president and the prime minister at any time.

12. Prime Minister Nakasone expressed his profound gratitude for the warm hospitality accorded by President Chun Tu-hwan and Mrs. Chun and by the Korean people.

The prime minister cordially invited the President and Mrs. Chun to visit Japan as state guests at their convenience. The president accepted the invitation with pleasure. The time of the visit will be determined by negotiations through diplomatic channels.

Appendix C ═══════════

Chun-Nakasone
Joint Communiqué,
September 8, 1984

1. His Excellency the President of the Republic of Korea and Mrs. Chun Doo Hwan paid, as state guests, an official visit to Japan for three days from September 6 to 8, 1984.

The president was accompanied by His Excellency Shin Byong Hyun, deputy prime minister and minister of the Economic Planning Board, His Excellency Lee Won-Kyung, minister of foreign affairs, His Excellency Bae Myung-In, minister of justice, His Excellency Kum Jin Ho, minister of trade and industry, His Excellency Lee Jin-Hie, minister of culture and information, His Excellency Lee Chung Oh, minister of science and technology, His Excellency Choi Kyung Nok, ambassador extraordinary and plenipotentiary to Japan, His Excellency Kang Kyung Shik, secretary general to the president, His Excellency Huh Chung Il, chief secretary to the president of the Democratic Justice Party, General Lee Ki Baek, chairman, Joint Chiefs of Staff, and other senior officials of the Government of the Republic of Korea.

2. After their arrival, President and Mrs. Chun Doo Hwan were warmly greeted by His Majesty the Emperor of Japan at a welcoming ceremony held at the State Guest House, and thereafter, met with the emperor at the Imperial Palace.

SOURCE: Information Office, Embassy of Korea, Washington, D.C.

3. President Chun Doo Hwan and Prime Minister Yashuhiro Nak-asone held summit talks in a most cordial and friendly atmosphere and exchanged frank views on the international situation with par-ticular reference to the East Asia, bilateral relations and other mat-ters of mutual interest.

The president and the prime minister shared the view that the official visit by Prime Minister Nakasone to the Republic of Korea in January 1983 and the first official visit to Japan by President Chun as the head of state of the Republic of Korea were very significant in the further development of good-neighborly relations based upon friend-ship and cooperation between the Republic of Korea and Japan by opening a new chapter in the history of the two countries' relations.

On the occasion of the president's historic visit to Japan, the pres-ident and the prime minister resolved to work together for the fur-ther development and consolidation of good-neighborly relations based upon friendship and cooperation between the Republic of Ko-rea and Japan, which will last for many generations to come. The two leaders shared the view that the maintenance and development of such cooperative relationship between the two countries in pursuit of their common ideals of freedom, peace and democracy will not only be beneficial to the peoples of the two countries, but also contributing to the world peace as well as the peace and stability of East Asia.

The president and the prime minister agreed that the Republic of Korea and Japan, as mature neighbors who uphold the principles of reciprocity, equality, mutual understanding and respect, should en-deavor to develop, from a global perspective, lasting good-neighborly relations based upon friendship and cooperation between them in accordance with the Treaty on Basic Relations between the Republic of Korea and Japan signed in 1965.

4. The president and the prime minister noted with satisfaction that on the occasion of the visit to the Republic of Korea by Prime Minister Nakasone last year, the matters of economic cooperation be-tween the two countries had been resolved and the projects were cur-rently being implemented and that various talks between the two Governments such as the regular ministerial meeting, the conference between the foreign ministers and the meeting of ministers of science and technology had been successfully held and had greatly contrib-uted to the promotion of the friendly and cooperative relations be-tween the two countries. The two leaders agreed to maintain closer consultations between the two Governments in the future.

The president and the prime minister, noting with satisfaction that the friendly and cooperative relations between the two countries had also been strengthened by the exchanges and cooperation between the parliamentarians as well as between the private sectors of the two countries, shared the view that such activities should continue and increase in the future and welcomed the establishment of a cultural exchange fund by the Parliamentarians' League of the two countries.

5. The president and the prime minister, sharing the view that the maintenance of peace and stability on the Korean peninsula is essential to those of the East Asia including Japan, reaffirmed their determination to continue to cooperate henceforth with each other with a view to promoting peace, stability and prosperity of this region.

The two leaders agreed that the Korean question should, basically, be resolved by peaceful means through direct talks between the authorities of the South and the North of Korea.

In this connection, the prime minister reconfirmed the position of the Government of Japan to support the efforts of the Republic of Korea for the realization of the dialogue between the South and the North in order to achieve peaceful reunification, including the proposal to hold direct talks between the highest authorities of the South and the North of Korea and the Proposal for Democratic Reunification through National Reconciliation, both advanced by the President. The prime minister highly appreciated that the defense efforts of the Government of the Republic of Korea in the face of the harsh realities surrounding the Korean peninsula, together with its efforts for dialogue, had contributed to the maintenance of peace on the Korean peninsula.

The president expressed the view that the admission of both the South and the North of Korea into the United Nations, as an interim measure pending the peaceful reunification of Korea, would contribute to easing tensions and help promote peace on the Korean peninsula. The prime minister stated that the government of Japan will support such a measure conducive to easing tensions and upholding the principle of universality of the United Nations.

6. The president and the prime minister, recalling the incidents of the shooting-down of a Korean Air Lines passenger plane and the terroristic bombing massacre in Rangoon last year, renewed their resolve to continue to work for the prevention of such use of force and act of terrorism.

7. The president and the prime minister, noting that one side's economic growth and prosperity contribute also to the economic

growth and prosperity of the other, shared the view that the promotion of wide-range expansion of cooperative relations in the economic field is important.

The president and the prime minister, concurring on the desirability of developing the bilateral trade toward balanced expansion, agreed to continue close consultations for the sound development of trade relations through periodical ministerial conferences, trade talks and other meetings.

In this regard, the president and the prime minister appreciated the planned dispatch of Japanese mission to the Republic of Korea for the promotion of imports, etc., by Japan on the occasion of the international trade fair to be held in Seoul beginning at the end of September this year.

The president and the prime minister, reconfirming the desirability of the expansion of industrial technology cooperation between the two countries, agreed to promote technology cooperation on the governmental level and to continue to hold consultations on the improvement of environment for the promotion of exchanges and cooperation in the private sectors.

In this regard, the president and the prime minister appreciated the training program in Japan of technicians of the Republic of Korea to be started sometime this fall.

The president and the prime minister concurred on the importance of investment expansion to the strengthening of cooperation in the economic and other fields, including industrial technology cooperation between the two countries.

The president and the prime minister expressed satisfaction at the achievements of the sixth meeting between the ministers of science and technology of the Republic of Korea and Japan held in Seoul in July this year and agreed on further promoting science and technology cooperation between governmental as well as public institutions of the two countries.

The president and the prime minister agreed to start negotiations at an early date with a view to concluding a treaty on science and technology cooperation between the two countries.

The president and the prime minister, expressing deep concern over the increasing protectionist trend in some parts of the world, also agreed to continue close cooperation in international forums in order to maintain and strengthen the free trade. The president and the prime minister confirmed their willingness to cooperate in initiating new rounds of multilateral trade negotiations in the framework of the General Agreement on Tariffs and Trade.

8. The president and the prime minister, sharing the view that the expansion of exchanges on nation-wide basis, respecting each other's national tradition and identity, is very important, from the long-term perspective, to the development of good-neighborly relations based upon friendship and cooperation between the Republic of Korea and Japan, reconfirmed their willingness to expand gradually, to this end, the cultural exchanges in scholarly, educational and sports areas. In particular, the two leaders, in view of the importance of mutual understanding between the younger generations of the two countries on the eve of the twenty first century, agreed on the desirability of accelerating the exchanges between the youth of the two countries.

The president and the prime minister, considering that next year marks the 20th anniversary of the normalization of the diplomatic relations between the two countries, also expressed the hope that the commemorative events which are currently being planned for the observation of the anniversary between the two countries should successfully take place and bring to fruition.

9. The president and the prime minister noted that, in view of the historical background of the question of the Korean residents in Japan, the improvement in their legal status and treatment is closely related to the promotion of friendly relations between the Republic of Korea and Japan.

The president, appreciating the measures taken so far by the Government of Japan in this regard, requested that the Government of Japan continue its efforts on this matter. The prime minister stated his willingness to make continued efforts.

10. The president and the prime minister, sharing the view that the 1988 Seoul Olympics, when held in the genuine Olympic spirit transcending differences in political system and ideology will serve as an important momentum for contributing to the world peace and the reconciliation among the peoples of the world, expressed their expectations and convictions that the Olympic games be held successfully with participation of all nations in the world.

11. The president and the prime minister, noting the increasingly interdependent relations among the Pacific-rim countries and the rapid development in this region, shared the view that the strengthening of cooperation in the Pacific region would contribute not only to the prosperity of this region but also to the peace and prosperity of the world.

The two leaders reaffirmed the need and importance of the promotion of cooperative relations through the expansion of various exchanges among the Pacific-rim countries.

12. The President and Mrs. Chun expressed, on behalf of their party, their profound appreciation for the warm reception and hospitality accorded to them by the Government and people of Japan.

Notes

1. These were some of the comments made by Japanese professors of moderate to conservative leaning at a two-day seminar held in Tokyo between September 5 and 6, 1973. The participants were Ichikawa Shin'ichi, Etō Shinkichi, Kajima Fuji, Koshima Kiyoshi, Kotani Shūjirō, Fujishima Taisuke, and Yano Tōru. For a verbatim text of the seminar, see Tōkyō Kankoku Kenkyūin and Kokusai Kankei Kyōdō Kenkyūjo, eds., *Nihon ni totte Kankoku to wa nanika* [What is South Korea to Japan?] (Tokyo, 1974).

2. See Tōkyō Kankoku Kenkyūin and Kokusai Kankei Kyōdō Kenkyūjo, eds., *Kankoku ni totte Nihon to wa nanika* [What is Japan to South Korea?] 3 vols. (Tokyo, 1977).

3. Key-hiuk Kim, *The Last Phase of the East Asian World Order: Korea, Japan, and the Chinese Empire, 1860–1882*, preface by Kwang-Ching Liu (Berkeley, 1980), p. xi.

4. Ibid., p. 331.

5. Cf. the comments of Professor Cho Soon of Seoul National University in Tōkyō Kankoku Kenkyūin and Kokusai Kankei Kyōdō Kenkyūjo, eds., *Kankoku ni totte Nihon to wa nanika* 1:38–42. Professor Cho and others who participated in the panel discussion in 1974 noted that not only had ancient Koreans paid no attention to Japan but also contemporary Koreans have very little knowledge about Japan. Most Koreans educated in the colonial

era do believe, however, that they have much knowledge about Japan simply because they speak Japanese.

6. Fukuzawa Yukichi, *An Outline of the Theory of Civilization*, trans. David A. Dilworth and G. Cameron Hurst (Tokyo, 1973), pp. 136–37.

7. For details, see Komori Tokuji, *Akashi Motojirō* (Taipei, 1928), 1: 86, 501–5. Akashi later served as governor-general of Taiwan.

8. Shakuo Shunjō, *Chōsen heigō-shi* [A history of the Korean annexation] (Tokyo, 1926), pp. 825–26.

9. For details, see Sŏnu Hun, *Minjok ŭi sunan: Paek-o-in sakŏn* [The suffering of the nation: The 105-person incident] (Seoul, 1955). For the proceedings of the trials of these men, see D. J. Evans, ed., *The Korean Conspiracy Trial: Full Proceedings* (Kobe, 1913).

10. Chōsen Kenpeitai Shireibu [Korean Gendarmerie Headquarters] and Chōsen Sōtokufu, Keimu-kyoku [Korean Government-General, Police Affairs Bureau], *Chōsen sōjō jiken ichiranhyō* [A table of the Korean uprising incident] (Seoul, April 1919), p. 2; and Henry Chung, *The Case for Korea* (New York and London, 1921), p. 346. Japanese atrocities against the demonstrators have been documented by Western missionaries in various parts of Korea (see the Federal Council of the Churches of Christ in America, Commission on Relations with the Orient, *The Korean Situation: Authentic Accounts of Recent Events by Eye Witnesses* [New York, 1919], and Chung, *The Case for Korea*).

11. Chōsen Sōtokufu [Korean Government-General], *Shisei sanjūnenshi* [A thirty-year history of administration] (Seoul, 1940), p. 824.

12. For this argument, see ibid., p. 752.

13. Ibid., pp. 790, 808–21, 827–32.

14. Ibid., pp. 780–81, 825.

15. Kim To-yŏn, *Na ŭi insaeng paeksŏ* [The white paper on my life] (Seoul, 1968), p. 143. For details, see also a longer account by Yi Hŭi-sŭng, "Chosŏn Ŏhakhoe Sakŏn" [The Korean Linguistic Society incident], *Sasangge* [World of thought], July 1959 to January 1960 (eight monthly installments).

16. For a moving account of Korean reaction by a novelist, see Richard Kim, *Lost Names* (New York, 1970).

17. Chōsen Sōtokufu [Korean Government-General], *Tōkei nempō* [Statistical annual report] (Seoul, 1932), p. 714 and (1942), p. 198; and Chōsen Sōtokufu, *Shisei sanjūnen-shi*, p. 810.

18. Chōsen Sōtokufu, Kōtō Hōin, Kenjikyoku [Korean Government-General, High Court, Prosecutors' Bureau], *Shisō ihō* [Thought report series], no. 16 (September 1938), p. 13.

19. Chōsen Sōtokufu, Keimukyoku [Korean Government-General, Police Affairs Bureau], *Saikin ni okeru Chōsen chian jōkyō* [Security conditions in Korea in the recent period] (Seoul, 1936), pp. 143, 148–49, and ibid. (1938), pp. 73–74, 76–77.

20. Ibid. (1934), pp. 121, 125, (1936), pp. 143, 148–49, (1938), pp. 73–74, 76–77, and (1938), p. 389.

21. For details, see ibid (1938), pp. 389–95; and Spencer J. Palmer, "Korean Christians and the Shinto Shrine Issue," in *Korea's Response to Japan: The Colonial Period: 1910–1945*, ed. C. I. Eugene Kim and Doretha E. Mortimore (Kalamazoo, Mich., 1974), pp. 146–47, 150.

22. *Saikin ni okeru Chōsen chian jōkyō* (1938), p. 24.

23. Naimushō [Ministry of Home Affairs], *Chōsen oyobi Taiwan no genkyō* [The present condition in Korea and Taiwan] (July 1942); reprinted in *Taiheiyō senka no Chōsen oyobi Taiwan* [Korea and Taiwan during the Pacific war], ed. Kondō Ken'ichi (Tokyo, 1961), pp. 32–33.

24. Mizuta Naomasa, "Shōwa jūkyūnendo Chōsen Sōtokufu yosan ni tsuite" [Concerning the budget of the Korean Government-General in 1944], in *Taiheiyō senka shūmatsuki Chōsen no chisei* [The administration of Korea during the Pacific war: The last period], ed. Kondō Ken'ichi (Tokyo, 1961), p. 23. See also *Chōsen oyobi Taiwan no genkyō*, pp. 35–36.

25. Tsuboe Senji, *Zai Nihon Chōsenjin no gaikyō* [The general condition of the Koreans in Japan] (Tokyo, 1965), p. 24.

26. Chōsen Sōtokufu [Korean Government-General], *Dai hachijūgokai Teikoku Gikai setsumei shiryō* [Explanatory material for the Eighty-fifth Imperial Diet]; reprinted in *Taiheiyō senka shūmatsuki Chōsen no chisei*, ed. Kondō Ken'ichi, pp. 152–53.

27. See Chōsen Sōtokufu, *Shisei sanjūnen-shi*, pp. 890–94.

28. Pak Kyŏng-sik [Boku Keishoku], *Chōsenjin kyōsei renkō no kiroku* [The record of forced mobilization of the Koreans] (Tokyo, 1965), pp. 20–98. For the Korean casualty figures, see ibid., pp. 90–96, and Chōsen Sōtokufu, *Dai hachijūgokai Teikoku Gikai setsumei shiryō*, p. 156.

29. The Japanese government vigorously opposes this view, which is held by many observers. Takeshi Nakamura, deputy consul general in New York, wrote in a letter to the editor of the *New York Times* on September 20, 1983, that "the Japanese government has repeatedly urged the Government of the Soviet Union to give favorable consideration to the applications of these Koreans [to be allowed to leave Sakhalin for their original homes], from a humanitarian standpoint," and that "the Japanese Government is doing all that it can to facilitate a solution to this problem" (see the *New York Times*, September 24, 1983). Nakamura's letter was prompted by a letter of Felice D. Gaer, executive director of the International League for Human Rights, who said, among other things, that "after the war, all Japanese on Sakhalin were allowed to return to Japan, but only 2,300 Koreans [out of 43,000] who had Japanese wives were allowed to leave. With the exception of only three persons, the remaining Koreans could not be repatriated, due largely to Japanese discrimination against ethnic Koreans." Gaer's letter was published on September 14, 1983.

30. Senda Kakō, "Chosŏn yŏja cheshindae ui chŏnmo" [The entire picture

of the Korean Women's Submit Body Unit], *Wŏlgan Taehwa* [Monthly dialogue], trans. O Ae-yong (Seoul), September 1977, pp. 174–96. This work is a translation of a portion of Senda's *Jūgun ianfu* [Comfort women for the army] (n.p., n.d.). Yamatani Tetsuo produced an 86-minute documentary film, *Okinawa no obasan: Shōgen Jūgun ianfu* [A grandmother in Okinawa: Testimony regarding comfort women for the army] in 1979, and it was shown in various Japanese cities in September 1979 (*Dong-a Ilbo*, September 21, 1979). Yamatani told a reporter that he had obtained the idea for the film from photographs of Teishin-tai members published in *Fukyoka shashinshū* [Prohibited photographs] by *Mainichi Shimbun*.

31. This can be seen from the decrease in Koreans paying land taxes. Between 1929 and 1938, the total number of Japanese residents in Korea paying land taxes, including taxes on residential land, increased from 86,908 to 114,161, an increase of 31.3 percent. The number of Koreans paying land taxes decreased from 3,917,722 to 3,730,197, a decrease of 4.8 percent. For other details, see Zenshō Eisuke, "Chōsen nōson keizai no dōkō" [A trend in the Korean farm economy], *Tōyō* [East Asia], November 1940, pp. 54–56. Zenshō's article is based on a study by the Chōsen Sōtokufu, Kanbō Bunshoka, Tōkei-kakari [Secretariat of the Korean Government-General, Document Division, Statistical Section].

32. The following table tells the story:

THE POOR AND INDIGENT IN KOREA, 1926–1937
(PERCENTAGE OF TOTAL POPULATION)

Year	Poor	Indigent	Total
1926	9.7	1.5	11.2
1930	17.1	4.3	21.4
1931	20.7	5.1	25.8
1933	21.2	8.8	30.0
1934	20.3	7.7	28.0
1937	18.9	6.6	25.5

NOTE: The poor (*saimin*) refers to those whose livelihood was extremely strained (*kyūhaku*). The indigent (*kyūmin*) required immediate relief for survival.

SOURCES: The data for 1926, 1930, and 1931 are from Yi Yŏ-sŏng and Kim Se-yong, eds., *Sucha Chosŏn yŏn'gu* [A statistical study of Korea] (Seoul, 1933), 4: 6. Data for 1933 and 1934 are from Chōsen Sōtokufu, Shakaika [Korean Government-General Social Section], *Saikyūmin oyobi furōsha matawa kojiki no shirabe* [A study of the poor, indigent, vagabonds, and beggars] (October 1934, Mimeographed). The data for 1937 are from Chōsen Sōtokufu Jikyoku Taisaku Chōsakai Shimon'an Sankōsho: Shakai shisetsu no kakujū ni kansuru ken [The Korean Government-General Study Group on Policies Toward Present Problems: Advisory proposal reference material on expansion of social facilities] (Seoul, September 1938), pp. 18–19.

33. For 1914, see Suzuki Masafumi, *Chōsen keizai no gendankai* [The present stage of the Korean economy] (Tokyo, 1938), pp. 437–39. For other years, see Chōsen Sōtokufu, *Tōkei nempo* (1939), pp. 76–77, (1944), pp. 42–43.

34. Chōsen Sōtokufu, Nōrinkyoku [Korean Government-General, Bureau

of Agriculture and Forestry], *Chōsen no nōgyō* [Agriculture in Korea] (Seoul, 1937), pp. 191–93; Naimushō, Kanrikyoku [Ministry of Home Affairs, Control Bureau], *Chōsen kankei shiryō: Dai hachijūrokukai, hachijūnanakai Teikoku Gikai shokuryō kankei setsumei shiryō* [Materials concerning Korea: Explanatory materials related to food grains for the Eighty-sixth and Eighty-seventh Imperial Diets]; reprinted in *Taiheiyō senka no Chōsen* [Korea during the Pacific war], ed. Kondō Ken'ichi (Tokyo, 1963), 4: 96.

35. Tōyō Keizai Shimpōsha [East Asia Economic News Company], *Chōsen sangyō no kyōeiken sanka taisei* [Korean industry's participation in the co-prosperity sphere] (Seoul, May 1942), pp. 35–36.

36. Naimushō, Keihokyoku [Ministry of Home Affairs, Police and Security Bureau], *Shōwa jūichinen ni okeru shakai undō no jōkyō* [The condition of social movements in 1936] (Tokyo, 1937), pp. 1484–485.

37. Maruyama Masao, *Thought and Behavior in Modern Japanese Politics*, trans. and ed. Ivan Morris (London, 1963), pp. 1, 9.

38. Ibid., p. 9.

CHAPTER 2

1. See John Lewis Gaddis, *Strategies of Containment: A Critical Appraisal of Postwar American National Security Policy* (Oxford and New York, 1982), chap. 2; and Robert E. Ward, ed., *Political Development in Modern Japan* (Princeton, N.J., 1968), p. 502.

2. John W. Dower, *Empire and Aftermath: Yoshida Shigeru and the Japanese Experience, 1878–1954* (Cambridge, Mass., 1979), pp. 273–74.

3. Ibid., pp. 225, 274.

4. Shigeru Yoshida, *The Yoshida Memoirs: The Story of Japan in Crisis*, trans. Kenichi Yoshida (London, 1961), pp. 277–78.

5. Yagi Nobuo, *Nihon to Kankoku* [Japan and South Korea] (Tokyo, 1978), p. 279.

6. Ibid., pp. 280, 281, 274. Yagi cites Ch'oe Rin, Yun Ch'i-ho, and Yi Kwang-su as leading Koreans who understood the spirit of "complete merger" of the two peoples. These three have been cited as prime examples of "pro-Japanese collaborators" in postliberation Korea. For recent Korean accounts of collaborators, see Yim Chong-guk, "Il-je-mal ŭi ch'in-Il gunsang" [The image of the pro-Japanese elements at the last stage of Japanese imperialism], *Wŏlgan Taehwa* [Monthly dialogue] (Seoul), August 1977, pp. 168–213, 321; and Ch'oe Min-ji and Kim Min-su, *Il-je-ha minjok ŏnronsa ron* [History of the national press under Japanese imperialism] (Seoul, 1978), pp. 217–320.

7. *Yomiuri Shimbun*, August 23, 1982.

8. Ibid.

9. For Kishi's career in Manchuria, see Tajiri Ikuzō, *Shōwa no yōkai Kishi Nobusuke* [A specter of the Showa era: Kishi Nobusuke] (Tokyo, 1979), pp. 9–93; and Chalmers Johnson, *MITI and the Japanese Miracle: The Growth of Industrial Policy, 1925–1975* (Stanford, 1982), pp. 125–56. Kishi had been designated a Class A war criminal and was incarcerated at Sugamo prison for three years, but was never tried as such. He was prohibited from engaging in political activities until April 1952. For Kishi's notions about Japan's role in Asia, see Tajiri, *Shōwa no yōkai*, pp. 163–67. It is relevant to note that Shiina Etsusaburō, who was to become the vice president of the Liberal Democratic Party and a kingmaker of the LDP cabinets, had been a deputy to Kishi in Manchukuo and in the Japanese Ministry of Commerce and Industry. The project to erect the monument had to be canceled in 1982 because of harsh denunciation from China (*Yomiuri Shimbun*, September 17, 1982).

10. "Korea-Japan Diplomacy," *Oriental Economist* (Tokyo), April 1958, p. 187. For a discussion of Terauchi as governor, see Chapter 1.

11. Chōsen Sōtokufu [Korean Government-General], *Jinkō chōsa kekka hōkoku* [Report on the result of the population census], May 1, 1944, pt. 2, pp. 142–43. The report indicated that 11.65 percent of males graduated from elementary school while 3.01 percent of females did so. An additional 1.11 percent of the population had attended elementary school but did not graduate. The percentage of children ages 7–14 attending school as of 1935 was 17.59 percent (27.26 percent male and 7.33 percent female). See Chōsen Kōsei Kyōkai [Korean Welfare Association], *Chōsen ni okeru jinkō ni kansuru sho tōkei* [Various statistics concerning population in Korea] (Seoul, 1943), p. 114.

12. "Korea-Japan Diplomacy," p. 187.

13. Ibid., p. 186.

14. *New York Times*, January 30, 1974.

15. *Tong-a Ilbo*, March 26, 1979.

16. Ibid., March 26, 1979.

17. Tsuboe Senji, *Zai Nihon Chōsenjin jōkyō* [Condition of the Koreans in Japan] (Tokyo, 1965), pp. 9–10.

18. Edward W. Wagner, *The Korean Minority in Japan* (New York, 1951), pp. 43–50, 60.

19. Ibid., 59.

20. For details, see ibid., pp. 64–72.

21. Ibid., p. 61.

22. Andrea Boltho, *Japan: An Economic Survey, 1953–1973* (London, 1975), p. 55n.

23. Memorandum of conversations between Assistant Secretary of State Dean Rusk and Korean Ambassador John M. Chang, January 17, 1951, *Foreign Relations of the United States*, 1951, vol. 7, pt. 1, p. 97.

24. From the "Rough Draft of Comment and Suggestions," written by President Rhee in 1951 (undated), in the private file of Robert T. Oliver.

25. Memorandum of Conversations, *Foreign Relations of the United States,* vol. 7, pt. 2, p. 97.

26. For the text of the peace treaty, see U.S. Department of State, *Treaty of Peace: Proceedings* (Washington, 1952), pp. 313–455.

27. On November 23, President Rhee instructed his ambassador in Washington, Chang Myun (John M. Chang), to press for Korea's right to participate in the San Francisco conference. If that was not possible, Chang was to seek a guarantee from the Allied powers that a "Korean-Japanese peace conference will be held later between the two countries." Rhee instructed his foreign minister, Pyun Yung Tai, on January 23, 1951, that in case the Allied Council did not wish to make such a guarantee, then "we must have an agreement signed by the Japanese to the effect that a separate peace conference between the two countries will be held at a certain date."

28. Koryŏ Taehakkyo Asea Munje Yŏn'guso [Asiatic Research Center, Korea University], ed., *Han-Il munje charyojip* [Materials on Korean-Japanese relations] (Seoul, 1976), 1: 86. Cited hereafter as *Materials on Korean-Japanese Relations.*

29. Foreign Minister Pyun wrote to Ambassador You Chan Yang [Yu Ch'an-yang] in Washington on August 14, 1951, saying "I understand that Mr. Rusk suggested in his letter to you that we had better conclude a fishery agreement with Japan before the Japanese Peace Treaty goes into effect."

30. Kimura Shūzō, "Nik-Kan kōshō no keii" [Circumstances of the Japanese–South Korean negotiations], in *Nik-Kan kankei no tenkai* [Development of Japanese–South Korean relations], ed. Nihon Kokusai Seiji Gakkai [Japanese Political Science Association] (Tokyo, 1963), p. 115.

31. Ibid., p. 114.

32. "Confidential Memorandum from President Rhee to All Diplomatic Representatives Abroad on Korean-Japanese Relations," undated draft, pp. 5–9.

33. For the text of the proclamation, see *Materials on Korean-Japanese Relations,* 1: 85–86. It is commonly assumed that the Rhee Line was suddenly decided by President Rhee because of his animosity toward the Japanese, but, according to two Korean reporters who delved into this question, Rhee had previously turned down his cabinet's proposal for such a line in September 1951. The National Assembly also had passed a resolution on April 24, 1951, to preserve the MacArthur Line, although I cannot determine the original source of the resolution. There is no doubt, in any event, that Rhee decided on the proclamation in reaction to presumed Japanese recalcitrance. See Yi Sŏk-yŏl and Cho Kyu-ha, "Han-Il hoedam chŏnmalsŏ" [An account of the Korean-Japanese talks], *Shin-dong-a,* June 1965, p. 102.

34. The exact wording of Kubota's statement of October 15, 1953, became a subject of controversy between the Japanese and South Korean delega-

tions. The statement cited here is from a summary of the Japanese Foreign Ministry's record prepared by an American foreign service officer in Tokyo and dispatched to the State Department on December 9, 1953. The six-page summary is entitled "'The Kubota Statement'—Summary of the Proceedings of the Second Meeting of the Claims Sub-Committee on October 15 and Plenary Sessions of October 20 and October 21, 1953: Japanese Foreign Ministry's Record," Decimal File 694.95B/12–953, Enclosure no. 1, U.S. National Archives, p. 3. For the Korean record of the Kubota statement, see *Materials on Korean-Japanese Relations*, 1: 108–11.

35. Yi Sŏk-yŏl and Cho Kyu-ha, "Han-Il hoedam chŏnmalsŏ," p. 10. The territorial line was altered to the Peace Line by the South Korean government after General Mark Clark, the commander of the United Nations forces, established a demarcation line for security purposes on September 20, 1952.

36. Robert Murphy, *Diplomat Among Warriors* (New York, 1964), p. 349. John Foster Dulles to Syngman Rhee, December 10, 1958, Decimal File 694.95B/11–1053, U.S. National Archives, p. 2. Secretary of State Dulles refers to a note sent by the U.S. government on the Rhee Line on February 11, 1952.

37. Murphy, *Diplomat Among Warriors*, p. 351. Although Premier Yoshida did not attend the luncheon, he evidently met President Rhee at a reception given in Rhee's honor by General Clark. Yoshida's only comment during the encounter, according to the aide-mémoire in the Oliver file, was "Our militarists were responsible." Hearing this, Rhee opened a long tirade against Japan: "You could express to the Koreans that the militarists were responsible for everything and from now on there will be no militaristic aggression on Korea, or some such statement would help the Koreans who still suspect and fear Japanese ambitions and attempts to control Korea again." Yoshida only smiled in response. Aide-mémoire of conference in Tokyo on January 8, 1953, in the private file of Robert T. Oliver.

38. "'The Kubota Statement'—Summary of Proceedings," p. 3.

39. Ibid., p. 4. It is interesting to note that the Japanese position on the effective date of Korean independence has not changed in subsequent years. Nakamura Takeshi, deputy consul general in New York, wrote in his letter to the editor of the *New York Times*, published on September 24, 1983, that "With the entry into force of the San Francisco Peace Treaty in 1952, Korea's separation from, and independence of, Japan was legally established." See also John M. Allison to the Secretary of State, October 21, 1953, telegram no. 1016, Decimal File 694.95B/10–2153, National Archives.

40. Foreign Office spokesman's statement, October 21, 1953. There is an unofficial translation in Decimal File 694.95B/10–2853, National Archives.

41. John M. Allison, *Ambassador from the Prairie or Allison Wonderland* (New York, 1973), pp. 258–59. Ambassador Allison repeatedly urged his government to exert pressure against President Rhee by such means as an announcement of the U.S. position on the Rhee Line or withholding of logistical

support from the South Korean navy. Copies of his telegrams are available in the Decimal File 694.95B, National Archives.

CHAPTER 3

1. For details, see David C. Cole and Princeton N. Lyman, *Korean Development: The Interplay of Politics and Economics* (Cambridge, Mass., 1971), pp. 22–30; and Hahn-Been Lee, *Korea: Time, Change, and Administration* (Honolulu, 1968), pp. 81–87.

2. See Anne O. Krueger, *The Developmental Role of the Foreign Sector and Aid* (Cambridge, Mass., 1979), p. 67.

3. Kawaguchi Tōru, *America no taigai enjo seisaku: Sono rinen to seisaku keisei* [Foreign aid policy of the United States: Its concept and policy formation] (Tokyo, 1980), pp. 49–50.

4. John M. Allison, *Ambassador from the Prairie or Allison Wonderland* (New York, 1973), p. 259.

5. *Asahi Shimbun*, September 9, 1960.

6. Yagi Nobuo, *Nihon to Kankoku* [Japan and South Korea] (Tokyo, 1978), p. 481.

7. Sŏng Hwang-yong, *Ilbon ui tae-Han chŏngch'aek* [Japan's South Korean policy] (Seoul, 1981), pp. 250–53.

8. Sungjoo Han, *The Failure of Democracy in South Korea* (Berkeley, 1974), pp. 171, 209.

9. *Asahi Shimbun*, February 4, 1961; and Kimura Shūzō, "Nik-Kan kōshō no keii" [Circumstances of the Japanese–South Korean negotiations], in *Nik-Kan kankei no tenkai* [Development of Japanese–South Korean Relations], ed. Nihon Kokusai Seiji Gakkai [Japanese Political Science Association] (Tokyo, 1963), p. 121.

10. Yagi Nobuo, *Nihon to Kankoku*, pp. 480–81; Kimura Shūzō, "Nik-Kan kōshō no keii," p. 122; and Sŏng Hwang-yong, *Ilbon ui tae-Han chŏngch'aek*, p. 257.

11. Sŏng Hwang-yong, *Ilbon ui tae-Han chŏngch'aek*, pp. 256–57.

12. Ōoka Eppei, " 'Jiyū Kankoku' o mamoru: Nik-Kan kaidan no mondaiten" [Defend "Free Korea": Searching for the problems in Japanese–South Korean talks], *Chūō Kōron*, January 1962, pp. 284, 285.

13. Ibid., p. 288.

14. Ibid., p. 284.

15. Se-jin Kim, *The Politics of Military Revolution in Korea* (Chapel Hill, N.C., 1971), pp. 96–97.

16. Ōoka Eppei, " 'Jiyū Kankoku' o mamoru," p. 287; and *New York Times*, June 23, 1961.

17. *New York Times*, June 23, 1961.

18. Ōoka Eppei, " 'Jiyū Kankoku' o mamoru," p. 289.

19. Ibid., pp. 287–88; Yagi Nobuo, *Nihon to Kankoku*, pp. 482–83; and Yi Sŏk-yŏl and Cho Kyu-ha, "Han-Il hoedam chŏnmalsŏ" [An account of the Korean-Japanese talks], *Shin-dong-a*, June 1965, pp. 113–15.

20. Ōoka Eppei, "'Jiyū Kankoku' o mamoru," pp. 288–89.

21. Japan agreed to provide a $300 million grant-in-aid, a $200 million long-term government loan, and a $100 million commercial loan. See Koryŏ Taehakkyo Asea Munje Yŏn'guso [Asiatic Research Center, Korea University], ed., *Han-Il munje charyojip* [Materials on Korean-Japanese relations] (Seoul, 1976), 1: 143.

22. For details, see Se-jin Kim, *The Politics of Military Revolution*, pp. 125–35.

23. Cf. Chong-Sik Lee, "Korea: Troubles in a Divided State," *Asian Survey*, January 1965, pp. 25–28.

24. Premier Ikeda reportedly told Foreign Secretary Alexander Douglas-Home of Great Britain, who was visiting Japan between March 28 and April 5, 1963, that "it would be better for South Korea to remain under the military regime rather than forcibly trying to bring about a civilian government" (Yi Sŏk-yŏl and Cho Kyu-ha, "Han-Il hoedam chŏnmalsŏ," p. 123).

25. For a vivid testimony by an insider, see Kim Hyŏng-uk and Pak Sa-wŏl, *Kim Hyŏng-uk jŭng-ŏn: Hyŏngmyŏng kwa usang* [Kim Hyŏng-uk's testimony: Revolution and idol] (Philadelphia, 1982), 1: 195–296.

26. Quoted in Yi Sŏk-yŏl and Cho Kyu-ha, "Han-Il hoedam chŏnmalsŏ," p. 123. Ōno Banboku saw President Park on December 18, 1963.

27. Chong-Sik Lee, "Korea: Troubles in a Divided State," pp. 25–26.

28. Cf. Donald C. Hellmann, "Basic Problems of Japanese–South Korean Relations," *Asian Survey*, May 1962, pp. 19–24. On the party platform, see "Japanese Socialist Party's Draft Action Policy for 1962," *Japan Socialist Review*, no. 4 (December 16, 1961), p. 63. For a summary of Socialist views, see *Nik-Kan kaidan: Sono teikoku shugi teki haikei* [Japanese–South Korean talks: Their imperialistic background], study ser. 17 (Tokyo, 1961).

29. *Asahi Shimbun*, November 26, 1961.

30. Hong Sŏng-u, "'Hyŏp-ryŏk' i'nya 'ch'imsik' i'nya: Han-Il kyŏngje kyosŏp ui naeil" ["Cooperation" or "erosion": The future of Korean-Japanese economic negotiations], *Shin-dong-a*, June 1965, p. 129.

31. Figures are drawn from Shūkan Tōyō Keizai [Weekly East Asian Economy], *Keizai tōkei nenkan* [Economic statistical annual] (1972), pp. 393–95. For analyses of the Japanese economy's postwar growth, see Hugh T. Patrick, "The Phoenix Arisen from the Ashes: Postwar Japan," in *Modern East Asia: Essays in Interpretation*, ed. James B. Crowley (New York, 1970), pp. 298–334; Edward F. Denison and William K. Chung, *How Japan's Economy Grew*

So Fast: The Sources of Postwar Expansion (Washington, D.C., 1976), *passim*; and *Economist* correspondents, *Consider Japan* (London, 1963).

32. See Yi Sŏk-yŏl and Cho Kyu-ha, "Han-Il hoedam chŏnmalsŏ," p. 120.

33. See Tajiri Ikuzō, *Shōwa no yōkai: Kishi Nobusuke* [The phantom of the Show era: Kishi Nobusuke] (Tokyo, 1979), pp. 28–29, 37–39.

34. For an observation of the relationship between Kishi and Ikeda, see Robert Scalapino and Junnosuke Masumi, *Parties and Politics in Contemporary Japan* (Berkeley, 1962), pp. 59, 141.

35. Yi Sŏk-yŏl and Cho Kyu-ha, "Han-Il hoedam chŏnmalsŏ," p. 121.

36. For the full text of the treaty, see *Materials on Korean-Japanese Relations*, 1: 153. U.N. General Assembly Resolution 195 (III) had stated that "there has been established a lawful government [the Government of the Republic of Korea] having effective control and jurisdiction over *that part of Korea* where the great majority of the people of Korea reside" (emphasis added). See Kim Se-jin, ed., *Korean Unification: Source Materials* (Seoul, 1976), pp. 109–10.

37. For details, see *Materials on Korean-Japanese Relations*, 1: 147–204.

38. C. I. Eugene Kim, "Korea in the Year of ŬLSA," *Asian Survey*, January 1966, pp. 34–37. A survey conducted by the Research Office of Educational Psychology of Sungmyong Women's University during student demonstrations on March 24 revealed that 31 percent of the respondents attributed the demonstrations to fear of Japanese economic and political exploitation, 20 percent to distrust of the Park regime, 15 percent to the "distasteful method of negotiation," and 13 percent to the removal of the Peace Line (ibid., p. 37). For an incisive analysis of the motives and behavior of the opposition forces, see Cole and Lyman, *Korean Development*, pp. 98–113.

39. *Tong-a Ilbo*, January 11–14, 1965 (cited in C. I. Eugene Kim, "Korea in the Year of ŬLSA," p. 37).

40. Nobutaka Ike, "Japan Twenty Years After Surrender," *Asian Survey*, January 1966, p. 27.

41. For an excellent discussion of the political situation within South Korea, see Cole and Lyman, *Korean Development*, pp. 70–77, 98–118.

42. The figures for 1944 are from Chōsen Sōtokufu [Korean Government-General], *Jinkō chōsa kekka hōkoku* [Report on the result of the census of population] (May 1, 1944), Part 2, pp. 142–43. The elementary school graduates for that year may include those who completed four-year courses. The figures for 1962 are from *Hapdong yŏn'gam* [United annual] (Seoul, 1967), pp. 800–801. They are based on data from the Economic Planning Board.

43. "Kiji mo tamago mo hina mo kutta Nihon" [Japan that has eaten the pheasant, the egg, and the chick] (Minutes of the Thirteenth Joint Standing Committee Meeting of the Japan–South Korean Cooperation Society), *Asahi jyānaru*, May 27, 1977, p. 37. The meeting was held December 8–9, 1975.

44. For a very detailed account of these events, see Kim Hyŏng-uk and Pak Sa-wŏl, *Kim Hyŏng-uk jŭng'ŏn*, 2: 41–47.

45. For details, see Cole and Lyman, *Korean Development*, p. 160. For another excellent overview of South Korea's economic development, see Edward D. Mason et al., *The Economic and Social Modernization of the Republic of Korea*, (Cambridge, Mass., 1980). Chapter 5 deals with industrialization and foreign trade. See also Wontack Hong and Anne O. Krueger, eds., *Trade and Development in Korea* (Seoul, 1975), *passim*.

46. Details are provided by Kim Chin-bae and Pak Ch'ang-rae in their investigatory article, "Ch'agwan" [Loans], *Shin-dong-a*, December 1968, pp. 215–48. Since the authors took a critical position on the mushrooming Japanese loans, they were subjected to investigation by the Korean Central Intelligence Agency. Finding the information accurate, however, both authors were released. The government then pressured the Dong-a Daily News Company, the publisher of the magazine, to dismiss the two reporters. See Kim Hyŏng-uk and Pak Sa-wŏl, *Kim Hyŏng-uk jŭng-ŏn*, 2: 277–84.

47. Chang Key-young, "Problems Between South Korea and Japan and the South Korean Position" (Speech delivered at the Inaugural Meeting of the Japan–South Korea Cooperation Committee [Chairman Kishi Nobusuke], Tokyo, February 13, 1969), in *Ttwimyŏnsŏ saenggak haetta: Chang Ki-yŏng Chŏn Buch'ongri tokchu samnyŏn ui ilhwajip* [I thought as I ran: Anecdotes of three years of former premier Chang Key-young's single-handed running], ed. Ch'oe Sŏng-yŏl (Seoul, 1969), pp. 427, 431. Pages 421–42 contain the full text of the important speech.

48. Ibid., pp. 427, 436–37.

CHAPTER 4

1. Richard Nixon, "Asia After Viet Nam," *Foreign Affairs* 46, no. 1 (October 1967), pp. 121, 111–25.

2. Henry Kissinger, *White House Years* (Boston, 1979), p. 324.

3. Chae-Jin Lee and Hideo Sato, *U.S. Policy Toward Japan and Korea* (New York, 1982), p. 44.

4. See Koryŏ Taehakkyo Asea Munje Yŏn'guso [Asiatic Research Center, Korea University], ed., *Han-Il munje charyojip* [Materials on Korean-Japanese relations] (Seoul, 1976), 2: 633, 632–69.

5. Ch'oe Sŏng-yŏl, ed., *Ttwimyŏnsŏ saenggak haetta: Chang Ki-yŏng Chŏn Buch'ongri tokchu samnyŏn ui ilhwajip* [I thought as I ran: Anecdotes of three years of former premier Chang Key-young's single-handed running] (Seoul, 1969), p. 437. The full text of the speech is on pp. 421–42.

6. Kissinger, *White House Years*, p. 324.

7. Lee and Sato, *U.S. Policy Toward Japan and Korea*, pp. 40–41.

8. Kubo Takuya, "Kinchō yurundemo yojibō wa yaru" [Even if tension subsides, the fourth defense buildup plan will be implemented], *Asahi jyānaru*, October 20, 1972, p. 10.

9. Miyoshi Osamu, "Amerika ni hōri dasareta Nihon" [Japan discarded by America], *Bungei shunjū*, September 1971, p. 105.

10. Seki Hiroharu, "Yoshida aryū jidai no owari" [The end of the Yoshida followers], *Chūō kōron*, February 1972, p. 71.

11. Chalmers Johnson, "Japan: The Year of 'Money Power' Politics," *Asian Survey*, January 1975, pp. 26–27.

12. Makoto Momoi, "Basic Trends in Japanese Security Policies," in *The Foreign Policy of Modern Japan*, ed. Robert A. Scalapino (Berkeley, 1977), p. 347.

13. Defense Secretary Melvin Laird issued in August 1971 a memorandum calling for the reduction of the Second Infantry Division in Korea to one brigade by the end of fiscal year 1974. In 1972 the target date was extended to the end of 1975, but this plan was thwarted by Henry Kissinger (Lee and Sato, *U.S. Policy Toward Japan and Korea*, p. 103, citing House Committee on Armed Services, *Hearings on Review of the Policy Decision to Withdraw United States Ground Forces from Korea* [Washington, D.C., 1978], p. 89).

14. For details, see Chong-Sik Lee, "The Detente and Korea," in *The World and the Great-Power Triangles*, ed. William E. Griffith (Cambridge, Mass., 1975), pp. 321–96.

15. Mushakōji Kinhide, "Namboku Chōsen to Nihon gaikō" [North-South Korea and Japanese diplomacy], *Sekai*, November 1975, pp. 10–22.

16. Soon-Sung Cho, "Japan's Two Koreas Policy and the Problems of Korean Unification," *Asian Survey*, October 1967, pp. 719–22.

17. Nixon, "Asia After Viet Nam," p. 121.

18. Kissinger, *White House Years*, p. 328.

19. Lee and Sato, *U.S. Policy Toward Japan and Korea*, pp. 40–41.

20. Kubo Takuya, "Kinchō yurundemo yojibō wa yaru," p. 10.

21. *Sankei Shimbun*, October 27, 1971, cited in Fujishima Udai, "Nihon o yusaburu Kankoku no seiji fuan" [Political insecurity in South Korea that shakes Japan], *Chūō kōron*, April 1972, p. 82.

22. *Tong-a Ilbo*, August 31, 1974; and *Asahi Shimbun*, August 20, 1974.

23. *Asahi Shimbun*, August 30 and September 6, 1974. For the full text of the resolution, see Se-jin Kim, ed., *Korean Unification: Source Materials* (Seoul, 1976), pp. 109–10. For an account of the background to the resolution, see Soon-Sung Cho, *Korea in World Politics, 1940–1950* (Berkeley, 1967), pp. 204–11. For a detailed account of the different interpretations of the conditional phrase by Japanese and Korean officials, see Soon-Sung Cho, "Japan's Two Koreas Policy," pp. 703–8.

24. Ajia Keizai Kenkyūjo [Institute of Developing Economies], *Ajia dōkō nempō* [Asian trend annual] (Tokyo, 1973), p. 83.

25. Ibid.; and Koryŏ Taehakkyo Asea Munje Yŏn'guso [Asiatic Research Center, Korea University], ed., *Han-Il munje charyojip* [Materials on Korean-Japanese relations], 2: 651–53.

26. Fujishima Udai, "Nihon o yusaburu Kankoku no seiji fuan," p. 82.

27. Komaki Teruo, "Nit-Chō bōeki no genkyō to kadai" [The present condition and the tasks ahead in Japan–North Korea trade], *Sekai*, November 1975, p. 128.

28. Yi To-hyŏng [Ri Do-kyŏ], *Nihon no Kankoku hōdō wa shinjirarenai* [Japanese reports on South Korea cannot be trusted] (Tokyo, 1981), p. 92.

29. *Tong-a Ilbo*, May 17, 1972; and *Washington Post*, January 8, 1972.

30. *Chung-ang Ilbo*, January 31 and February 1, 1972.

31. I have consulted numerous Japanese and Korean newspaper and magazine articles dealing with various aspects of the incident.

32. *Tong-a Ilbo*, August 22, 1974, cited the NHK-TV commentary of August 15, the *Asahi Shimbun* editorial of August 17, and the *Yomiuri Shimbun* editorial of August 18.

33. See Richard Halloran's dispatches from Tokyo in the *New York Times*, September 4, 13, 15, and 20, 1974. Japanese and Korean newspapers, of course, provided detailed coverage of every step of the negotiations.

34. Economic Planning Board, Republic of Korea, *Major Statistics of the Korean Economy, 1977* (Seoul, 1977), pp. 200–205, and *Oegukin t'uja paeksŏ* [White paper on investment by foreign nationals] (Seoul, 1981), pp. 126–29, 136–37.

35. Kae H. Chung, "Industrial Progress in South Korea," *Asian Survey*, May 1974, pp. 439–55.

36. *Tong-a Ilbo*, September 5, 1972.

37. Ibid., December 27, 1973. An additional $45 million was to be provided during the fiscal year as had been agreed at the previous meeting.

38. Chiku Isao, "Sekiyu panikku ka no Nikkan kyōryoku rosen" [The Japanese–South Korean cooperative line during the oil panic], *Korea hyōron*, March 1974, pp. 14–16.

39. *Tong-a Ilbo*, September 6, 1972.

40. Lee and Sato, *U.S. Policy Toward Japan and Korea*, p. 103.

41. See Richard Halloran, "Japanese Fearful of Conflict in Korea," *New York Times*, May 14, 1975; Rowland Evans and Robert Novak, "Japan and the Korean Domino," *Washington Post*, June 7, 1975; and Takashi Oka, "Japan Watches Korea," *Christian Science Monitor*, June 10, 1975.

42. *Peking Review*, April 25, 1975, p. 17.

43. Young C. Kim, "The Democratic People's Republic of Korea in 1975," *Asian Survey*, January 1976, p. 84.

44. *New York Times*, June 1975; *Department of State Bulletin*, May 26, 1975, p. 669, and ibid., June 2, 1975; *New York Times*, June 26, 1975; *Tong-a Ilbo*, August 21 and 23, 1975.

45. Takashi Oka, "Japan Watches Korea."

46. Ōe Kanzaburō, "Nise no kotoba o kyofu suru" [Deny the false words], *Sekai*, November 1975, p. 26.

47. Edward Seidensticker, "Japan After Vietnam," *Commentary*, September 1975, p. 56.

48. *Tong-a Ilbo*, May 13, 1975; "Dokyumento: Kin Dai-chū shi rachi jiken" [Document: The kidnap incident of Mr. Kim Dae-jung], *Sekai*, July 1975, pp. 169–70. Miyazawa reaffirmed the Korea clause upon his return to Tokyo. For his remark of April 15 at the Foreign Affairs Committee of the upper house, see ibid., pp. 171–72. *Sekai*, the popular liberal magazine, carried a series of detailed chronology, documentaries, and commentaries on Japanese-Korean relations under the title "Document: The Kidnap Incident" in many of its monthly issues after July 1975. Its commentaries have been highly critical of the Park regime in South Korea while voicing no criticism of the Pyongyang regime.

49. *Tong-a Ilbo*, May 29, 1975; and *Sekai*, July 1975, p. 186.

50. *Tong-a Ilbo*, July 11 and 12, 1975; and *Sekai*, September 1975, pp. 193–96.

51. *Tong-a Ilbo*, May 29, 1975.

52. *Sekai*, October 1975, pp. 206–7. *Sekai* referred to Utsunomiya's mission to Pyongyang as that of an unofficial "special envoy" (*tokushi*). Premier Kim Il-sŏng became president in 1972 after the constitution was revised in the DPRK. The visit by the Tamura delegation is also covered in Hong N. Kim, "Japanese–South Korean Relations in the Post-Vietnam Era," pp. 988–89. On Miki's talk with Ford, see *Sekai*, October 1975, p. 201.

53. *New York Times*, August 7, 1975. On July 22, Premier Miki conferred with Foreign Minister Miyazawa and Deputy Minister Tōgō on his forthcoming visit to Washington. It was announced after the meeting that the Korea clause would not be reaffirmed. Hence the Japanese draft of the Miki-Ford joint communiqué did not mention either Japan or Korea but stated simply that "the maintenance of peace on the Korean peninsula is essential to the peace of Asia." The U.S. side insisted on further elaboration (*Sekai*, October 1975, p. 201). As noted before, both Miki and Miyazawa confirmed the Korea clause.

54. *Sekai*, November 1975, p. 156; and Hong N. Kim, "Japanese–South Korean Relations," p. 989.

55. *Tong-a Ilbo*, June 2, 1975.

56. *Mainichi Shimbun*, November 16, 1975; and *New York Times*, August 21, 1975.

57. *Tong-a Ilbo*, September 15, 16, and 17, 1975. See also *Asahi Shimbun*, September 17, 1975.

58. For a detailed account of President Carter's plan to withdraw U.S. combat troops and its implications, see Lee and Sato, *U.S. Policy Toward*

Japan and Korea, pp. 104–17. See also Chalmers Johnson, "Carter in Asia: McGovernism Without McGovern," *Commentary*, January 1978, p. 36.

59. See U.S. House of Representatives, *Investigation of Korean-American Relations: Report of the Subcommittee on International Organizations of the Committee on International Relations* (Washington, D.C., 1978), pp. 3–5; and U.S. Senate, *Korean Influence Inquiry: Report of the Select Committee on Ethics* (Washington, D.C., 1978), pp. 1–3.

60. Bernard Weinraub, "Japan Ponders Its Own Defenses as U.S. Prepares Korea Pullout," *New York Times*, August 1, 1977; and Scott Thompson, "Japan Debates Security as U.S. Pulls out of Korea," *Christian Science Monitor*, August 12, 1977.

61. Lee and Sato, *U.S. Policy Toward Japan and Korea*, pp. 106–7.

62. Ibid., pp. 111, 112.

63. Ibid., pp. 113, 110.

64. Ibid., p. 116.

65. Ibid., pp. 122, 124.

66. Sungjoo Han, "South Korea 1977: Preparing for Self-Reliance," *Asian Survey*, January 1978, pp. 50–51. The Japanese press and publication industry in 1977 was inundated with charges of Japanese–South Korean collusion (*Nikkan yuchaku*) and Japanese–South Korean scandal (*Nikkan giwaku*). For examples, see Senda Kakō, "Giwaku kyūmei no tameno 'kasetsu' no susume" [A suggestion for a 'hypothesis' for clarification of the scandal], *Asahi jyānaru*, April 8, 1977, pp. 91–93; and Nakagawa Nobuo, *Tāgetto: Nik-Kan Giwaku no kōzō to ronri* [Target: The structure and logic of the Japanese–South Korean scandal] (Tokyo, 1978), *passim*.

67. *Tong-a Ilbo*, April 28 and 30, 1979, and May 2, 1979. See also *Korea Herald*, May 1, 1979, and July 24, 26, and 27, 1979.

68. For details, see "South Korea 1979: Confrontation, Assassination, and Transition," *Asian Survey*, January 1980, pp. 63–76.

69. See *Nihon Keizai Shimbun*, October 27, 1979, for some of the favorable Japanese comments on Park Chung Hee.

70. See Gerald L. Curtis, "The Tyumen Oil Development Project and Japanese Foreign Policy Decision-Making," in *The Foreign Policy of Modern Japan*, pp. 147–73.

71. Cf. Donald C. Hellmann, "Japanese Security and Postwar Japanese Foreign Policy," in *The Foreign Policy of Modern Japan*, p. 329.

CHAPTER 5

1. *Yomiuri Shimbun*, February 4, 1981.

2. For an excellent account of these events, see Lee W. Farnworth, "Japan in 1980: Conservative Resurgence," *Asian Survey*, January 1981, pp. 70–83.

3. Chong-Sik Lee, "South Korea in 1980: The Emergence of a New Authoritarian Order," *Asian Survey*, January 1981, pp. 126–29.

4. *Yomiuri Shimbun*, August 15, 1980; and *Asahi Shimbun*, September 16, 1980.

5. Lee, "South Korea in 1980," pp. 131–32.

6. *New York Times*, May 23, 1980.

7. *Yomiuri Shimbun*, September 18, 1980.

8. Ibid., November 26, 1980.

9. "Profit Motive Seen Behind Tokyo Stand," *Korea Herald*, November 29, 1980. For Sōhyō's announcement, see *Yomiuri Shimbun*, November 27, 1980.

10. For the text of the Reagan-Chun communiqué, see *Department of State Bulletin*, March 1981, pp. 14–15. On President Reagan's defense strategy, see Fred I. Greenstein, *The Reagan Presidency: An Early Assessment* (Baltimore, Md., 1983); and Samuel F. Wells, Jr., "A Question of Priorities: A Comparison of the Carter and Reagan Defense Programs," *Orbis*, Fall 1983, pp. 641–66.

11. For the text of the joint communiqué, see the *New York Times*, May 9, 1981.

12. See, for example, *Yomiuri Shimbun*, July 23, 1981.

13. Ibid., May 13, 1981.

14. Steven R. Weisman, "Japanese Vow 'Even Greater Efforts' on Defense," *New York Times*, May 9, 1981; and "Ripping of the Premier's Double Tongue," *Yomiuri Shimbun*, May 17, 1981.

15. Chūma Kiyofuku, "Restored, the Republic of Korea Is the Next," *Asahi jyānaru*, August 7, 1981, p. 25.

16. Ibid., p. 26; and *Korea Herald*, July 23, 1981.

17. Chūma Kiyofuku, "Restored," p. 26.

18. Seki Kensaburō, "Japanese Aid, South Korea's Logic," *Yomiuri Shimbun*, August 6, 1981.

19. Kamata Mitsuto, "Nik-Kan keizai kyōryoku no mondaiten" [Problems in Japanese–South Korean economic cooperation], *Korea Hyōron* [Korea review], April 1982, p. 12.

20. *Asahi Shimbun*, May 17, 1981.

21. Takashi Oka, "Sonoda Rivets Japan to Peace Goal," *Christian Science Monitor*, July 19, 1978.

22. Ibid.

23. *Yomiuri Shimbun*, July 28 and August 9, 1981.

24. Ibid., August 15, 1981; and *Mainichi Shimbun*, August 19, 1981.

25. *Tong-a Ilbo*, August 20 and 21, 1981; and *Asahi Shimbun*, August 20, 1981. Sonoda's first two points were matters of opinion although not at all diplomatic in tone. His third point, however, was not based on an accurate historical understanding. For my discussion of the Empress Jingū, see Chapter 6.

26. "Inside Story of the '$6 billion' Negotiations," *Shūkan Asahi*, October 30, 1981, p. 161.

27. *Yomiuri Shimbun*, August 22, 1981.

28. Ibid., August 27, 1981.

29. Ibid., September 3, 1981.

30. Ibid., August 25, 1981.

31. *Tong-a Ilbo*, August 29, 1981.

32. *Yomiuri Shimbun*, September 10, 1981.

33. For details, see *Asahi Shimbun*, September 17, 1981.

34. See Table 9 and the tables on export commodities in Tsūshō Sangyō-shō [Ministry of International Trade and Industry], ed., *Tsūshō hakusho* [Trade white paper], 1981 and 1982. Japanese exports in 1980 were (in billions of U.S. dollars) (1) United States, 31.36, (2) West Germany, 5.75, (3) South Korea, 5.36, (4) Taiwan, 5.14, and (5) China, 5.07. The exports in 1981 were (1) United States, 38.6, (2) West Germany, 5.96, (3) Saudi Arabia, 5.87, (4) South Korea, 5.65, (5) Taiwan, 5.40, (6) Hong Kong, 5.31, and (7) China, 5.09. On Japanese investments, see Tables 7 and 8.

35. For details, see *Nihon Keizai Shimbun*, January 10, 1983; *Chosŏn Ilbo*, January 12, 1983; and the *Tong-a Ilbo* editorial, "Export and Foreign Debts," February 17, 1983. South Korea lost much of its advantages in the export market because of its high rate of inflation and the competition for skilled labor that pushed up average wages in the manufacturing sector. This occurred in spite of the very rapid rise in labor productivity. The following table tells the story:

COST OF LABOR IN THE MANUFACTURING SECTOR, 1975–1980

Country	Items	1975	1976	1977	1978	1979	1980
Korea	Nominal wages	100	134.7	180.2	242.1	311.4	382.2
	Labor productivity	100	107.5	118.7	132.9	153.9	170.3
	Real price of labor	100	125.3	151.8	182.2	202.3	224.4
Japan	Nominal wages	100	112.3	121.9	129.1	138.7	149.3
	Labor productivity	100	112.3	118.0	127.4	142.8	156.0
	Real Price of labor	100	100.0	103.3	101.3	97.1	95.7
Taiwan	Nominal wages	100	117.5	135.6	157.4	139.1	166.2
	Labor productivity	100	116.2	128.1	158.8	117.1	126.7
	Real price of labor	100	101.1	105.9	99.1	118.1	131.1
U.S.	Nominal wages	100	108.1	117.6	127.5	99.3	108.2
	Labor productivity	100	104.7	107.4	111.7	91.3	91.9
	Real price of labor	100	103.2	109.5	114.1	108.7	117.7

SOURCE: Economic Planning Board, Republic of Korea, "5 ch'a 5 kaenyŏn kyehoek Nosa kwangye bumun kyehoek" [Fifth five-year plan, plan on labor relations], cited in *Tong-a Ilbo*, September 13, 1982. For data on labor productivity and real price of labor between 1966 and 1972, see Wontack Hong and Anne O. Krueger, eds., *Trade and Devel-*

opment in Korea (Seoul, 1975), p. 136. The real price of labor had risen from 100 in 1966 to 208.9 in 1972, that is, it had more than doubled during those years. The table above shows that the real cost of labor rose by 2.2 times between 1975 and 1981.

36. *Yomiuri Shimbun*, October 2, 1981.

37. *Korea Herald*, October 20, 1981.

38. See, for example, *Mainichi Shimbun*, November 3, 1981; *Yomiuri Shimbun*, November 3, 1981; and *Tong-a Ilbo*, November 2, 1981.

39. *Yomiuri Shimbun*, December 2, 1981.

40. Ibid. South Korea received a total of 249.68 billion yen in ODA loans between 1970 and 1980. The annual breakdown, in billions of yen, was 1970, 7.20; 1971, 38.04; 1972, 21.60; 1973, 21.60; 1974, 31.32; 1975, 23.42; 1976, 23.50; 1977, 24.00; 1978, 21.00; 1979, 19.00; 1980, 19.00 (*Yomiuri Shimbun*, August 20, 1981).

41. *Asahi Shimbun*, December 4 and 5, 1981; and *Mainichi Shimbun*, December 5, 1981.

42. *Yomiuri Shimbun*, January 6 and 8, 1982; *Tong-a Ilbo*, January 9, 1982; and *Nihon Keizai Shimbun*, January 29, 1982.

43. *Yomiuri Shimbun*, February 16, 1982; *Asahi Shimbun*, February 17, 1982; and *Mainichi Shimbun*, April 7, 1982.

44. *Yomiuri Shimbun*, April 20 and 30, 1982.

45. Ibid., April 30, 1982; and *Tong-a Ilbo*, April 30, 1982.

46. *Korea Herald*, May 1, 1982.

47. *Yomiuri Shimbun*, May 1, 1982.

48. *Asian Wall Street Journal Weekly*, April 19, 1982, p. 18.

49. *Korea Herald*, June 26, 1982.

50. *Tong-a Ilbo*, July 26, 1982.

51. Dae-Sok Suh, "South Korea in 1982: A Centennial Year," *Asian Survey*, January 1983, pp. 95–99.

52. Japan was willing to grant an additional $700 million soft loan fund that could be used to augment domestic Korean funds for labor and other costs, but it was not willing to yield any further. The ODA fund was to remain $1.5 billion. See *Asahi Shimbun*, July 2, 1982; and *Yomiuri Shimbun*, July 13, 1982.

53. For details, see *Yomiuri Shimbun*, January 19, 1983.

54. Foreign Broadcast Information Service, *Daily Report*, 4 (December 2, 1982), p. C1.

55. *Yomiuri Shimbun*, January 9, 1983.

56. Kim Dae-jung's death sentence was commuted to a life sentence in January 1981. In March 1982, the sentence was reduced to a twenty-year imprisonment. The only comment Premier Nakasone and the Japanese government issued on Kim Dae-jung's release was to welcome it on "humanitar-

ian grounds." None of the details concerning Kim's liberation have been released by the governments involved.

57. *Asahi Shimbun*, January 12, 1983; and *Tong-a-Ilbo*, January 13, 1983.

58. *Yomiuri Shimbun*, January 11, 1983; and *Tong-a Ilbo*, January 13, 1983.

59. The full text of the joint communiqué is reproduced in the Appendix.

60. The translation used here is the one used by the Korean side. The Japanese text says "The premier stated [he] has the intention [*ito ga aru mune*] of providing all possible cooperation under the basic principle of Japanese economic cooperation." For the Japanese text, see *Asahi Shimbun*, January 13, 1983, p. 4.

61. Frank Kowalski, "An Inoffensive Rearmament" (Unpublished English manuscript published in Japanese translation as *Nihon saigunbi* [Rearmament of Japan] [Tokyo, 1969]), quoted in J. W. Dower, *Empire and Aftermath: Yoshida Shigeru and the Japanese Experience, 1878–1954* (Cambridge, Mass., 1979), pp. 388–89.

62. Kamata, "Nik-Kan keizai," p. 12.

63. Japan objected to the Chinese proposal to mention both nations' opposition to "hegemony over the area by any power." The issue became a subject of major controversy within Japan, and was used by many different groups for political purposes. This caused a prolonged deadlock over the treaty. It was signed in August 1978, after three years of negotiations, when the Chinese agreed with the Japanese position that the antihegemony clause neither is aimed at a particular third country nor would bind Japan to undertake joint military action with China in case of conflict. In 1981 Premier Suzuki declared that the term "alliance" (*dōmei*) did not have any military connotations with regard to U.S.-Japanese relations, a position contradicted by Foreign Minister Itō Masayoshi, who eventually resigned over the content of the joint communiqué.

64. *Yomiuri Shimbun*, March 1 and 3, 1981.

CHAPTER 6

1. For details, see R. P. Dore, "Textbook Censorship in Japan: The Ienaga Case," *Pacific Affairs*, Winter 1970–71, pp. 548–56, particularly pp. 548–49. For a useful chronology of the development of the laws and regulations concerning textbook certification, see *Yomiuri Shimbun*, April 9, 1982, which also carries a round-table discussion of the Ienaga case.

2. Dore, "Textbook Censorship," p. 550.

3. *Yomiuri Shimbun*, April 9, 1982. Nihon Minshutō (Japanese Democratic Party), a predecessor of the Liberal Democratic Party, had published a white paper bearing the same title in 1955.

4. See, for example, Yomiuri Shimbunsha, ed., *Aikokushin ni tsuite* [On patriotism] (Tokyo, 1980), 292 pp.

5. Based on accounts given in "The Textbooks That Provoke Laughter: The Most Ingenious Technique for 'Interference,'" a round-table discussion by textbook writers, *Asahi jyānaru*, July 10, 1981, pp. 10–18.

6. Yayama Tarō, "Kyōkasho o meguru shimbun kyōsōkyoku" [Frenzied clamor of newspapers surrounding textbooks], *Chūō Kōron*, November 1982, pp. 108–17.

7. *Tong-a Ilbo*, July 22, 1982.

8. *Asahi Shimbun*, July 24, 1982.

9. See, for example, *Tong-a Ilbo*, July 24, 1982.

10. Okada Hidehiro, "Textbook Certification Is China's Domestic Problem," *Chūō Kōron*, October 1982, pp. 89–90; and *Yomiuri Shimbun*, July 27, 1982.

11. *Korea Herald*, July 30, 1982; and *Tong-a Ilbo*, August 4, 1982.

12. *Korea Herald*, July 27 and 30, 1982.

13. Okada, "Textbook Certification," p. 90.

14. *Korea Herald*, August 4, 1982; and *Yomiuri Shimbun*, August 4, 1982.

15. *Korea Herald*, July 27, 1982; and *Tong-a Ilbo*, July 27, 1982.

16. *Yomiuri Shimbun*, August 7, 14, and 17, 1982.

17. Ibid., August 5, 1982.

18. Ibid., August 12, 1982; and *Tong-a Ilbo*, August 13, 1982.

19. A summary of President Chun's speech was reported in the Japanese press. See, for example, *Yomiuri Shimbun*, August 16, 1982. His speech was notable in that, for the first time in history, a Korean president acknowledged Korea's past weakness as a factor that had resulted in Korea's subjugation by Japan.

20. *Tong-a Ilbo*, August 10, 1982; and *Yomiuri Shimbun*, August 11, 1982.

21. *Yomiuri Shimbun*, August 13, 1982.

22. Ibid., August 15 and 18, 1982. This idea was first proposed by Arishima Shigetake, chairman of the Education Committee (Bunkyōbu) of Kōmeitō, on August 14. See ibid., August 15, 1982.

23. Ibid., August 21 and 22, 1982.

24. For the full text of the press conference, see ibid., August 24, 1982.

25. Ibid., August 27, 1982.

26. For the English text of the statement, see *Korea Herald*, August 28, 1982.

27. *Yomiuri Shimbun*, August 29 and 31, and September 10, 1982. See also *Tong-a Ilbo*, August 31, 1982.

28. For an evaluation of the Suzuki trip, see *Yomiuri Shimbun*, September 29, 1982. The Japanese wished to commemorate the visit with a joint press

release as was done on the occasion of Premier Ōhira's visit in November 1979. They sent the Chinese a draft two weeks prior to Premier Suzuki's visit, but the Chinese summarily turned down the proposal. See ibid., September 26, 1982.

29. Ibid., September 5, 18, and 28, 1982.

30. For this information, I am indebted to Professor G. Cameron Hurst III, for his unpublished paper "Weaving the Emperor's New Clothes: the Japanese Textbook 'Revision' Controversy," pp. 9–10. Hurst cites Tanaka Masaaki, "Kyōkasho kentei mondai ni tsuite no ankēto" [Inquiry concerning the textbook authorization problem], *Gaikō jihō* [Diplomatic review], November 1982, pp. 29–33.

31. Yayama Tarō, "Frenzied Clamor," p. 112.

32. Hurst, "Weaving the Emperor's New Clothes," p. 7.

33. See, for example, *Tōkyō Shimbun*, July 23, 1982; and *Yomiuri Shimbun*, July 29 and August 27, 1982.

34. *Yomiuri Shimbun*, October 11, 1982. Seventy-one percent of the people surveyed answered questions.

35. *Tong-a Ilbo*, August 5, 1982, reprinted the entire list in two full pages.

36. On the Japanese, see Edwin O. Reischauer, *The United States and Japan* (Cambridge, Mass., 1958), p. 109; and W. G. Beasley, *The Modern History of Japan* (New York, 1965), p. 310. On the Koreans, see Yoon Woo-kon, "Korean Bureaucrats' Behavior," *Korea Journal*, 1974, p. 27.

37. Masataka Kosaka, "International Economic Policy of Japan," in *The Foreign Policy of Modern Japan*, ed. Robert A. Scalapino (Berkeley, 1977), p. 223. See also Hiroshi Kitamura, *Psychological Dimensions of U.S.-Japanese Relations*, Harvard Center for International Affairs Occasional Papers, no. 28 (Cambridge, Mass., 1971), p. 11.

38. Edwin O. Reischauer, *The Japanese* (Cambridge, Mass., 1977), p. 165.

39. Okada Hidehiro, *Wakoku* [The country of Wa] (Tokyo, 1977), pp. 147–55.

40. Scholarly works and commentaries on this subject are too numerous to list. I have consulted Inoue Hideo, "Mimana Nihonfu no gyōsei soshiki" [Administrative organization of the Japanese-fu in Mimana], in *Nihonshoki kenkyū* [Study of Japanese chronicles], ed. Mishina Shōhei (Tokyo, 1966), pp. 186–243; Ueda Masaaki, "Nis-Sen 'dōsoron' no keibo" [Genealogy of the "theory of identical ancestry" of Japan and Korea], *Sanzenri* [Three thousand ri], no. 14 (May 1978), pp. 28–36; Inoue Mitsusada, *Nihon kokka no kigen* [The origins of the Japanese state] (Tokyo, 1960); Okada Hidehiro, *Wakoku*; and Inoue Hideo, *Kodai Chōsen* [Ancient Korea] (Tokyo, 1972), pp. 82–98. The place indicated as Mimana is where the Kaya, Karak, or Imna confederacy existed, according to Korean history. Thousands of stoneware ceramics excavated from this area indeed establish an intimate relationship with the numerous *sueki* ceramics of Wa-Yamato-Japanese tumuli from the fourth to

tenth centuries. But the relationship here seems the other way round, since Kaya ceramics seem the source from which *sueki* ceramics derive, according to Gregory Henderson. Both differ radically from Chinese pottery of the time. Much the same can be said for the great tumuli themselves. I am indebted to Professor Henderson for this information.

41. Inoue Hideo and Ueda Masaaki, eds., *Nihon to Chōsen no nisennen* [Two thousand years of Japan and Korea] (Tokyo, 1969), 1: 153.

42. Hatada Takashi, *Nihonjin no Chōsenkan* [Japanese views of Korea] (Tokyo, 1969), pp. 12–13; and Inoue and Ueda, *Nihon to Chōsen no nisennen*, pp. 256–59.

43. Inoue and Ueda, *Nihon to Chōsen no nisennen*, 1: 253–56; and Ryusaku Tsunoda, William T. de Bary, and Donald Keene, eds., *Sources of Japanese Tradition* (New York, 1958), p. 305. On Hayashi Razan, see Donald H. Shively, "Tokugawa Tsunayoshi, the Genroku Shogun," in *Personality in Japanese History*, ed. Albert M. Craig and D. H. Shively (Berkeley, 1970), p. 114. On Fujiwara and Hayashi, see Nomura Kentarō, *Tokugawa jidai no shakai keizai shisō gairon* [Introduction to the social and economic thought of the Tokugawa period] (Tokyo, 1949), pp. 88–89.

44. On this point, see the excellent work by Ronald P. Toby, *State and Diplomacy in Early Modern Japan* (Princeton, N.J., 1984), chap. 3. I wish to thank Professor Gari Ledyard for bringing this work to my attention. On the Korean diplomatic missions, see also Inoue and Ueda, *Nihon to Chōsen no nisennen*, 1: 239–43; Yi Chin-hŭi, *Richō no tsūshinshi: Edo jidai no Nihon to Chōsen* [Diplomatic missions of the Yi dynasty: Japan and Korea in the Edo era] (Tokyo, 1976); and Ueda Masaaki, "Yugamerareta Nit-Chō kankeishi o toi neosu" [To correct the warped history of Japanese-Korean relations], *Asahi jyānaru*, April 20, 1979, pp. 96–98.

45. Toby, *State and Diplomacy*, pp. 260–63; Hatada Takashi, "Nihonjin no Chōsenkan" [Japanese views of Korea] in Hatada Takashi et al., *Nihon to Chōsen* [Japan and Korea], Ajia-Afurica Kōza (Tokyo, 1965), 3: 14.

46. Ibid., pp. 15, 16–23. See also Hilary Conroy, *The Japanese Seizure of Korea, 1868–1910* (Philadelphia, 1960), pp. 17–77.

47. *Kojiki* was believed to have been written in A.D. 712, but some historians now think it was produced at least a century later (see Okada Hidehiro, *Wakoku*, p. 147).

48. Hatada Takashi, *Nihonjin no Chōsenkan*, pp. 184–91. This work was first edited by the History Office of the Office of the Premier [Taiseikan Shūshikan] in 1877 under the title *Nihonshi ryaku* [Brief history of Japan]. It was re-edited in 1885 by the Cabinet History Bureau (Naikaku Shūshikyoku). It was first published in 1890 and went through many editions.

49. See Ueda Masaaki, "Genealogy of the 'Theory of Identical Ancestry,'" pp. 28–36; and Takashi Hatada, "An Interpretation of the King Kwang-gaet'o Inscription," trans. W. Dixon Morris, in *Korean Studies* (University of Hawaii), no. 3 (1979), p. 9.

50. Ueda Masaaki attributed this to Kita Sadakichi, who was the most active proponent of the theory of identical ancestry of the Japanese and Korean peoples and the author of *Kankoku no heigō to kokushi* [The Korean annexation and Japanese history] (Tokyo, 1910). See Ueda's "Genealogy of the 'Theory of Identical Ancestry,'" p. 31.

51. Hatada Takashi, *Nihonjin no Chōsenkan*, pp. 190–93.

52. See, for example, Mizuno Yū, *Nihon kodai no kokka keisei* [Formation of the state in ancient Japan] (Tokyo, 1967), pp. 102–71; and Okada Hidehiro, *Wakoku*, pp. 147–58.

53. Quoted from Inoue Mitsusada, *Nihon kokka no kigen*, p. 128.

54. See Nakatsuka Akira, "Kindai Nihon shigakushi ni okeru Chōsen mondai: Tokuni 'Kōkaitoō ryōhi o megutte,'" [The Korean problem in modern Japanese historiography: Particularly "Concerning the stele of King Kwang-gae-t'o"], *Shisō* [Thought], March 1971, pp. 350–51.

55. Kim Sŏk-hyŏng, "Sam-Han samguk ui Ilbon yŏltonae pun'guk dŭl e taehayŏ" [On the three Korean kingdoms' branches in Japan], *Ryŏksa kwahak* [Historical science], no. 1 (1963), pp. 1–32. This article was translated into Japanese and published in *Rekishi hyōron* [Historical review], nos. 5, 8, and 9 (1964). Kim Sŏk-hyŏng's book, *Ch'ogi Cho-Il kwan'gye yŏn'gu* [Study of early Korean-Japanese relations] (Pyongyang, 1966), was translated as *Kodai Chō-Nichi kankeishi: Yamato seiken to Mimana* [A History of Korean-Japanese relations of antiquity: The Yamato regime and Mimana] (Tokyo, 1969).

56. Pak Shi-hyŏng, *Kwang-gae-t'o-wang nŭng-bi* [The King Kwang-gae-t'o stele] (Pyongyang, 1966). An abstracted translation was published in *Chōsen kenkyū nempō* [Korean studies annual], no. 9 (1968).

57. Nakatsuka Akira, "Kindai Nihonshigakushi ni okeru Chōsen mondai," p. 348; and Yi Chin-Hŭi, "Kōkaitoōhi to kindai shigaku" [The King Kwang-gae-t'o stele and modern historiography], *Sanzenri*, no. 7 (Autumn 1976), p. 55.

58. Tōma Shodai, "Genzai ni okeru shisō jōkyō no kadai to shite: Kim Sŏk-hyŏng, 'Kodai Chō-Nichi Kankeishi' ni tsuite" [As a problem of thought condition at present: On Kim Sŏk-hyŏng's "A History of Korean-Japanese Relations of Antiquity"], *Rekishigaku kenkyū*, no. 361 (June 1970), pp. 23–25.

59. Nakatsuka Akira, "Kindai Nihonshigakushi ni okeru Chōsen mondai," pp. 348, 359–60. Minabuchi Shoan supposedly went to Sui as a member of the Japanese mission in 607 and stopped by Chi-an in Manchuria on his return to read King Kwang-gae-t'o's stele. Hence the book printed the text of the entire inscription without a single missing word. This version of the inscription, of course, substantiated the claims of the General Staff. In 1933, Professor Kuroita Katsumi of Tokyo Imperial University declared the three-volume work attributed to Minabuchi a forgery and aroused considerable interest and controversy. For details, see Saeki Arikiyo, *Kōkaitoōhi to sambō hombu* [The King Kwang-gae-t'o stele and the general staff] (Tokyo, 1976),

pp. 134–35. Saeki lists two articles published in the 1930s that supported Kuroita.

60. See Inumaru Giichi, "Kindaishika no mita kodaishi ronsō" [Controversy on ancient history as seen by a modern historian], *Sanzenri*, no. 7 (Autumn 1976), pp. 42–49. There are exceptions. Inumaru noted that Professor Inoue Mitsusada of Tokyo University, "the citadel of official academism," seems to adhere to the fourth-century theory. Inoue's *Kodaishi kenkyū no sekai* [The world of ancient historical studies] (Tokyo, 1975) is cited as an example. For Inoue's other views, see my references to his *Nihon kokka no kigen*. Inoue's views were enormously important in Japan not only because of his scholarly prestige but also because of his family background. Professor Inoue, who died in 1982, was a great-grandson of Inoue Kaoru, one of the most illustrious names in modern Japanese history. Inoue was one of the prominent leaders from Chōshū who headed the anti-Tokugawa revolt. He led the Meiji regime as minister of finance and minister of internal affairs. He was in Korea in 1876 to conclude the treaty of amity and friendship with the old Korean government.

61. Hatada Takashi, *Nihonjin no Chōsenkan*, p. 7. For Yi Chin-hŭi's writings, see "Kōkaitoō ryōhibun no nazo: Shoki Chō-Nichi kankeishijō no mondaiten" [The puzzle of the King Kwang-gae-t'o stele: Problems in the early relations between Korea and Japan], *Shisō*, May 1972, pp. 75–101; *Kōkaitoō ryōhi no kenkyū* [A study of the King Kwang-gae-t'o stele] (Tokyo, 1972); and *Kōkaitoōhi no nazo* [The puzzle of the King Kwang-gae-t'o stele] (Tokyo, 1973). Saeki Arikiyo casts some doubts about Yi Chin-hŭi's argument. See his *Kōkaitoōhi to sambō hombu*, pp. 180–209 (this section of the book was originally published in *Rekishigaku kenkyū* [Historical studies], no. 401 [October 1973]). Wang Jian-qun, Director of the Jilin Province Anthropological Research Center in Changchun and a student of the stele, also disagreed with Yi's argument. See his interview with a Japanese reporter in *Yomiuri Shimbun*, January 10, 1984. Yomiuri Shimbun Company sponsored an international symposium, including Wang Jian-qun and others from China, on January 11–12, 1985, in Tokyo. Summary of the discussion was published in *Yomiuri Shimbun*, January 14, 1985.

62. Okada Hidehiro, for example, treats *Nihon Shoki* and the story about Empress Jingū as a myth, but he uncritically accepts the earlier interpretations of Wa's subjugation of Silla and Paekche as "recorded in the Kwang-gae-t'o stele." See *Wakoku*, pp. 130–34.

63. See Kim Tal-su et al., *Kyōkasho ni kakareta Chōsen* [Korea as written in textbooks] (Tokyo, 1977); *Sanzenri*, no. 12 (Winter 1977) (a special issue on the subject), and ibid., no. 14 (Summer 1978), pp. 206–31 (three articles).

64. As noted before, Kita Sadakichi was the leading exponent of colonialist historical views. For details about him and his theory, see Ueda Masaaki, "'Nissen Dōsoron' no keibo" [Genealogy of the "theory of identical ancestry of Japan and Korea"], *Sanzenri*, no. 14 (Summer 1978), pp. 28–36. The quotation is from p. 34.

65. Gari Ledyard, "Horserider Theory," *Kodansha Encyclopedia of Japan* (Tokyo, 1983), 3: 229.

66. Ibid., p. 230. For Egami's own account, see his *Kiba minzoku kokka* [Horse-riding people's state] (Tokyo, 1967). See also Inoue Hideo, *Nihon kokka no kigen*, pp. 199–202, and Okuno Takeo, "Kodai wa Nihon mo Chōsen mo nakkatta: Tennō wa Chōsenkei de aru" [Neither Japan nor Korea existed in antiquity: The emperors were of Korean origin], *Sanzenri*, no. 7 (Fall 1976), pp. 72–76.

67. The excavation received wide public attention in the Japanese and Korean mass media, and throngs of Japanese and foreigners visited the site. For a collection of symposium papers on the subject, see Inoue Mitsusada, ed., *Takamatsuzuka kofun to Asuka* [The Takamatsu tomb and Asuka] (Tokyo, 1972).

68. J. Edward Kidder, Jr., professor of art history and archaeology at International Christian University, Tokyo, concluded his article, "The Newly Discovered Takamatsuzuka Tomb" (*Monumenta Nipponica*, Autumn 1972, pp. 245–51), by saying, "It would probably have been the tomb of a Korean associated with the court of Empress Jitō, the builder of the new city of Fujiwara, and the paintings were done by artists familiar with both the Korean tradition and T'ang style of China."

69. Kobayashi Yukio, archaeologist at Kyoto University, is one of the leading opponents of Egami's theory. He accepts the traditional reading of the inscription on the King Kwang-gae-t'o stele with all its implications. See his *Kofun no hanashi* [The story of the ancient tombs] (Tokyo, 1959), pp. 27–31.

70. Inoue Mitsusada, *Nihon kokka no kigen*, pp. 190–204. Professor Mizuno Yū of Waseda University also believes that the horseback-riding people reached Japan sometime after the second century B.C. See *Nihon kodai no kokka keisei* [The formation of the state of ancient Japan] (Tokyo, 1967), p. 197.

71. Inoue Mitsusada, *Nihon kokka no kigen*, pp. 104, 128, 210–21.

72. Okada Hidehiro, *Wakoku*, pp. vi, 115–17.

73. For an American contribution to this debate, see Gari Ledyard, "Galloping Along with the Horseriders," *Journal of Japanese Studies*, vol. 1, no. 2 (Spring 1975), pp. 217–54.

74. Okada Hidehiro, *Wakoku*, p. v.

75. Ibid., p. 199.

76. Yi Man-yŏl, "Samguk ui hangjaeng gwa Koguryŏ wa Su Tang kwa ŭi ch'ungdol" [The struggle among the three kingdoms and the clash between Koguryŏ and Sui-Tang], in *Han'guksa* [History of Korea], ed. Kuksa P'yŏnch'an Wiwŏnhoe [Committee for the Compilation of National History] (Seoul, 1978), 2: 468. "Japan must have ruled the peninsula with great might since Empress Jingū to require Koguryŏ to dispatch 50,000 troops," a Japa-

nese author writing under the General Staff's auspices argued (see Saeki Ari-kiyo, *Kōkaitoōhi to sambō hombu*, p. 21).

77. Ro Chung-guk, "Samguk munhwa ka Ilbon e kkich'in yŏnghyang" [The influence of the culture of the three kingdoms on Japan], *Han'guksa*, 2: 421–59; and Inoue and Ueda, *Nihon to Chōsen no nisennen*, 1: 86–102.

78. Roy A. Miller, "Plus ça change . . ." *Journal of Asian Studies*, August 1980, pp. 773–780. Miller cites the *Biographic Dictionary of Japanese Literature* (Tokyo, 1976), pp. 47–48, edited by Hisamatsu Sen'ichi and others and published by the International Society for Educational Information; and Katō Shūichi, *A History of Japanese Literature*, trans. David Chibett (Tokyo, 1979), pp. 175.

79. Ibid., pp. 773, 776–80.

CHAPTER 7

1. According to a report by the Japanese Publishing Industries Trade Union [Shuppan Rōdō Remmei] on high school social subjects textbooks, issued June 14, 1984, the textbook censors continued to favor embellishment of Japanese colonial policies in Korea although the March First movement of 1919 was no longer described as "riots." The censors irritated the Koreans further by changing the designation of the Korea Strait (the body of water lying between the Korean peninsula and Tsushima Island) to the Western Waterway of the Tsushima Strait (Tsushima Kaikyō Seisuidō) (*Han'guk Ilbo*, April 11, 1984 [editorial], and April 15, 1984; see also the *Tong-a Ilbo* editorial of April 12, 1984, on the Korea Strait).

2. *Yomiuri Shimbun*, April 11 and 24, 1984.

3. *Korea Herald*, March 13, 1984.

4. For the text of Emperor Hirohito's remarks to Chun, see the *New York Times*, September 7, 1984. For Premier Nakasone's remark, see ibid., September 8, 1984.

5. *Yomiuri Shimbun* published a series entitled "Rikai e no michi" [The Road to Understanding] by Shiba Ryōtarō, beginning on February 21, 1984. Under the same title, the newspaper carried the text of a round-table discussion on Japanese and Korean culture in nineteen installments between July 7 and 18, 1982. The round table was attended by Shiba, Professors Mori Kō-ichi and Kim Tal-su from Japan, and Professors Ko Pyŏng-ik and Sŏn'u Hwi from Seoul. The first installment, on the Middle Ages, occupied three-quarters of the front page. The series was republished in 1983 as a book, *Nik-Kan rikai e no michi* [The road to Japanese–South Korean understanding] (Tokyo, 1983). Shiba, Kim Tal-su, and Professor Ueda Masaaki of Kyōto University participated in many round tables of a similar nature organized by Nihon no naka no Chōsen Bunka-sha [Korean Culture in Japan Company]

since 1969. At least four collections of these round tables were published by the Chū-ō Kōron Company, publisher of the important journal *Chū-ō Kōron* [Central Review].

6. See Kikuchi Masato (Seoul correspondent for *Yomiuri Shimbun*), "Seoul Dansō" [Fragmentary Recollection of Seoul], *Korea Hyōron* [Korea Review], June 1984, pp. 18–20.

7. The Japanese Foreign Ministry was optimistic about the establishment of the cultural committee as of August 15, according to *Asahi Shimbun* (August 16, 1984), but the plan was abandoned on August 25. See *Korea Times*, August 26, 1984; and *Han'guk Ilbo*, August 26, 1984.

8. *Korea Times*, August 26, 1984.

9. On Sino-Japanese relations before 1975, see Chae-Jin Lee, *Japan Faces China* (Baltimore and London, 1976), pp. 64–82, 141–158.

10. See *Yomiuri Shimbun*, April 3 and 6, 1984.

11. Kim Il-sŏng, "Let us promote the building of socialism by vigorously carrying out the three revolutions," speech at the meeting of active industrial workers, March 3, 1975, in Kim Il Sung, *Selected Works* (Pyongyang, 1979), 7: 178.

12. For my prognosis of North Korean policies in the 1980s, see "P'alsim-nyŏn-dae Puk-Han ŭi tae'oe chŏng'ch'aek" [External Policies of North Korea in the 1980s] in Tong-a Ilbo-sa, ed., *P'alsimnyŏn-dae ŭi sagang kwa Han pando* [The four major powers and the Korean peninsula in the 1980s] (Seoul, 1978), pp. 276–319.

13. The shipbuilding industry in Japan, for example, suffered from a declining demand for oil tankers and competition from Brazil, Taiwan, and South Korea. Total tonnage sold declined from 17.0 million gross tons in 1975 to 6.3 million in 1978 (Ira C. Magazineer and Thomas M. Hout, *Japanese Industrial Policy* [Berkeley, 1980], p. 85). Twenty-eight small and medium-sized shipbuilders went into bankruptcy in the year ending March 1978. The larger, conglomerate-associated companies survived. Japanese shipbuilders charged South Korea with unfair competition, citing government subsidies, but the Koreans were simply copying the Japanese model. The Japanese shipbuilding industry had grown with heavy government support and subsidy since the early 1950s. For the Japanese experience, see Chalmers Johnson, *MITI and the Japanese Miracle: The Growth of Industrial Policy, 1925–1975* (Stanford, 1982), p. 232.

14. Imai Chōhachirō, "Sōgo rikai o fukumeta Nik-Kan Minkan Keizai Kaigi" [The Japanese–South Korean Economic Conference that deepened mutual understanding], *Korea Hyōron* [Korea Review], June 1983, pp. 15–16. In spite of its reputation, the Japanese government is not always successful in persuading industries to accept its advice. Some electronic companies refused MITI's request to share technological information with Western nations. See "Japanese Technology: A Survey," *The Economist*, June 19, 1982, p.

14; and Ken'ichi Ohmae, "Inside Japanese Business," *The McKinsey Quarterly*, Spring 1982, p. 32.

15. Ole R. Holsti, "Cognitive Dynamics and Images of the Enemy," in *Image and Reality in World Politics*, ed. John C. Farrell and Asa P. Smith (New York and London, 1967), p. 18.

16. Tanaka Akira, "Seoul ni shokuhatsu sareta dansō" [Fragmentary thoughts of my Seoul visit], *Korea Hyōron* [Korea Review], October 1983, p. 37.

Index